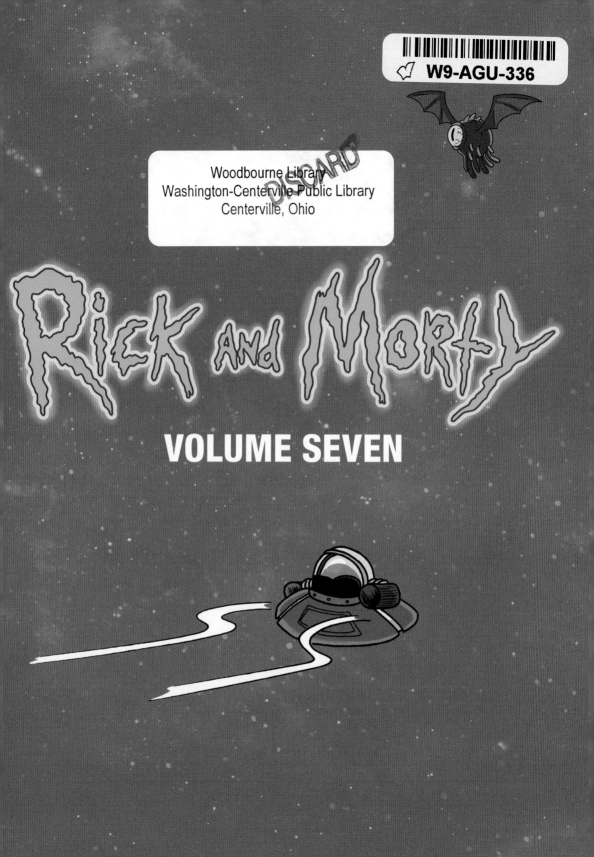

Rick and Morty

VOLUME SEVEN

PRESS

AN ONI PRESS PUBLICATION

[adult swim]

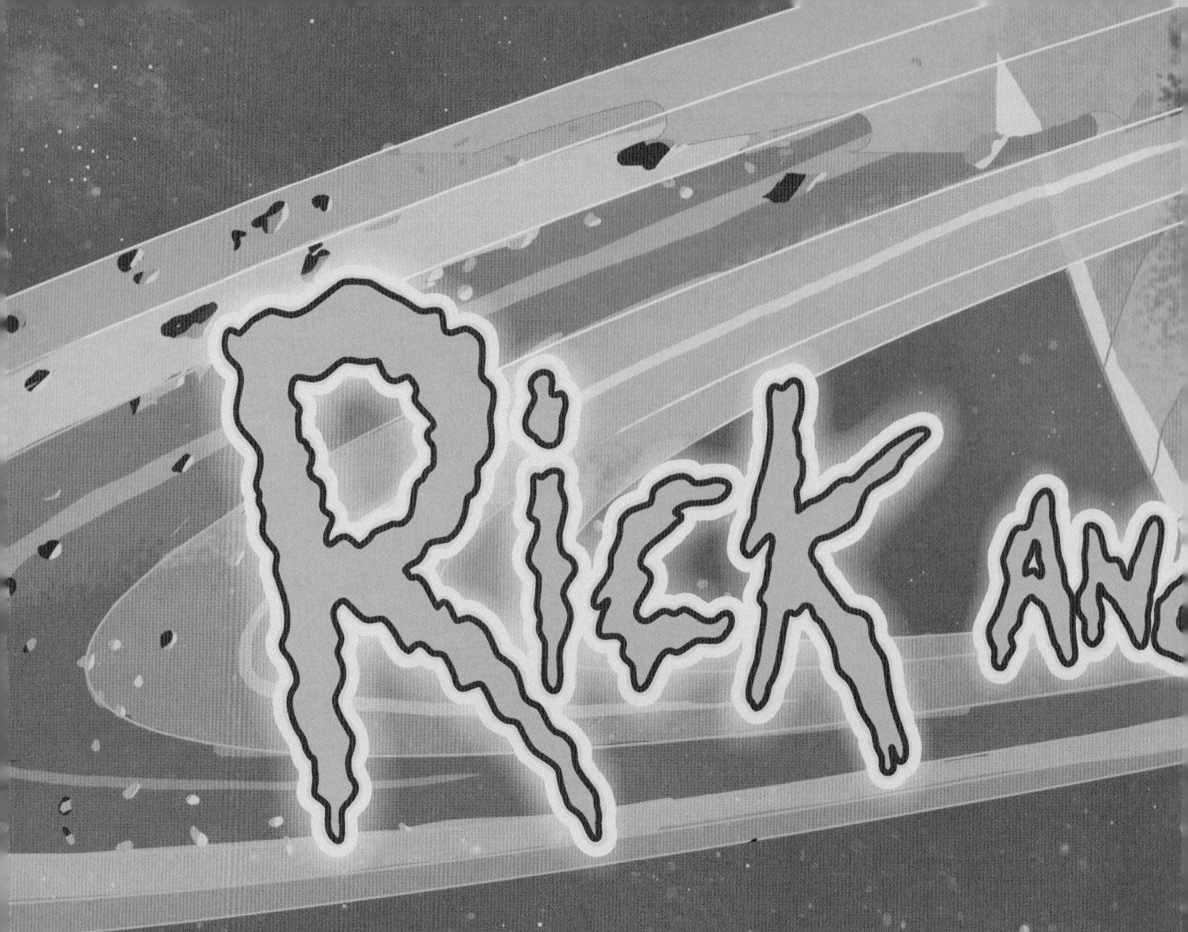
RICK

VOLUME SEVEN

RICK AND MORTY™ CREATED BY **DAN HARMON** AND **JUSTIN ROILAND**

RETAIL COVER BY

CJ CANNON AND **KATY FARINA**

ONI EXCLUSIVE COVER BY

JULIETA COLÁS

EDITED BY
ARI YARWOOD

DESIGNED BY
HILARY THOMPSON

ONI PRESS

[adult swim]

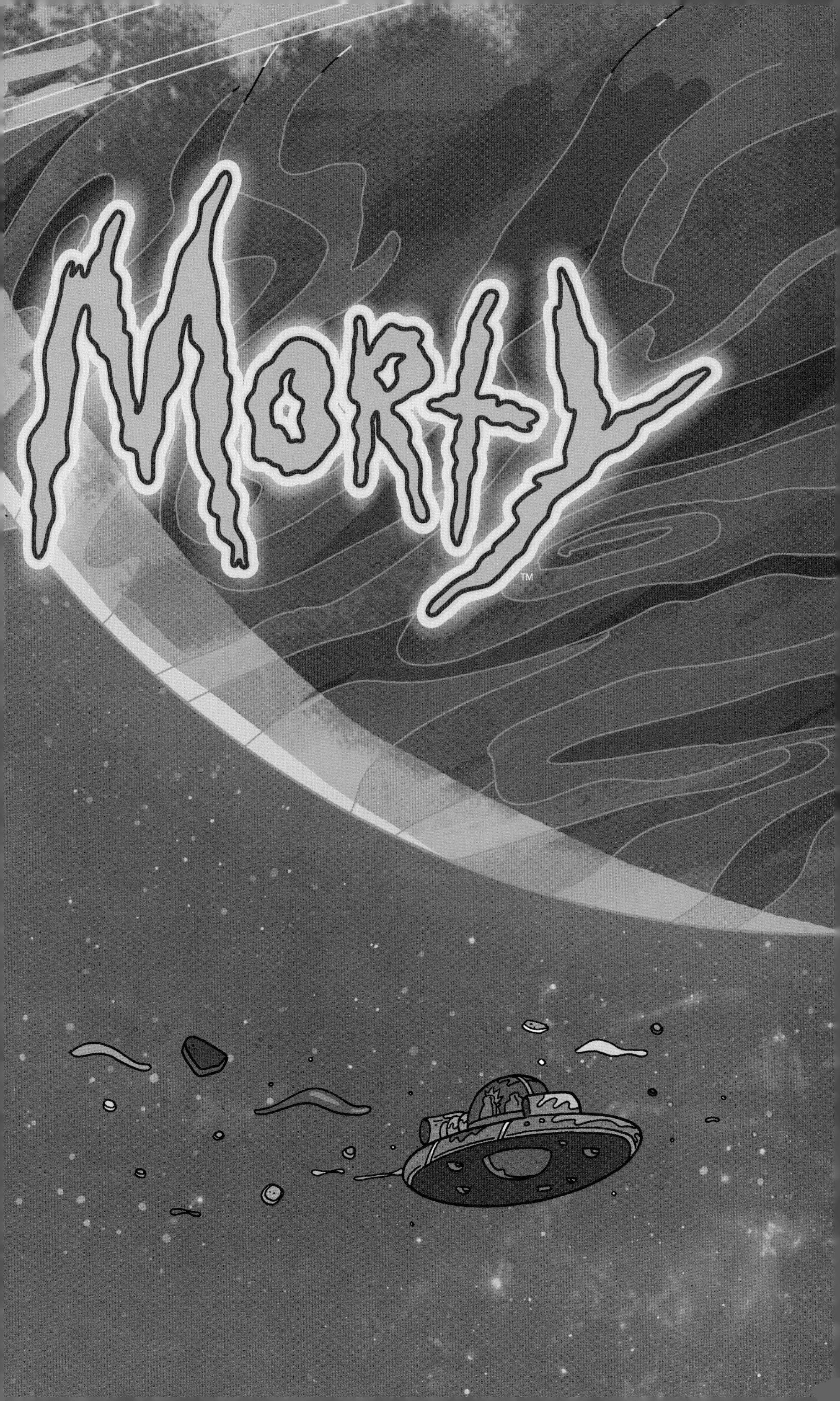
Morty™

PUBLISHED BY ONI PRESS, INC.
JOE NOZEMACK FOUNDER & CHIEF FINANCIAL OFFICER
JAMES LUCAS JONES PUBLISHER
CHARLIE CHU V.P. OF CREATIVE & BUSINESS DEVELOPMENT
BRAD ROOKS DIRECTOR OF OPERATIONS
MELISSA MESZAROS DIRECTOR OF PUBLICITY
MARGOT WOOD DIRECTOR OF SALES
AMBER O'NEILL SPECIAL PROJECTS MANAGER
TROY LOOK DIRECTOR OF DESIGN & PRODUCTION
HILARY THOMPSON SENIOR GRAPHIC DESIGNER
KATE Z. STONE GRAPHIC DESIGNER
SONJA SYNAK JUNIOR GRAPHIC DESIGNER
ANGIE KNOWLES DIGITAL PREPRESS LEAD
ARI YARWOOD EXECUTIVE EDITOR
ROBIN HERRERA SENIOR EDITOR
DESIREE WILSON ASSOCIATE EDITOR
ALISSA SALLAH ADMINISTRATIVE ASSISTANT
JUNG LEE LOGISTICS ASSOCIATE
SCOTT SHARKEY WAREHOUSE ASSISTANT

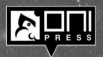

ONIPRESS.COM
FACEBOOK.COM/ONIPRESS
TWITTER.COM/ONIPRESS
ONIPRESS.TUMBLR.COM
INSTAGRAM.COM/ONIPRESS
ADULTSWIM.COM
TWITTER.COM/RICKANDMORTY
FACEBOOK.COM/RICKANDMORTY

THIS VOLUME COLLECTS ISSUES #31–35
OF THE ONI PRESS SERIES *RICK AND MORTY*™.

FIRST EDITION: MAY 2018

ISBN 978-1-62010-509-2
EISBN 978-1-62010-510-8
ONI EXCLUSIVE ISBN 978-1-62010-511-5

PRINTED IN USA.

LIBRARY OF CONGRESS CONTROL NUMBER: 2017960331

1 2 3 4 5 6 7 8 9 10

SPECIAL THANKS TO JUSTIN ROILAND, DAN HARMON, MARISA MARIONAKIS, MIKE MENDEL, AND JANET NO.

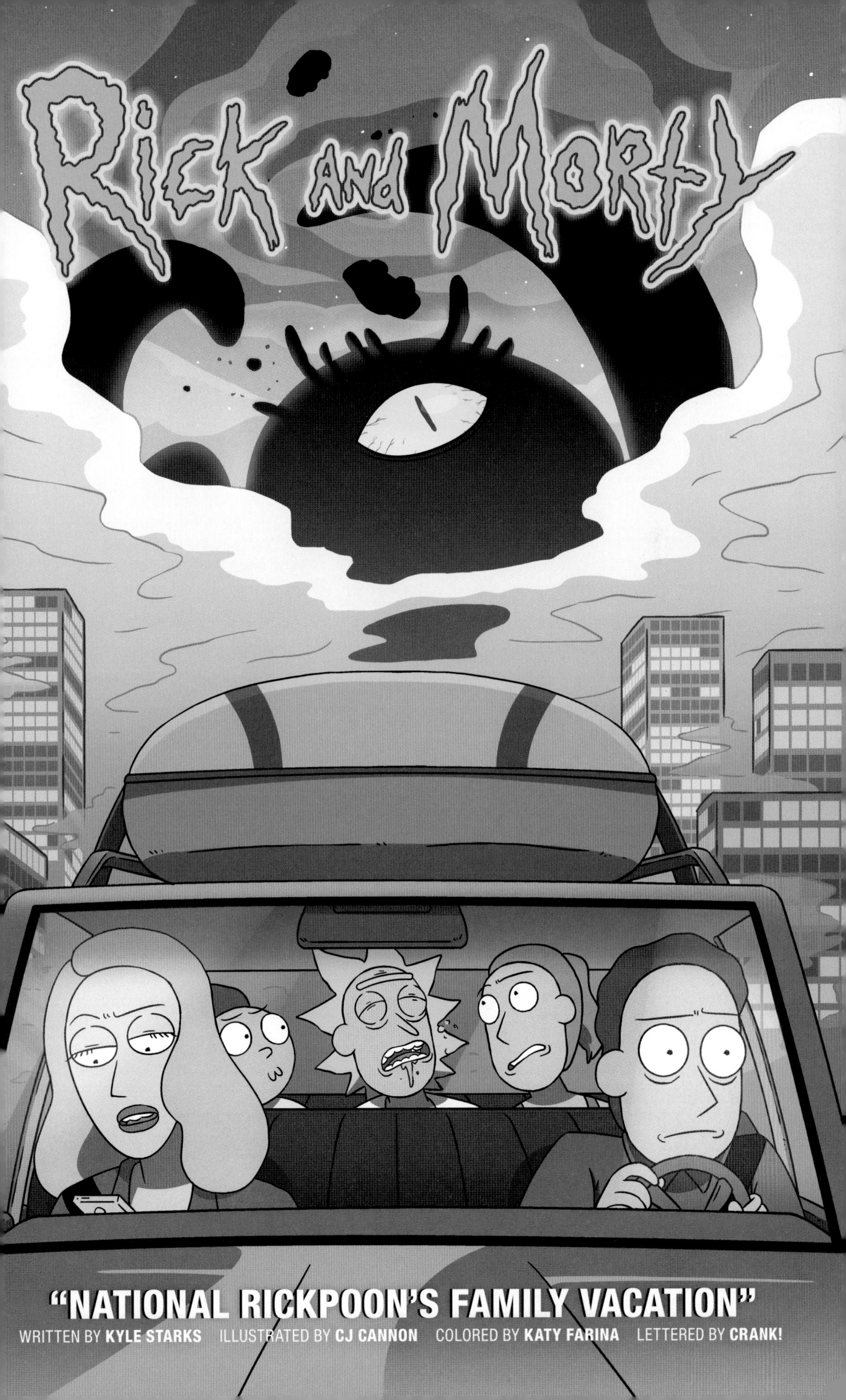
Rick and Morty

"NATIONAL RICKPOON'S FAMILY VACATION"

WRITTEN BY **KYLE STARKS** ILLUSTRATED BY **CJ CANNON** COLORED BY **KATY FARINA** LETTERED BY **CRANK!**

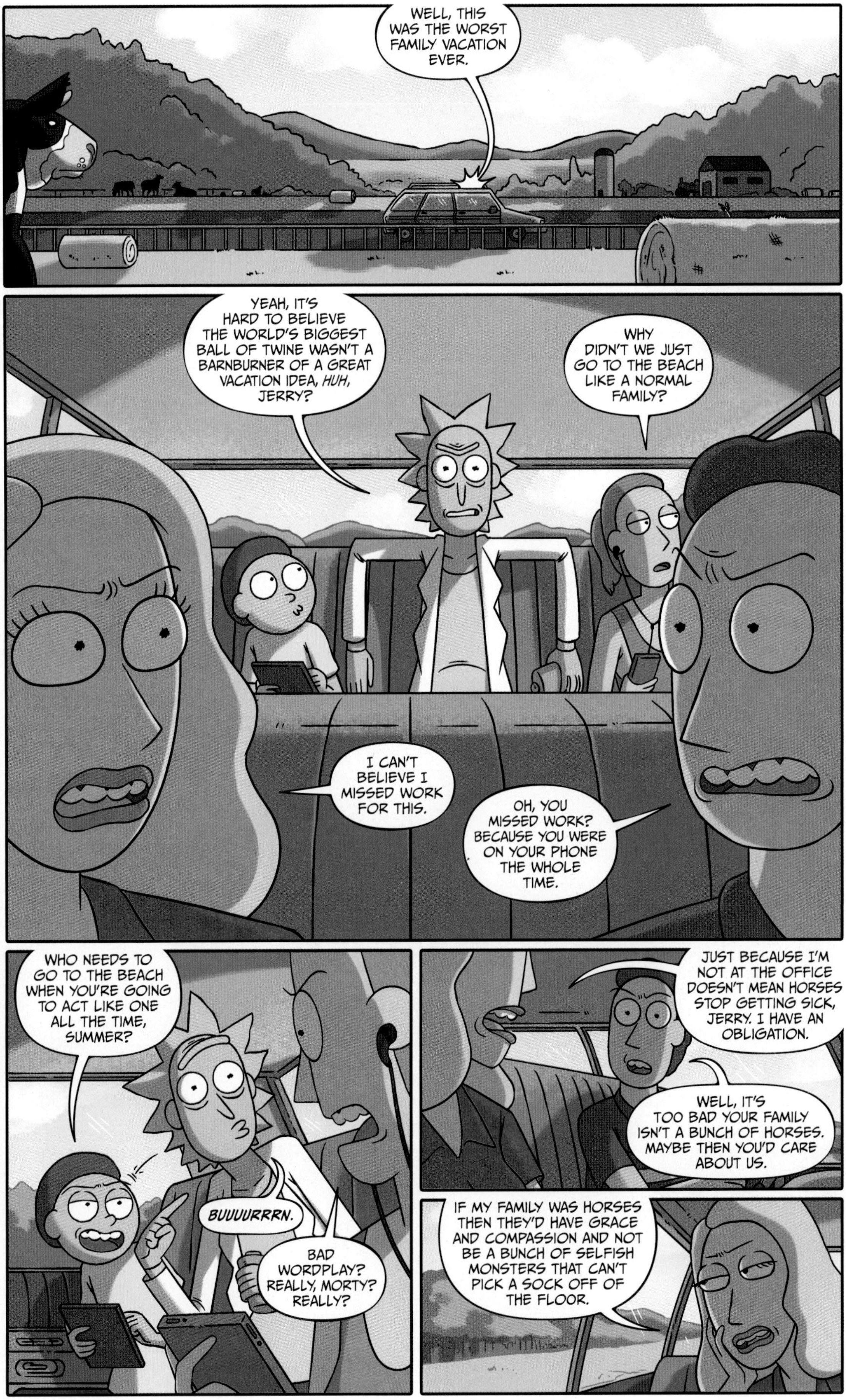
WELL, THIS WAS THE WORST FAMILY VACATION EVER.
YEAH, IT'S HARD TO BELIEVE THE WORLD'S BIGGEST BALL OF TWINE WASN'T A BARNBURNER OF A GREAT VACATION IDEA, *HUH*, JERRY?
WHY DIDN'T WE JUST GO TO THE BEACH LIKE A NORMAL FAMILY?
I CAN'T BELIEVE I MISSED WORK FOR THIS.
OH, YOU MISSED WORK? BECAUSE YOU WERE ON YOUR PHONE THE WHOLE TIME.
WHO NEEDS TO GO TO THE BEACH WHEN YOU'RE GOING TO ACT LIKE ONE ALL THE TIME, SUMMER?
BUUUURRRN.
BAD WORDPLAY? REALLY, MORTY? REALLY?
JUST BECAUSE I'M NOT AT THE OFFICE DOESN'T MEAN HORSES STOP GETTING SICK, JERRY. I HAVE AN OBLIGATION.
WELL, IT'S TOO BAD YOUR FAMILY ISN'T A BUNCH OF HORSES. MAYBE THEN YOU'D CARE ABOUT US.
IF MY FAMILY WAS HORSES THEN THEY'D HAVE GRACE AND COMPASSION AND NOT BE A BUNCH OF SELFISH MONSTERS THAT CAN'T PICK A SOCK OFF OF THE FLOOR.

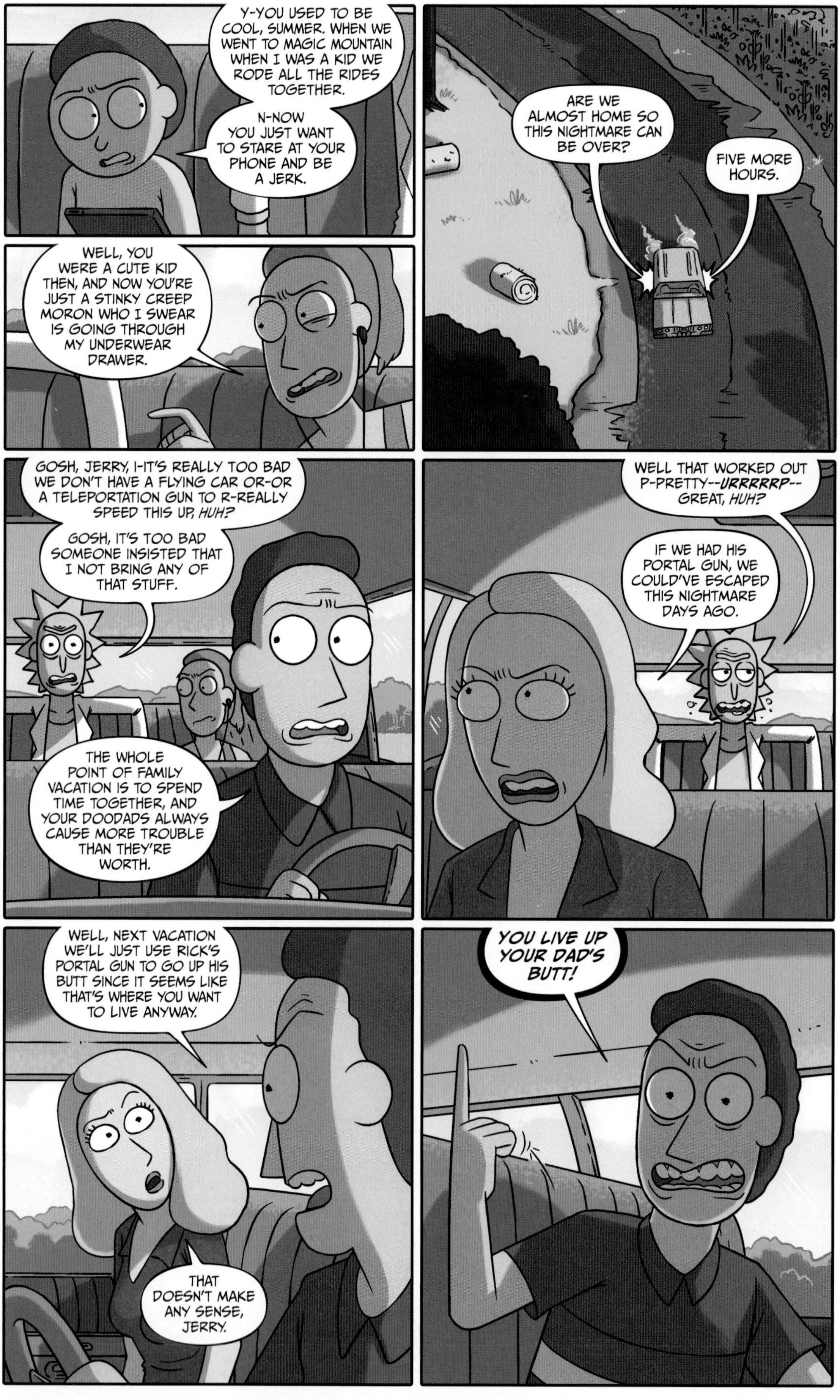
Y-YOU USED TO BE COOL, SUMMER. WHEN WE WENT TO MAGIC MOUNTAIN WHEN I WAS A KID WE RODE ALL THE RIDES TOGETHER.
N-NOW YOU JUST WANT TO STARE AT YOUR PHONE AND BE A JERK.
WELL, YOU WERE A CUTE KID THEN, AND NOW YOU'RE JUST A STINKY CREEP MORON WHO I SWEAR IS GOING THROUGH MY UNDERWEAR DRAWER.
ARE WE ALMOST HOME SO THIS NIGHTMARE CAN BE OVER?
FIVE MORE HOURS.
GOSH, JERRY, I-IT'S REALLY TOO BAD WE DON'T HAVE A FLYING CAR OR-OR A TELEPORTATION GUN TO R-REALLY SPEED THIS UP, HUH?
GOSH, IT'S TOO BAD SOMEONE INSISTED THAT I NOT BRING ANY OF THAT STUFF.
THE WHOLE POINT OF FAMILY VACATION IS TO SPEND TIME TOGETHER, AND YOUR DOODADS ALWAYS CAUSE MORE TROUBLE THAN THEY'RE WORTH.
WELL THAT WORKED OUT P-PRETTY--URRRRRP--GREAT, HUH?
IF WE HAD HIS PORTAL GUN, WE COULD'VE ESCAPED THIS NIGHTMARE DAYS AGO.
WELL, NEXT VACATION WE'LL JUST USE RICK'S PORTAL GUN TO GO UP HIS BUTT SINCE IT SEEMS LIKE THAT'S WHERE YOU WANT TO LIVE ANYWAY.
THAT DOESN'T MAKE ANY SENSE, JERRY.
YOU LIVE UP YOUR DAD'S BUTT!

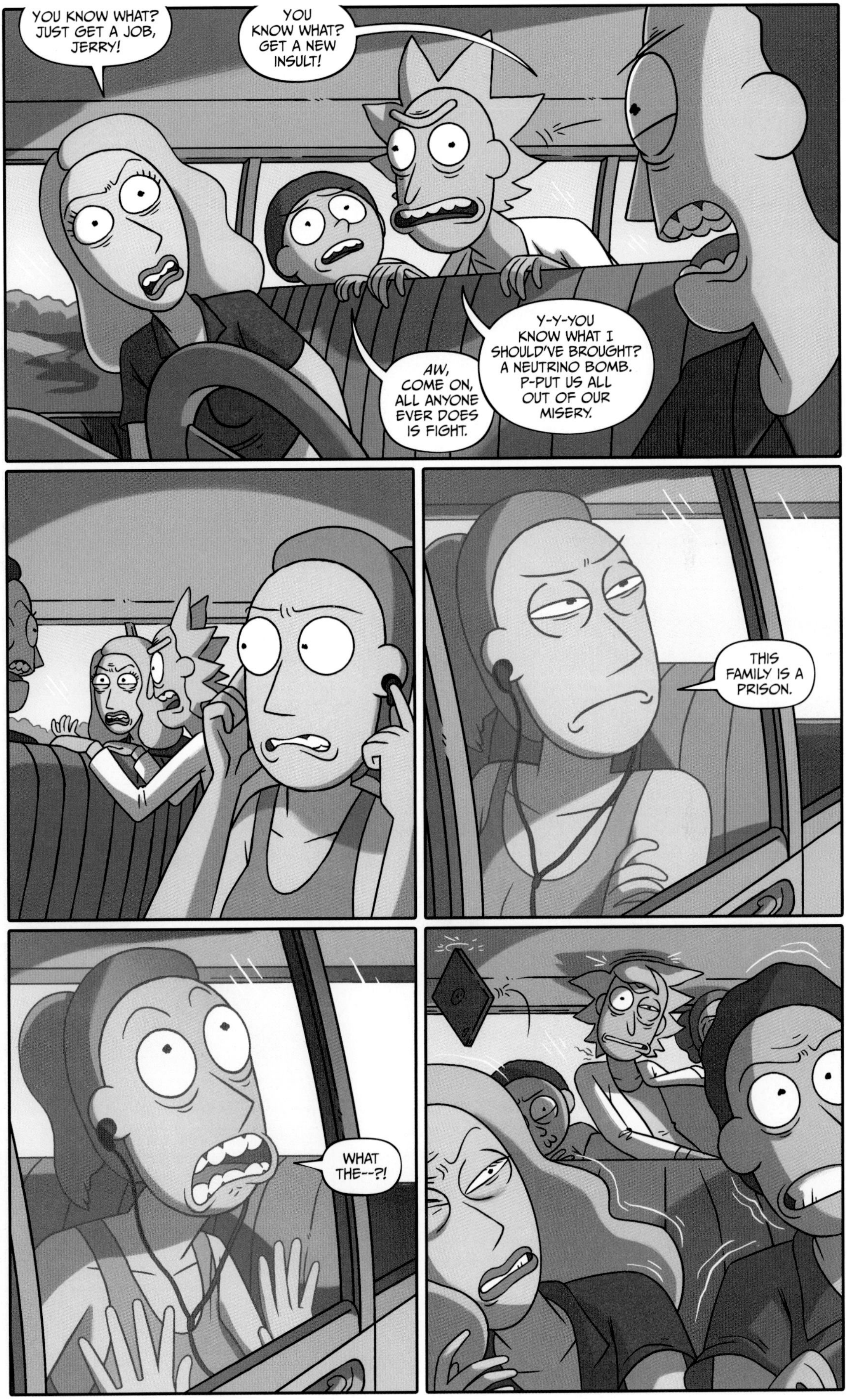
YOU KNOW WHAT? JUST GET A JOB, JERRY!
YOU KNOW WHAT? GET A NEW INSULT!
AW, COME ON, ALL ANYONE EVER DOES IS FIGHT.
Y-Y-YOU KNOW WHAT I SHOULD'VE BROUGHT? A NEUTRINO BOMB. P-PUT US ALL OUT OF OUR MISERY.
THIS FAMILY IS A PRISON.
WHAT THE--?!

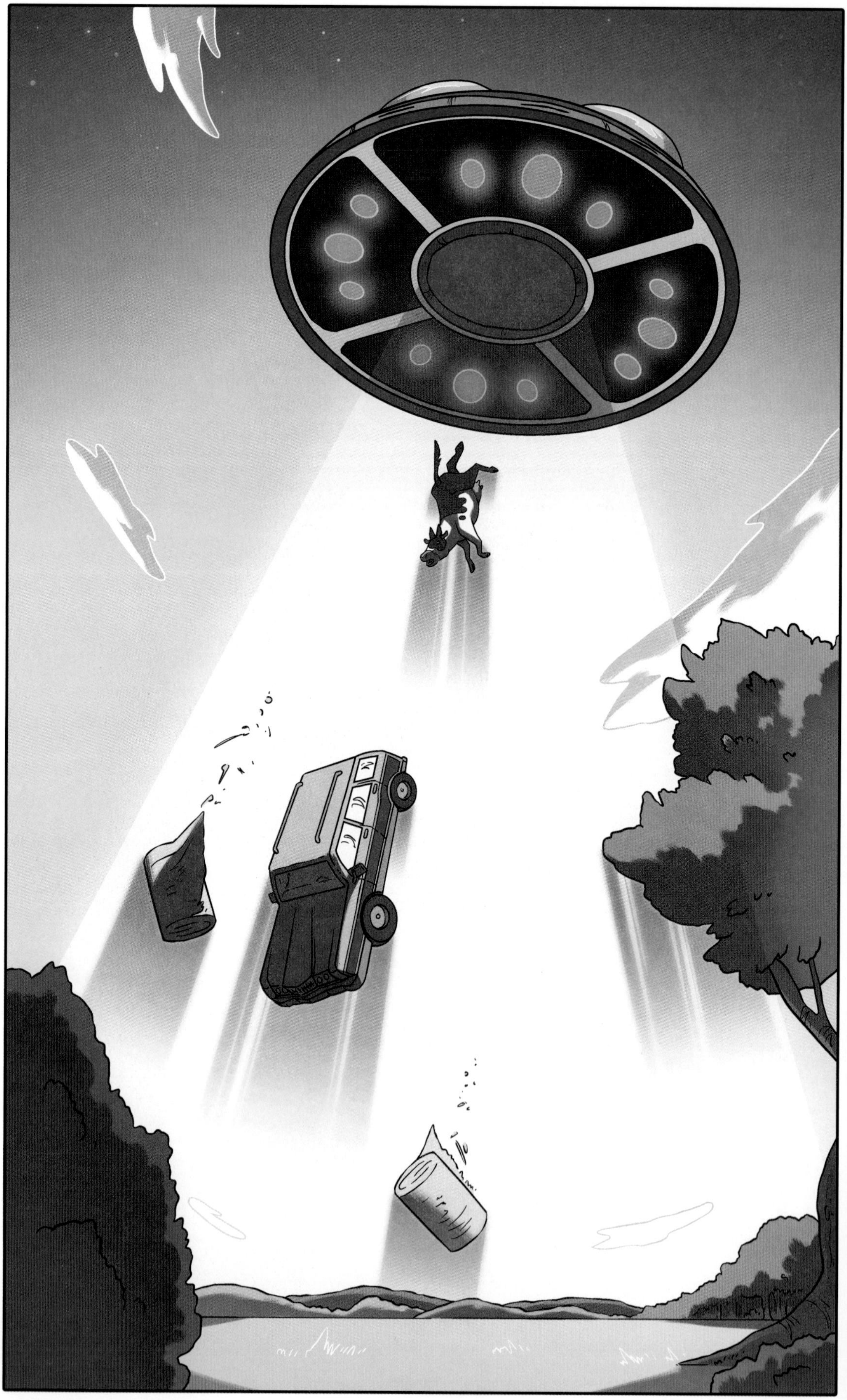

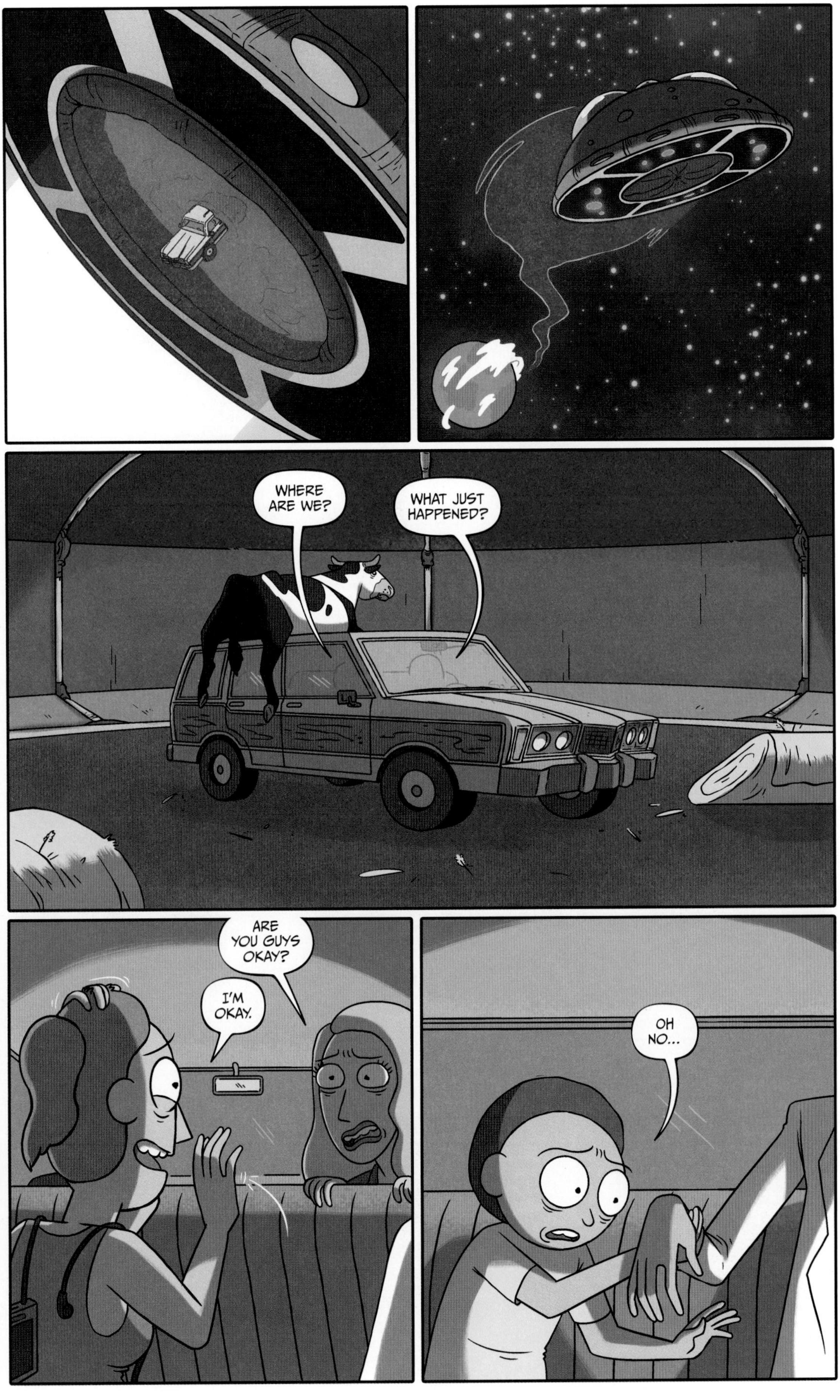
WHERE ARE WE?
WHAT JUST HAPPENED?
ARE YOU GUYS OKAY?
I'M OKAY.
OH NO...

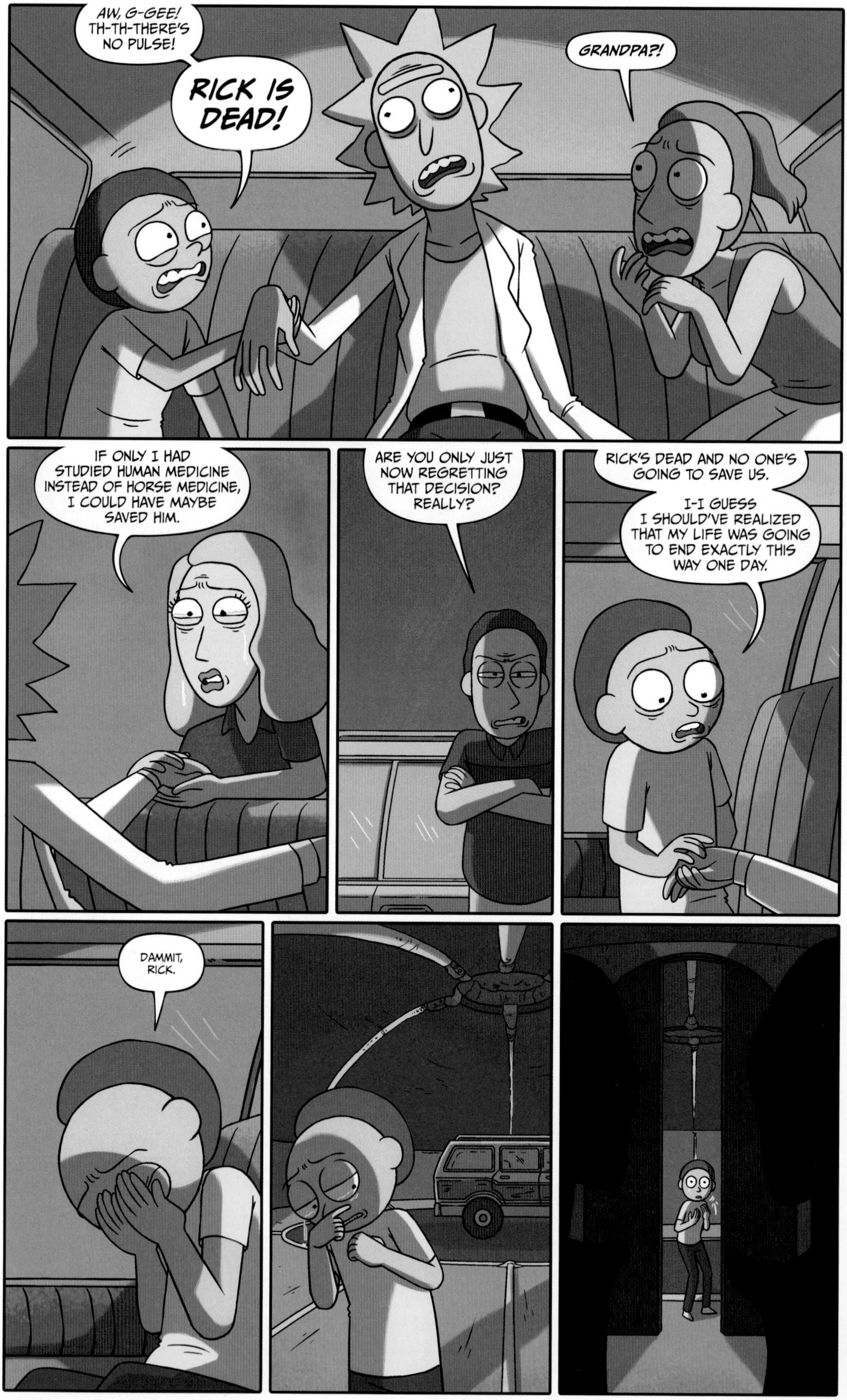
AW, G-GEE! TH-TH-THERE'S NO PULSE!
RICK IS DEAD!
GRANDPA?!
IF ONLY I HAD STUDIED HUMAN MEDICINE INSTEAD OF HORSE MEDICINE, I COULD HAVE MAYBE SAVED HIM.
ARE YOU ONLY JUST NOW REGRETTING THAT DECISION? REALLY?
RICK'S DEAD AND NO ONE'S GOING TO SAVE US.
I-I GUESS I SHOULD'VE REALIZED THAT MY LIFE WAS GOING TO END EXACTLY THIS WAY ONE DAY.
DAMMIT, RICK.

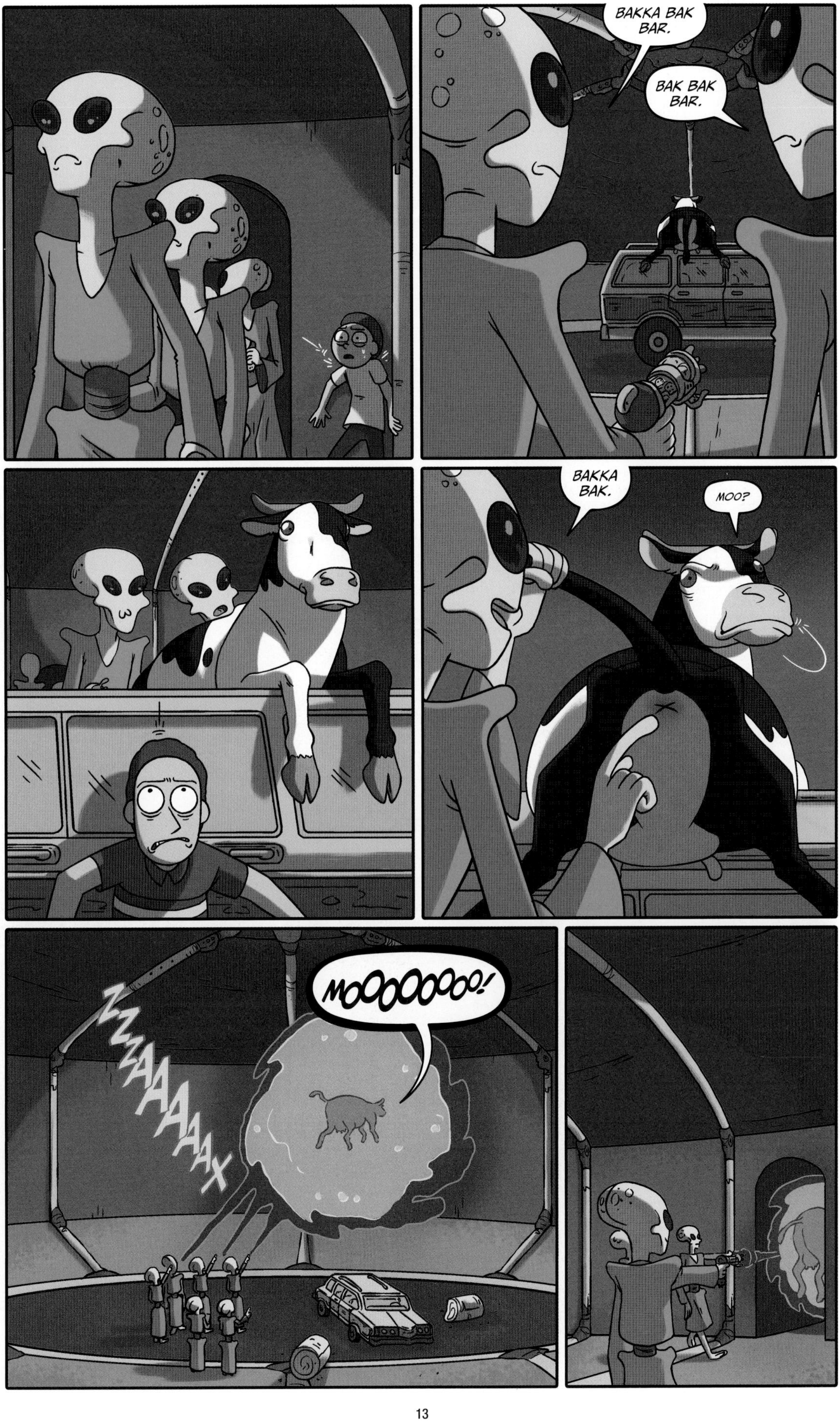
BAKKA BAK BAR.
BAK BAK BAR.
BAKKA BAK.
MOO?
MOOOOOOOO!
ZZZAAAAAAX

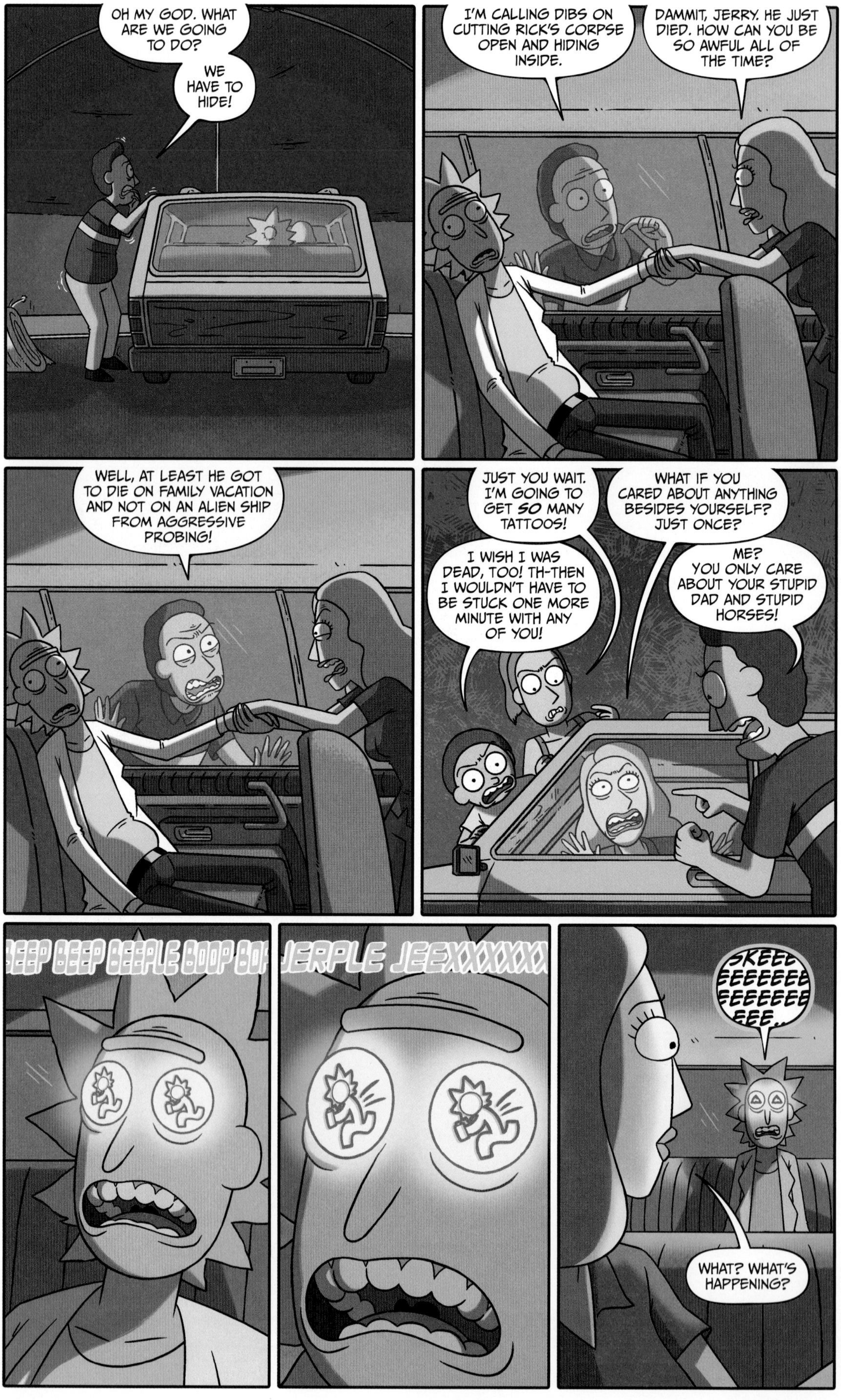
OH MY GOD. WHAT ARE WE GOING TO DO?
WE HAVE TO HIDE!
I'M CALLING DIBS ON CUTTING RICK'S CORPSE OPEN AND HIDING INSIDE.
DAMMIT, JERRY. HE JUST DIED. HOW CAN YOU BE SO AWFUL ALL OF THE TIME?
WELL, AT LEAST HE GOT TO DIE ON FAMILY VACATION AND NOT ON AN ALIEN SHIP FROM AGGRESSIVE PROBING!
JUST YOU WAIT. I'M GOING TO GET SO MANY TATTOOS!
WHAT IF YOU CARED ABOUT ANYTHING BESIDES YOURSELF? JUST ONCE?
I WISH I WAS DEAD, TOO! TH-THEN I WOULDN'T HAVE TO BE STUCK ONE MORE MINUTE WITH ANY OF YOU!
ME? YOU ONLY CARE ABOUT YOUR STUPID DAD AND STUPID HORSES!
BEEP BEEP BEEPLE BOOP BOP
JERPLE JEEXXXXXX
SKEEEEEEEEEEEEEEEEEEEEE...
WHAT? WHAT'S HAPPENING?

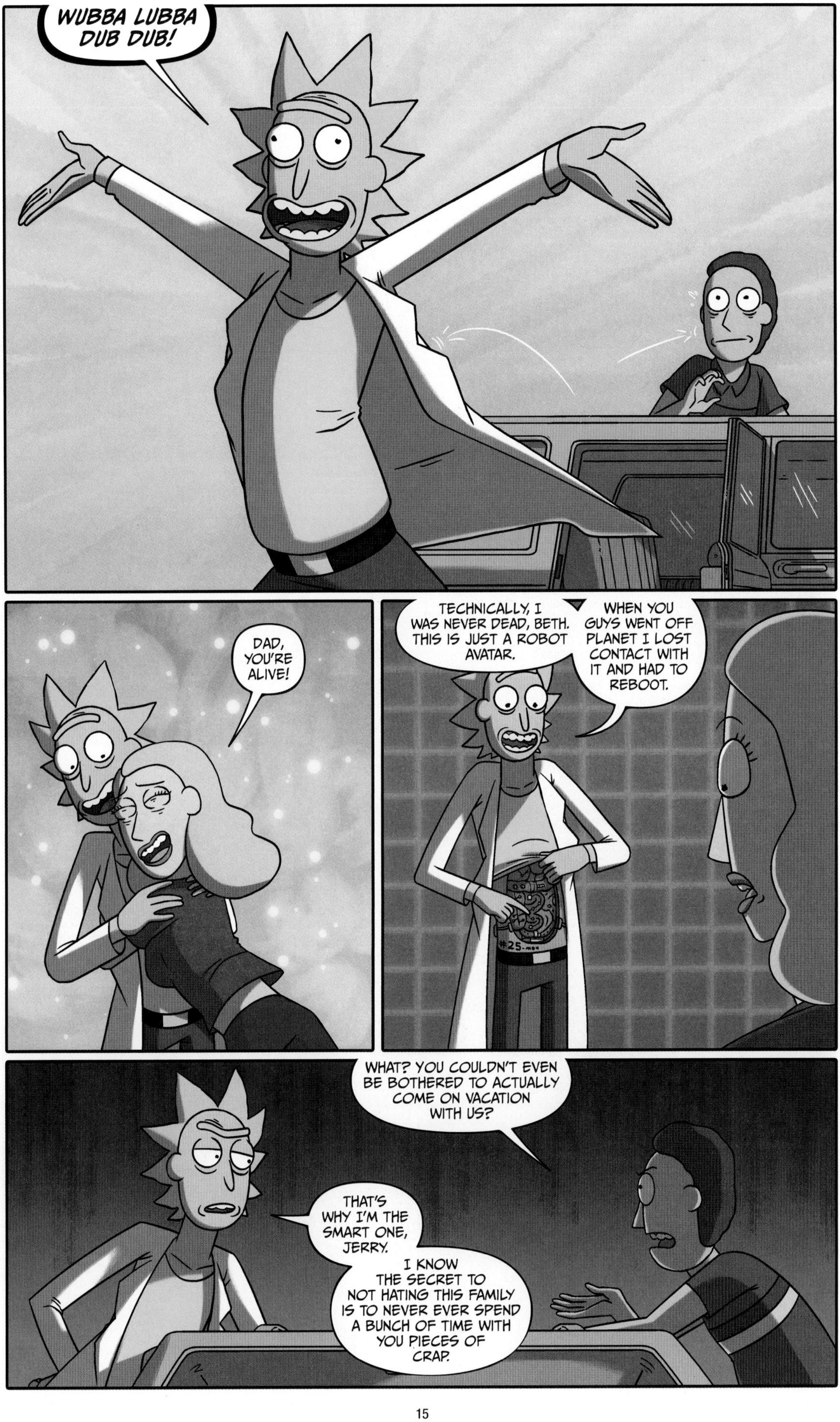
WUBBA LUBBA DUB DUB!
DAD, YOU'RE ALIVE!
TECHNICALLY, I WAS NEVER DEAD, BETH. THIS IS JUST A ROBOT AVATAR.
WHEN YOU GUYS WENT OFF PLANET I LOST CONTACT WITH IT AND HAD TO REBOOT.
#25
WHAT? YOU COULDN'T EVEN BE BOTHERED TO ACTUALLY COME ON VACATION WITH US?
THAT'S WHY I'M THE SMART ONE, JERRY.
I KNOW THE SECRET TO NOT HATING THIS FAMILY IS TO NEVER EVER SPEND A BUNCH OF TIME WITH YOU PIECES OF CRAP.

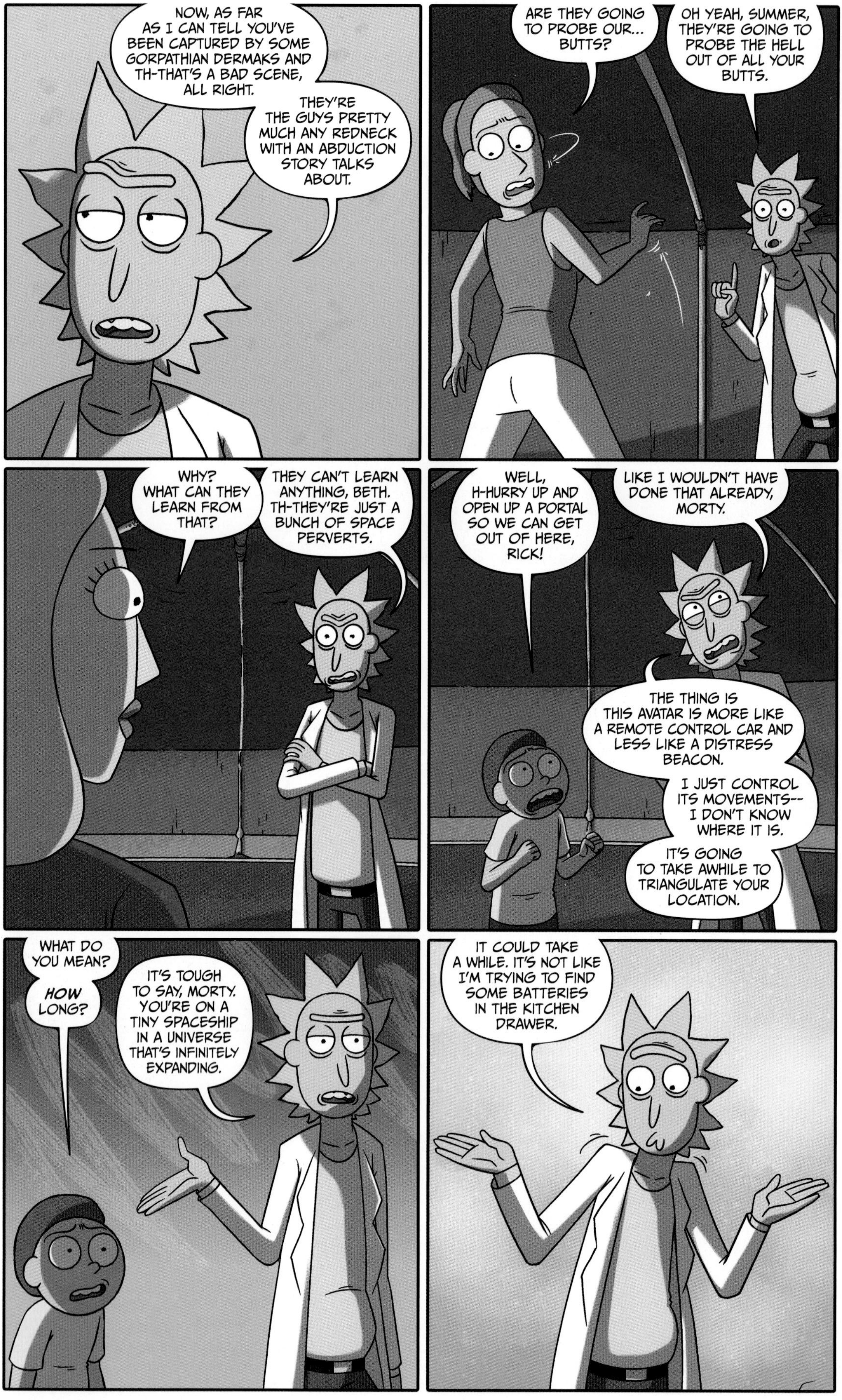
NOW, AS FAR AS I CAN TELL YOU'VE BEEN CAPTURED BY SOME GORPATHIAN DERMAKS AND TH-THAT'S A BAD SCENE, ALL RIGHT.
THEY'RE THE GUYS PRETTY MUCH ANY REDNECK WITH AN ABDUCTION STORY TALKS ABOUT.
ARE THEY GOING TO PROBE OUR... BUTTS?
OH YEAH, SUMMER, THEY'RE GOING TO PROBE THE HELL OUT OF ALL YOUR BUTTS.
WHY? WHAT CAN THEY LEARN FROM THAT?
THEY CAN'T LEARN ANYTHING, BETH. TH-THEY'RE JUST A BUNCH OF SPACE PERVERTS.
WELL, H-HURRY UP AND OPEN UP A PORTAL SO WE CAN GET OUT OF HERE, RICK!
LIKE I WOULDN'T HAVE DONE THAT ALREADY, MORTY.
THE THING IS THIS AVATAR IS MORE LIKE A REMOTE CONTROL CAR AND LESS LIKE A DISTRESS BEACON.
I JUST CONTROL ITS MOVEMENTS-- I DON'T KNOW WHERE IT IS.
IT'S GOING TO TAKE AWHILE TO TRIANGULATE YOUR LOCATION.
WHAT DO YOU MEAN?
HOW LONG?
IT'S TOUGH TO SAY, MORTY. YOU'RE ON A TINY SPACESHIP IN A UNIVERSE THAT'S INFINITELY EXPANDING.
IT COULD TAKE A WHILE. IT'S NOT LIKE I'M TRYING TO FIND SOME BATTERIES IN THE KITCHEN DRAWER.

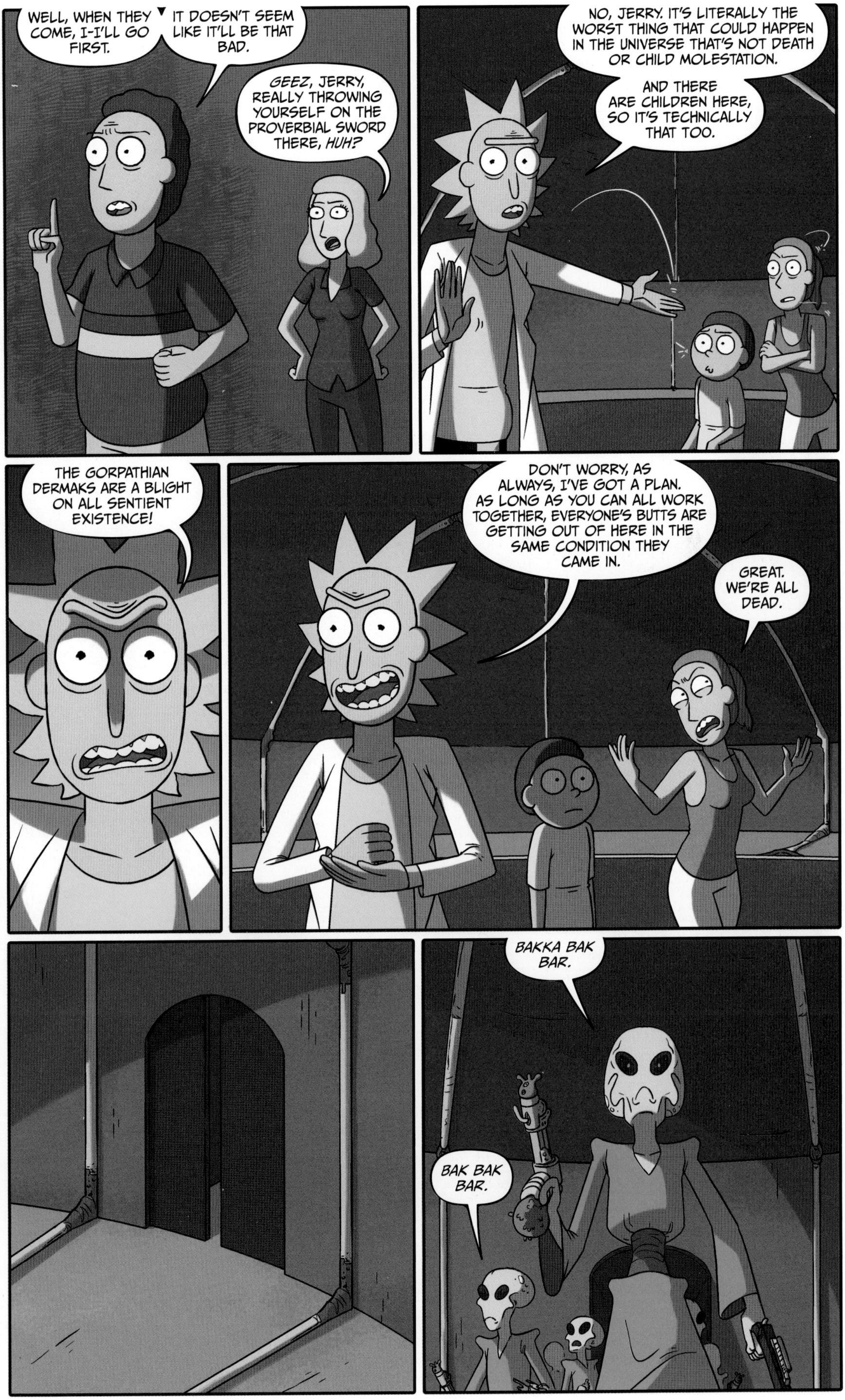

WELL, WHEN THEY COME, I-I'LL GO FIRST.
IT DOESN'T SEEM LIKE IT'LL BE THAT BAD.
GEEZ, JERRY, REALLY THROWING YOURSELF ON THE PROVERBIAL SWORD THERE, *HUH?*
NO, JERRY. IT'S LITERALLY THE WORST THING THAT COULD HAPPEN IN THE UNIVERSE THAT'S NOT DEATH OR CHILD MOLESTATION.
AND THERE ARE CHILDREN HERE, SO IT'S TECHNICALLY THAT TOO.
THE GORPATHIAN DERMAKS ARE A BLIGHT ON ALL SENTIENT EXISTENCE!
DON'T WORRY, AS ALWAYS, I'VE GOT A PLAN. AS LONG AS YOU CAN ALL WORK TOGETHER, EVERYONE'S BUTTS ARE GETTING OUT OF HERE IN THE SAME CONDITION THEY CAME IN.
GREAT. WE'RE ALL DEAD.
BAKKA BAK BAR.
BAK BAK BAR.

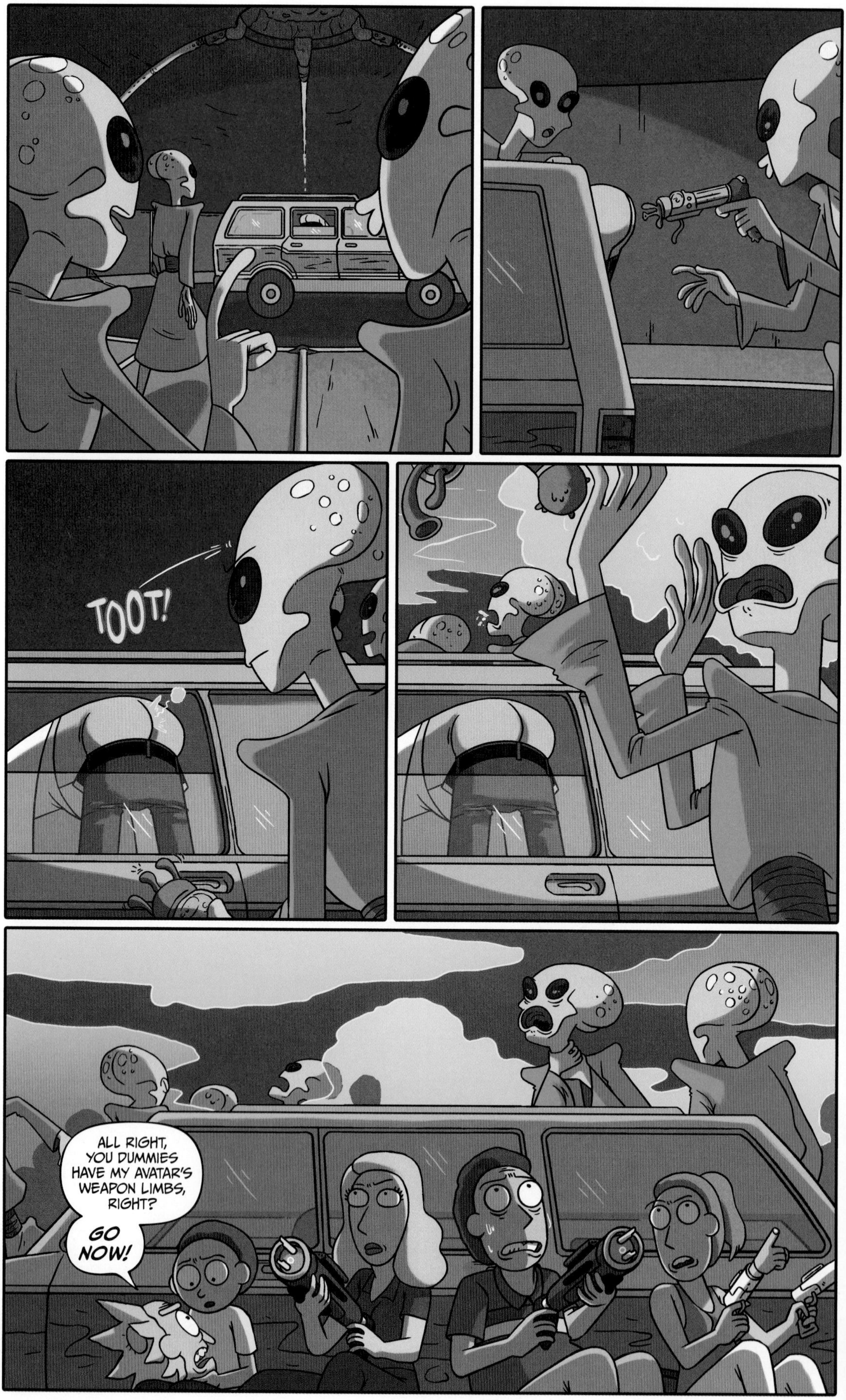
TOOT!
ALL RIGHT, YOU DUMMIES HAVE MY AVATAR'S WEAPON LIMBS, RIGHT?
GO NOW!

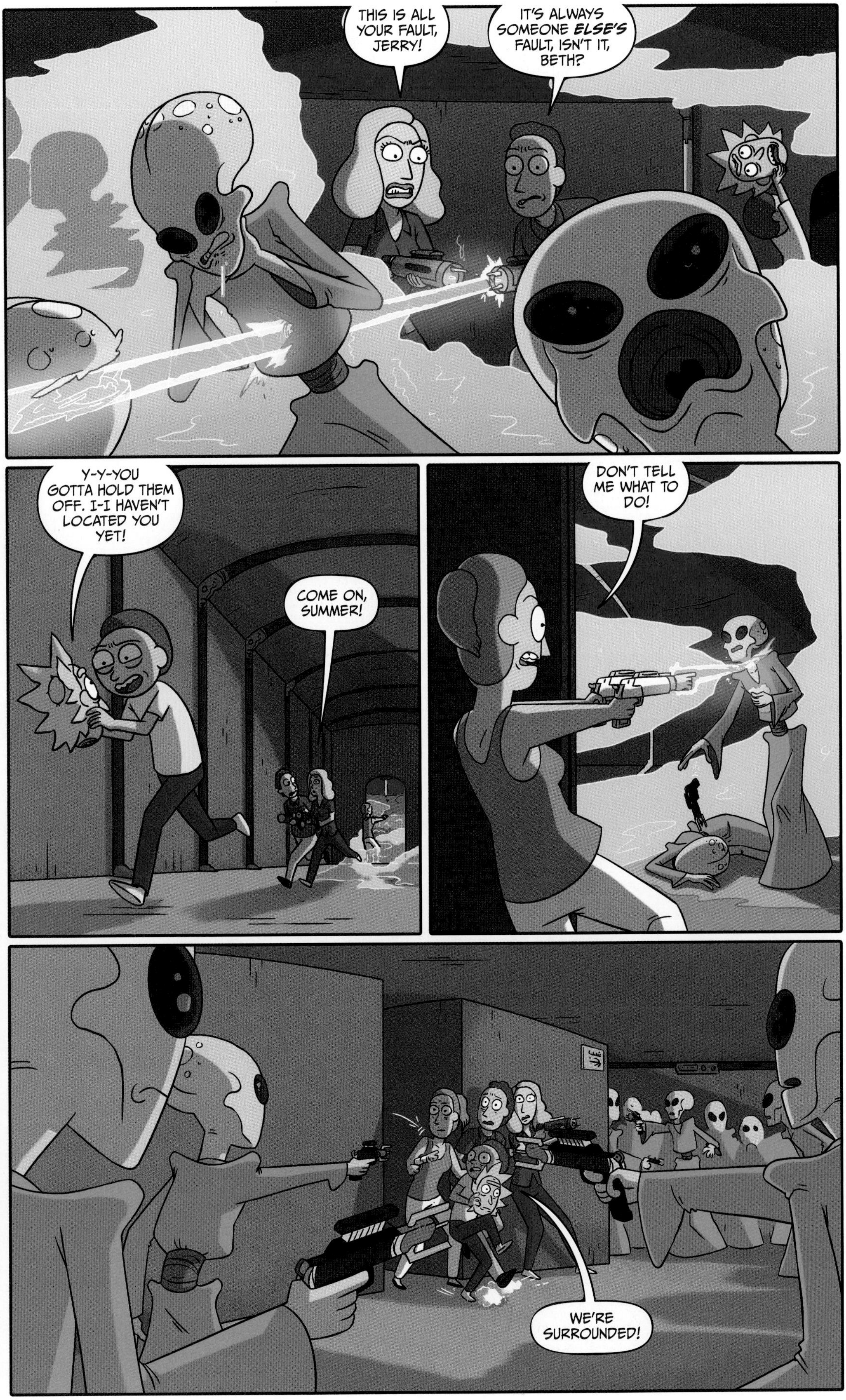
THIS IS ALL YOUR FAULT, JERRY!
IT'S ALWAYS SOMEONE ELSE'S FAULT, ISN'T IT, BETH?
Y-Y-YOU GOTTA HOLD THEM OFF. I-I HAVEN'T LOCATED YOU YET!
COME ON, SUMMER!
DON'T TELL ME WHAT TO DO!
WE'RE SURROUNDED!

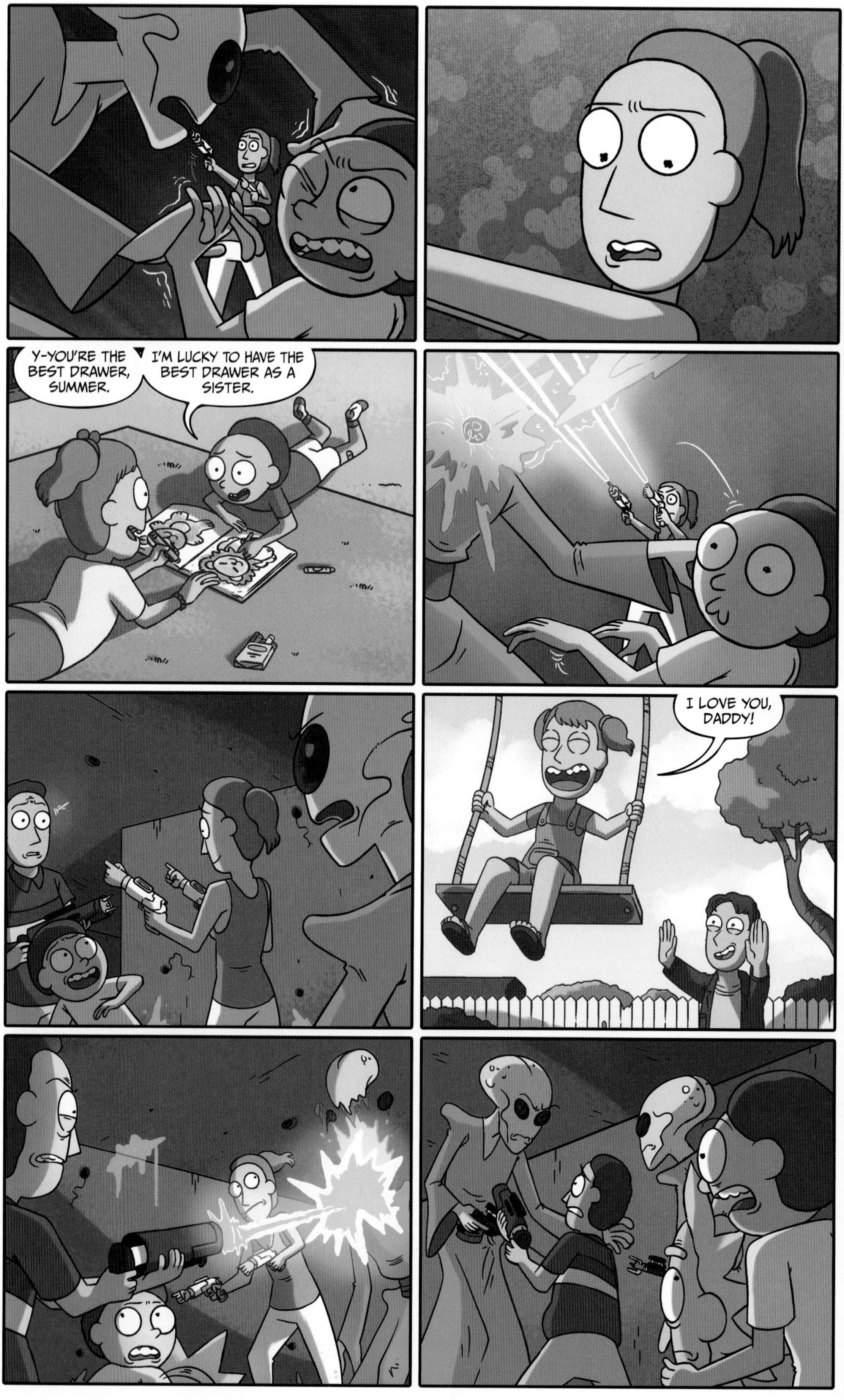
Y-YOU'RE THE BEST DRAWER, SUMMER.
I'M LUCKY TO HAVE THE BEST DRAWER AS A SISTER.
I LOVE YOU, DADDY!

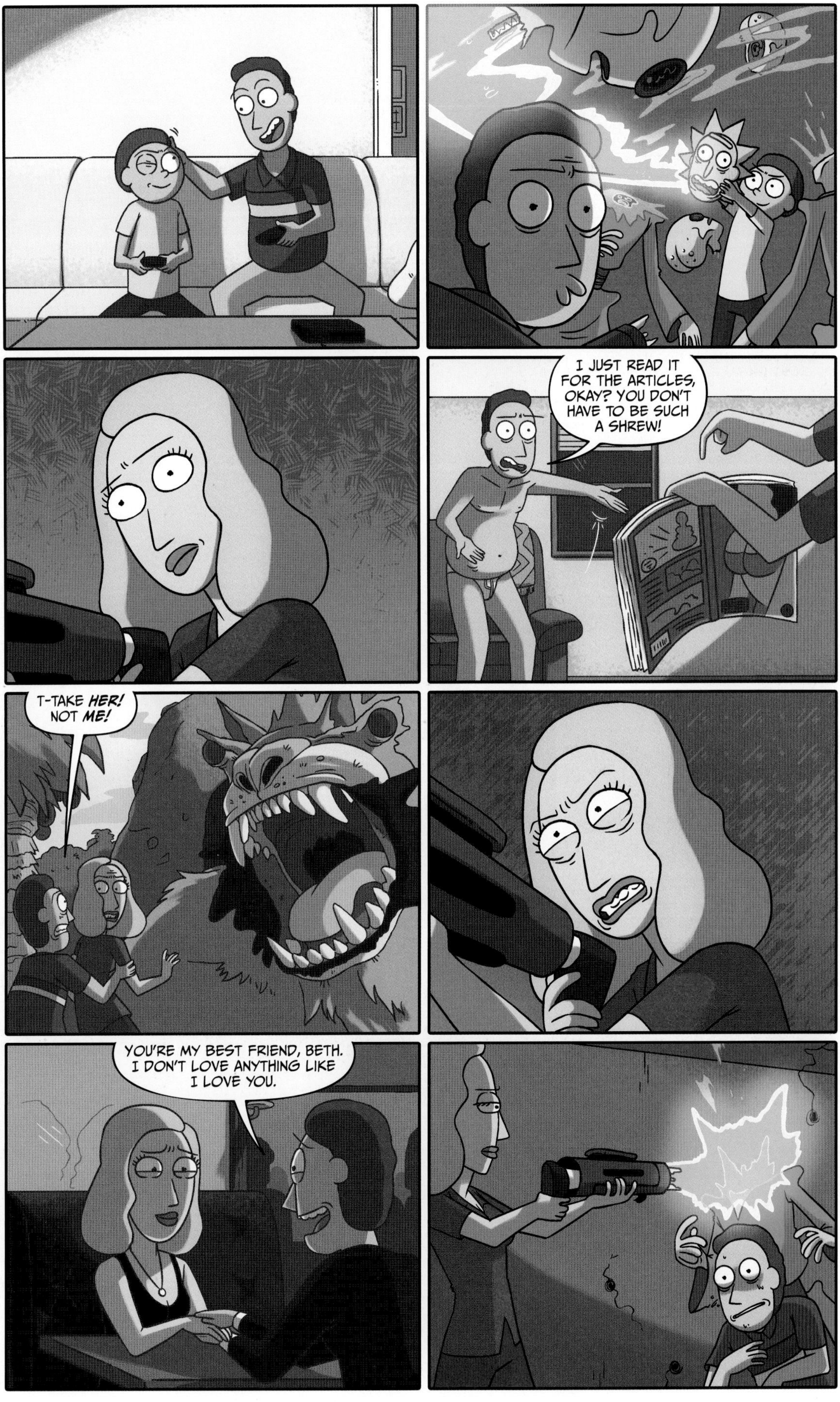
I JUST READ IT FOR THE ARTICLES, OKAY? YOU DON'T HAVE TO BE SUCH A SHREW!
T-TAKE HER! NOT ME!
YOU'RE MY BEST FRIEND, BETH. I DON'T LOVE ANYTHING LIKE I LOVE YOU.

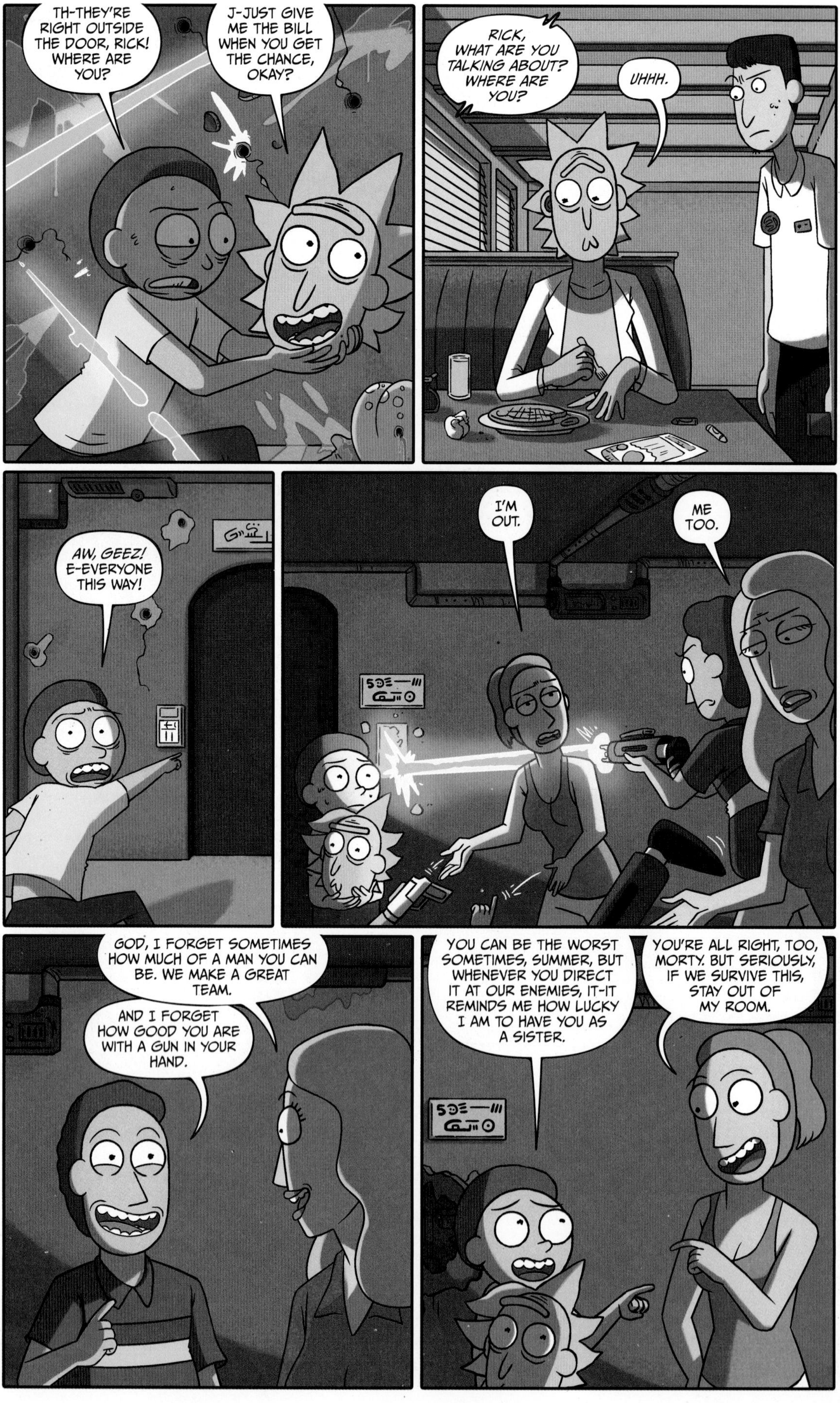
TH-THEY'RE RIGHT OUTSIDE THE DOOR, RICK! WHERE ARE YOU?
J-JUST GIVE ME THE BILL WHEN YOU GET THE CHANCE, OKAY?
RICK, WHAT ARE YOU TALKING ABOUT? WHERE ARE YOU?
UHHH.
AW, GEEZ! E-EVERYONE THIS WAY!
I'M OUT.
ME TOO.
GOD, I FORGET SOMETIMES HOW MUCH OF A MAN YOU CAN BE. WE MAKE A GREAT TEAM.
AND I FORGET HOW GOOD YOU ARE WITH A GUN IN YOUR HAND.
YOU CAN BE THE WORST SOMETIMES, SUMMER, BUT WHENEVER YOU DIRECT IT AT OUR ENEMIES, IT-IT REMINDS ME HOW LUCKY I AM TO HAVE YOU AS A SISTER.
YOU'RE ALL RIGHT, TOO, MORTY. BUT SERIOUSLY, IF WE SURVIVE THIS, STAY OUT OF MY ROOM.

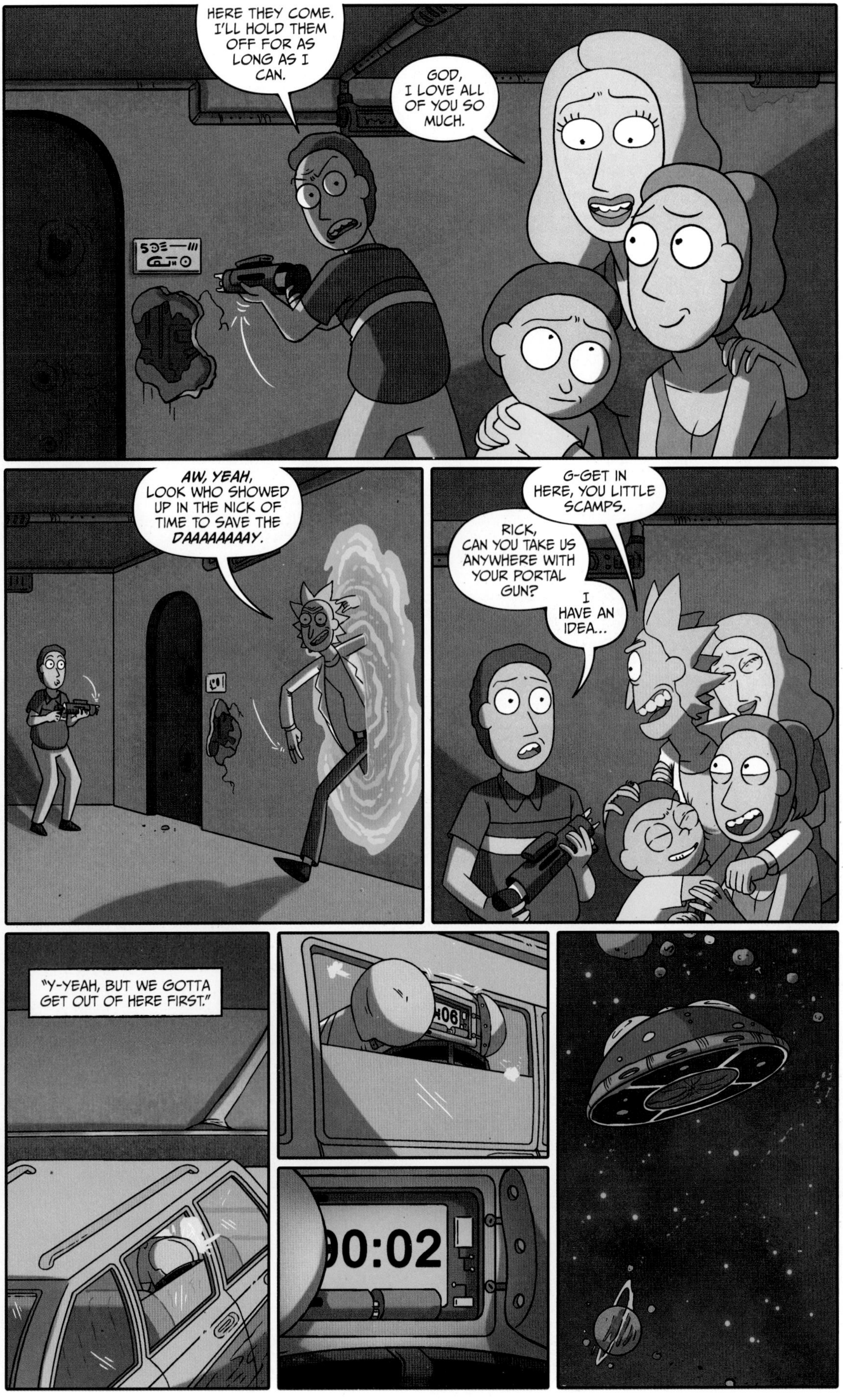
HERE THEY COME. I'LL HOLD THEM OFF FOR AS LONG AS I CAN.
GOD, I LOVE ALL OF YOU SO MUCH.
AW, YEAH, LOOK WHO SHOWED UP IN THE NICK OF TIME TO SAVE THE *DAAAAAAAAY.*
G-GET IN HERE, YOU LITTLE SCAMPS.
RICK, CAN YOU TAKE US ANYWHERE WITH YOUR PORTAL GUN?
I HAVE AN IDEA...
"Y-YEAH, BUT WE GOTTA GET OUT OF HERE FIRST."
00:02

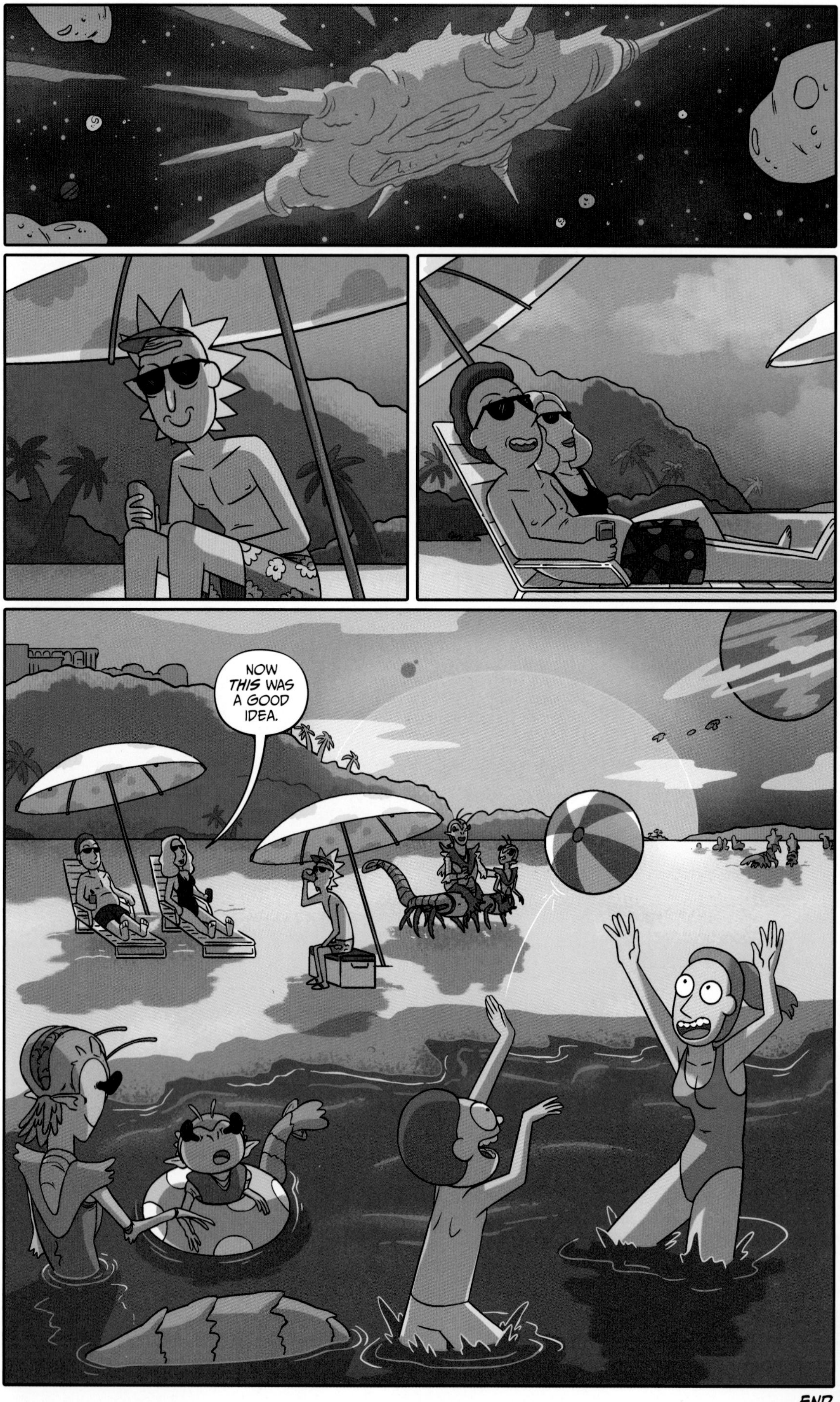
NOW *THIS* WAS A GOOD IDEA.

END.

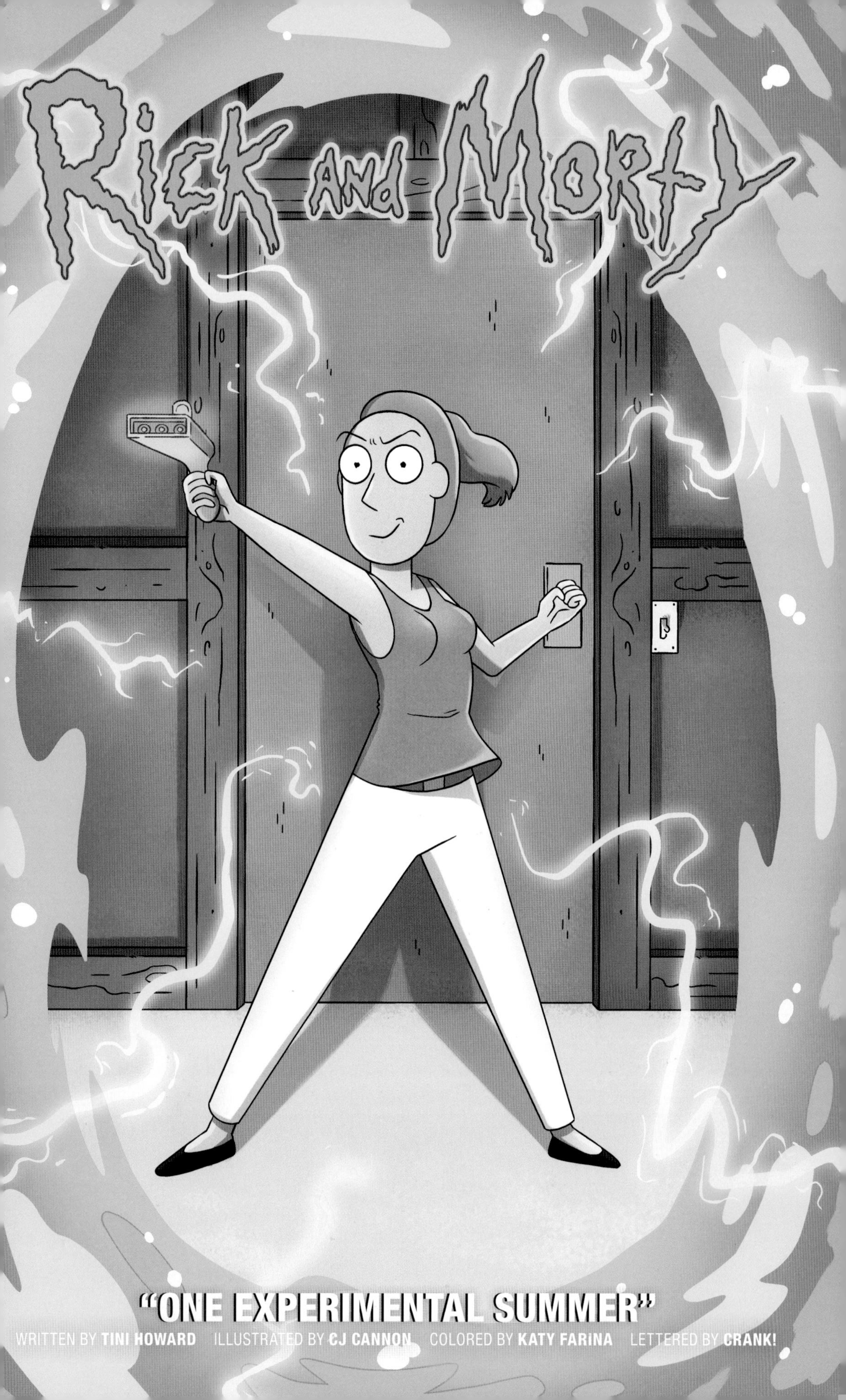
Rick and Morty

"ONE EXPERIMENTAL SUMMER"

WRITTEN BY **TINI HOWARD** ILLUSTRATED BY **CJ CANNON** COLORED BY **KATY FARINA** LETTERED BY **CRANK!**

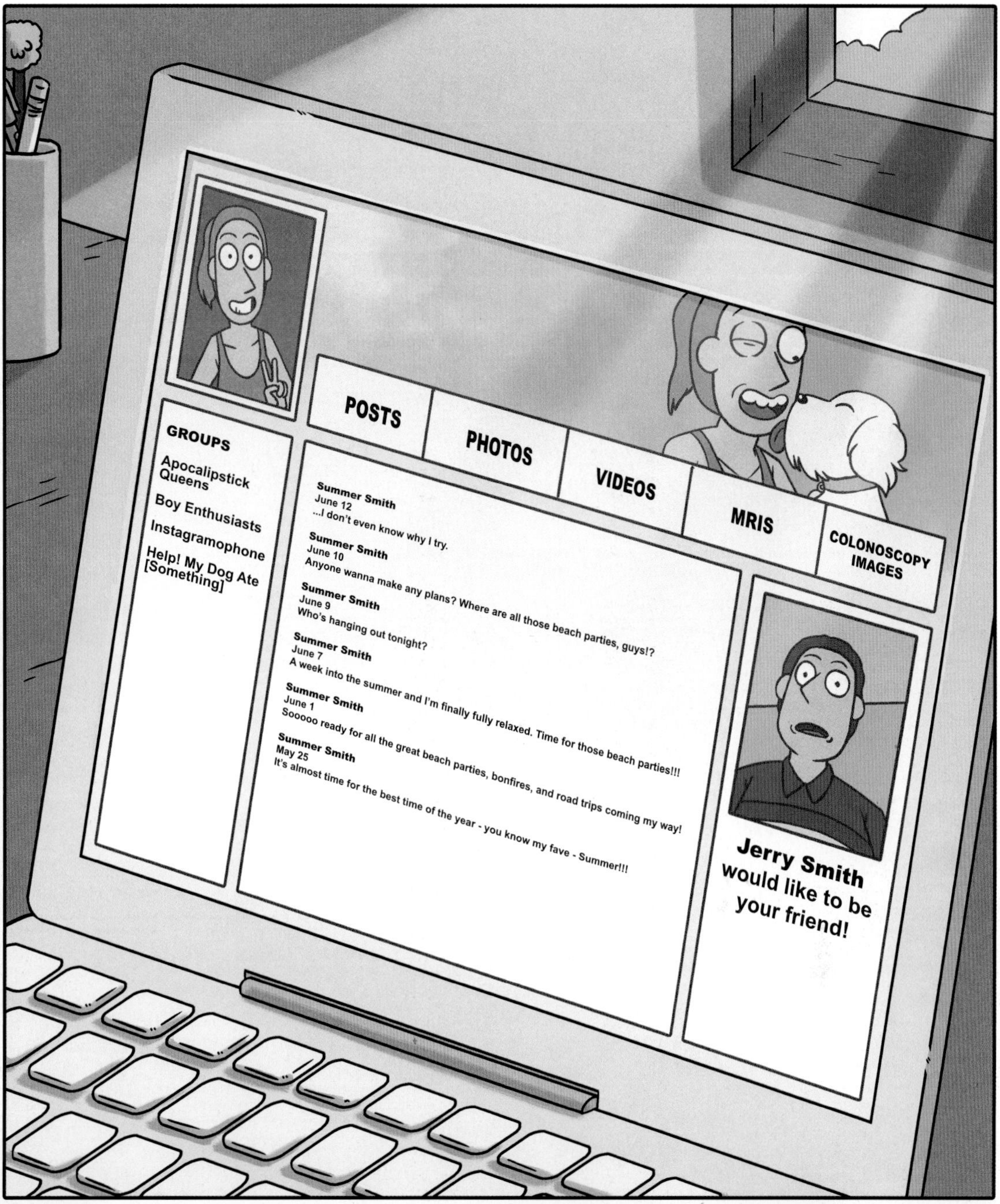
POSTS
PHOTOS
VIDEOS
MRIS
COLONOSCOPY IMAGES
GROUPS
Apocalipstick Queens
Boy Enthusiasts
Instagramophone
Help! My Dog Ate [Something]
Summer Smith
June 12
...I don't even know why I try.
Summer Smith
June 10
Anyone wanna make any plans? Where are all those beach parties, guys!?
Summer Smith
June 9
Who's hanging out tonight?
Summer Smith
June 7
A week into the summer and I'm finally fully relaxed. Time for those beach parties!!!
Summer Smith
June 1
Sooooo ready for all the great beach parties, bonfires, and road trips coming my way!
Summer Smith
May 25
It's almost time for the best time of the year - you know my fave - Summer!!!
Jerry Smith would like to be your friend!

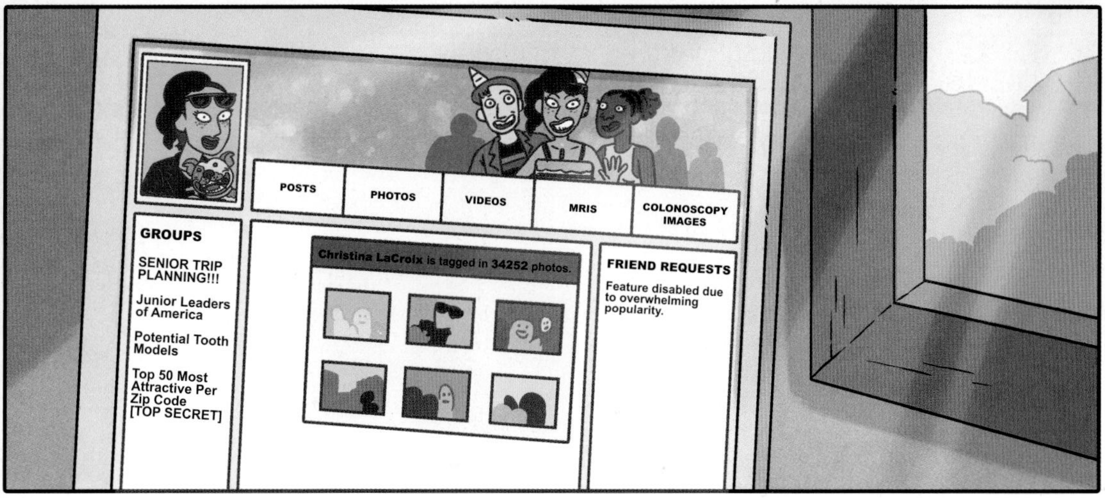
POSTS
PHOTOS
VIDEOS
MRIS
COLONOSCOPY IMAGES
GROUPS
SENIOR TRIP PLANNING!!!
Junior Leaders of America
Potential Tooth Models
Top 50 Most Attractive Per Zip Code [TOP SECRET]
Christina LaCroix is tagged in 34252 photos.
FRIEND REQUESTS
Feature disabled due to overwhelming popularity.

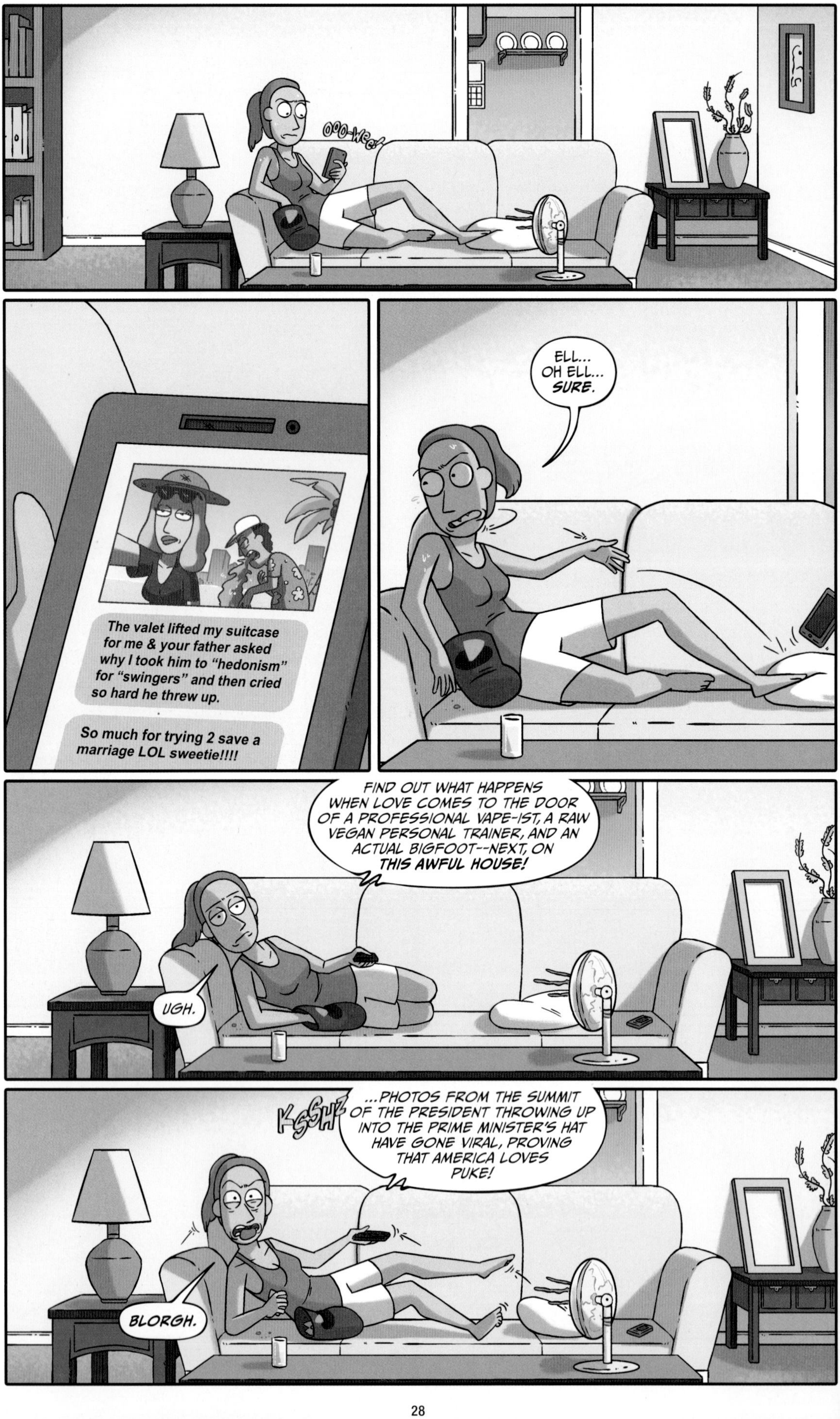
OOO-WEE!
The valet lifted my suitcase for me & your father asked why I took him to "hedonism" for "swingers" and then cried so hard he threw up.
So much for trying 2 save a marriage LOL sweetie!!!!
ELL... OH ELL... SURE.
FIND OUT WHAT HAPPENS WHEN LOVE COMES TO THE DOOR OF A PROFESSIONAL VAPE-IST, A RAW VEGAN PERSONAL TRAINER, AND AN ACTUAL BIGFOOT--NEXT, ON THIS AWFUL HOUSE!
UGH.
KSSHZ
...PHOTOS FROM THE SUMMIT OF THE PRESIDENT THROWING UP INTO THE PRIME MINISTER'S HAT HAVE GONE VIRAL, PROVING THAT AMERICA LOVES PUKE!
BLORGH.

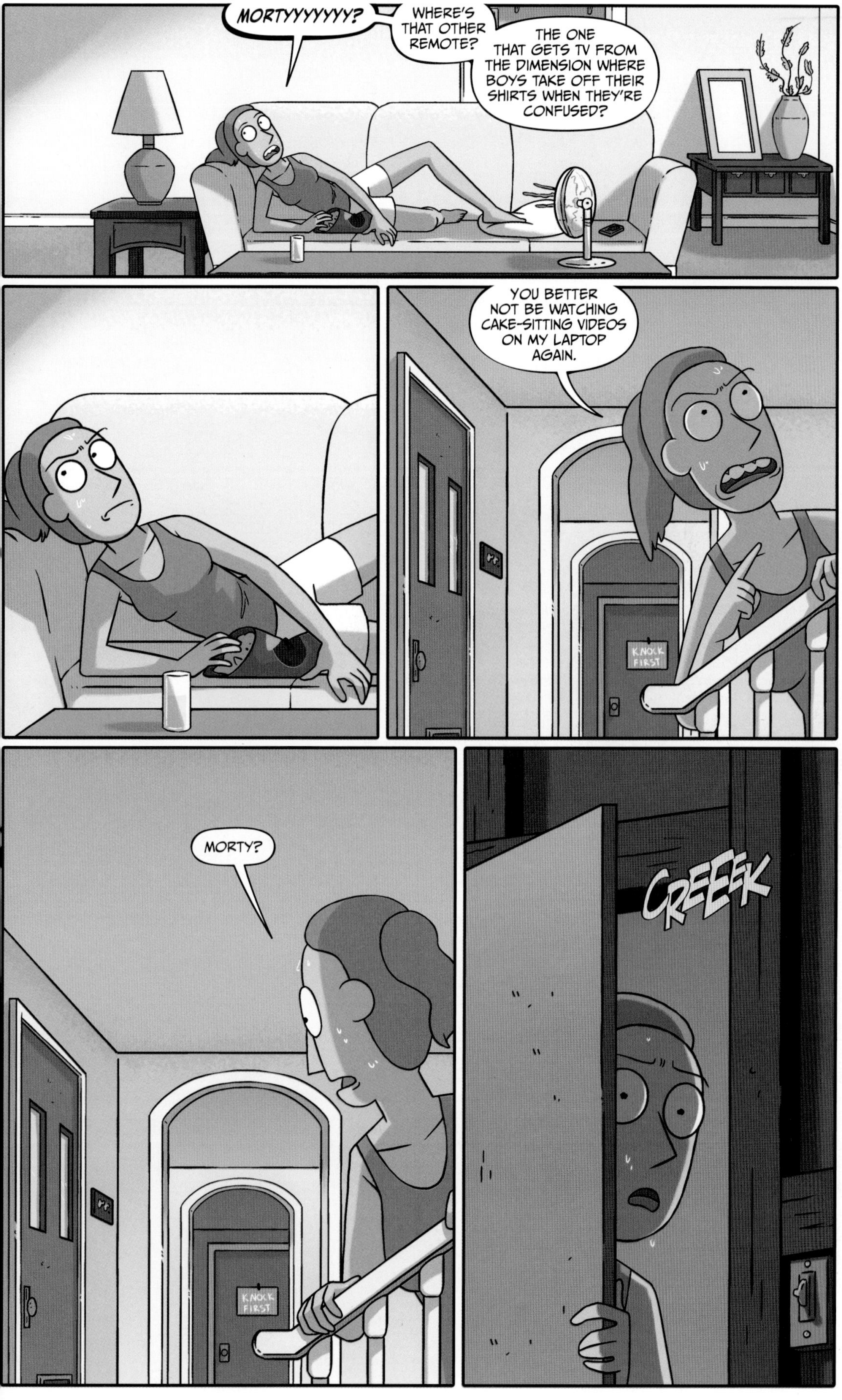
MORTYYYYYYY?
WHERE'S THAT OTHER REMOTE?
THE ONE THAT GETS TV FROM THE DIMENSION WHERE BOYS TAKE OFF THEIR SHIRTS WHEN THEY'RE CONFUSED?
YOU BETTER NOT BE WATCHING CAKE-SITTING VIDEOS ON MY LAPTOP AGAIN.
KNOCK FIRST
MORTY?
KNOCK FIRST
CREEEK

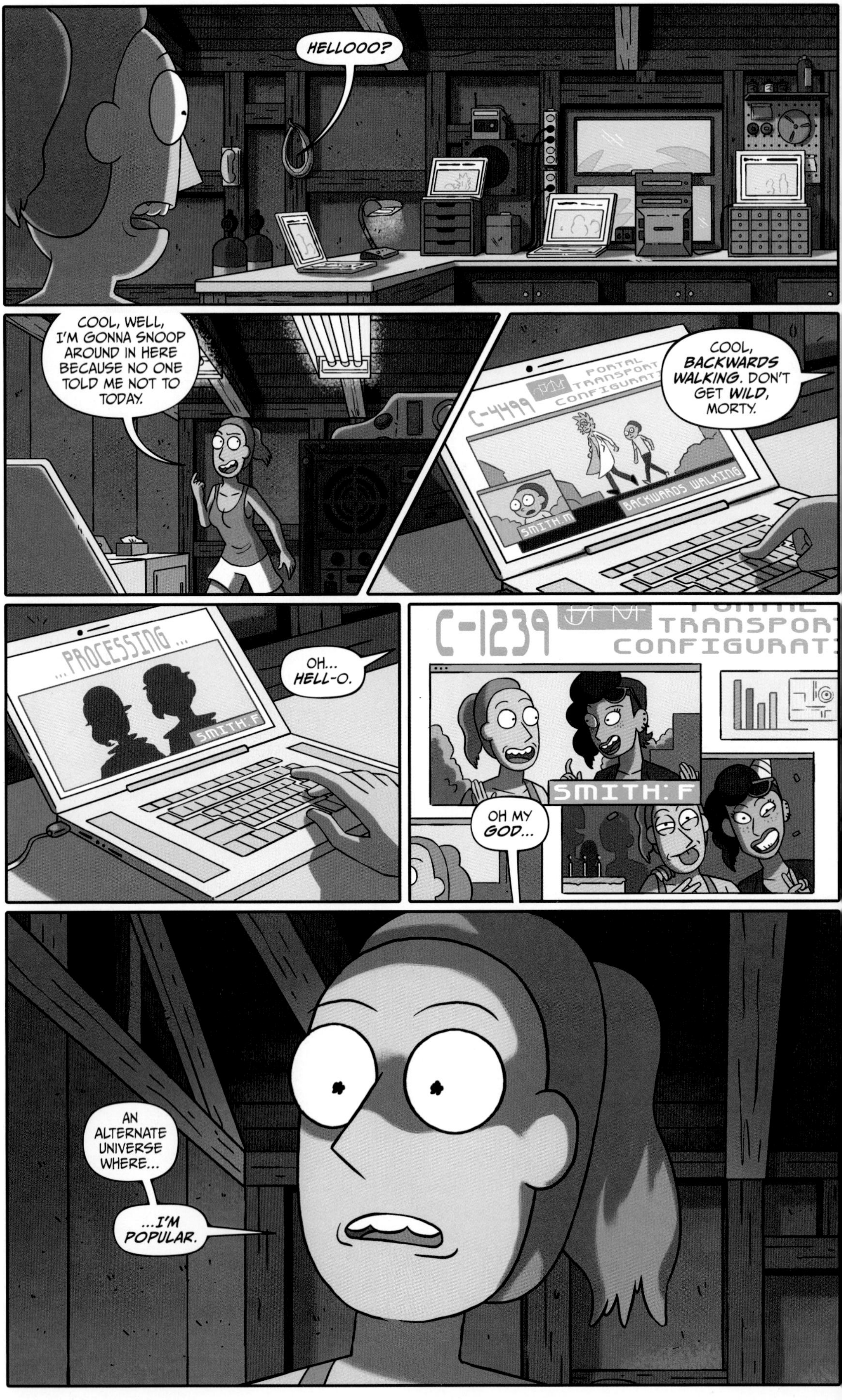
HELLOOO?
COOL, WELL, I'M GONNA SNOOP AROUND IN HERE BECAUSE NO ONE TOLD ME NOT TO TODAY.
C-4499
PORTAL TRANSPORT CONFIGURATI
SMITH.M
BACKWARDS WALKING
COOL, BACKWARDS WALKING. DON'T GET WILD, MORTY.
...PROCESSING...
SMITH: F
OH... HELL-O.
C-1239
TRANSPORT CONFIGURATI
SMITH: F
OH MY GOD...
AN ALTERNATE UNIVERSE WHERE...
...I'M POPULAR.

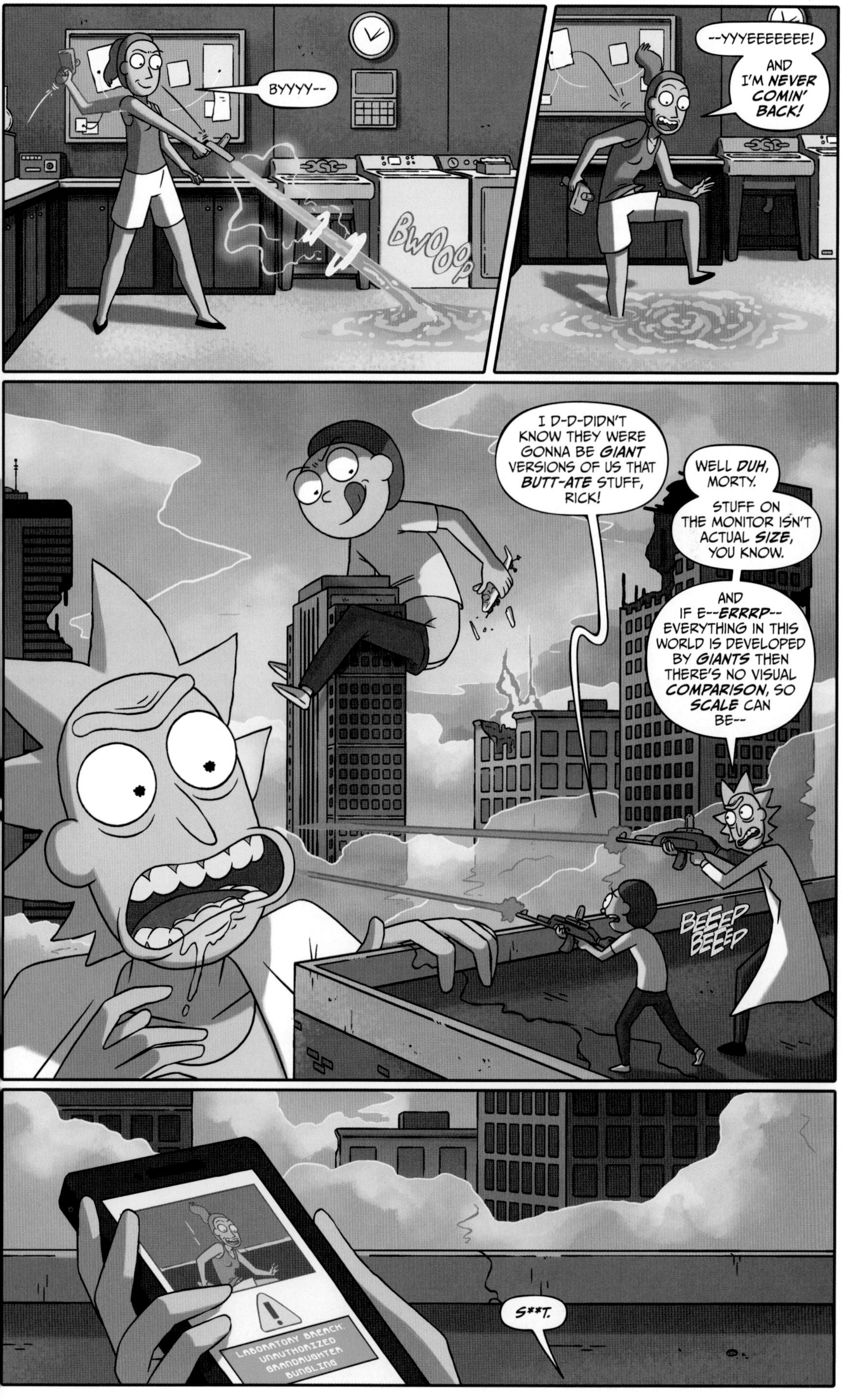
BYYYY--
--YYYEEEEEEE!
AND I'M NEVER COMIN' BACK!
BWOOOP
I D-D-DIDN'T KNOW THEY WERE GONNA BE GIANT VERSIONS OF US THAT BUTT-ATE STUFF, RICK!
WELL DUH, MORTY.
STUFF ON THE MONITOR ISN'T ACTUAL SIZE, YOU KNOW.
AND IF E--ERRRP--EVERYTHING IN THIS WORLD IS DEVELOPED BY GIANTS THEN THERE'S NO VISUAL COMPARISON, SO SCALE CAN BE--
BEEEP BEEEP
LABORATORY BREACH: UNAUTHORIZED GRANDDAUGHTER BUNGLING
S**T.

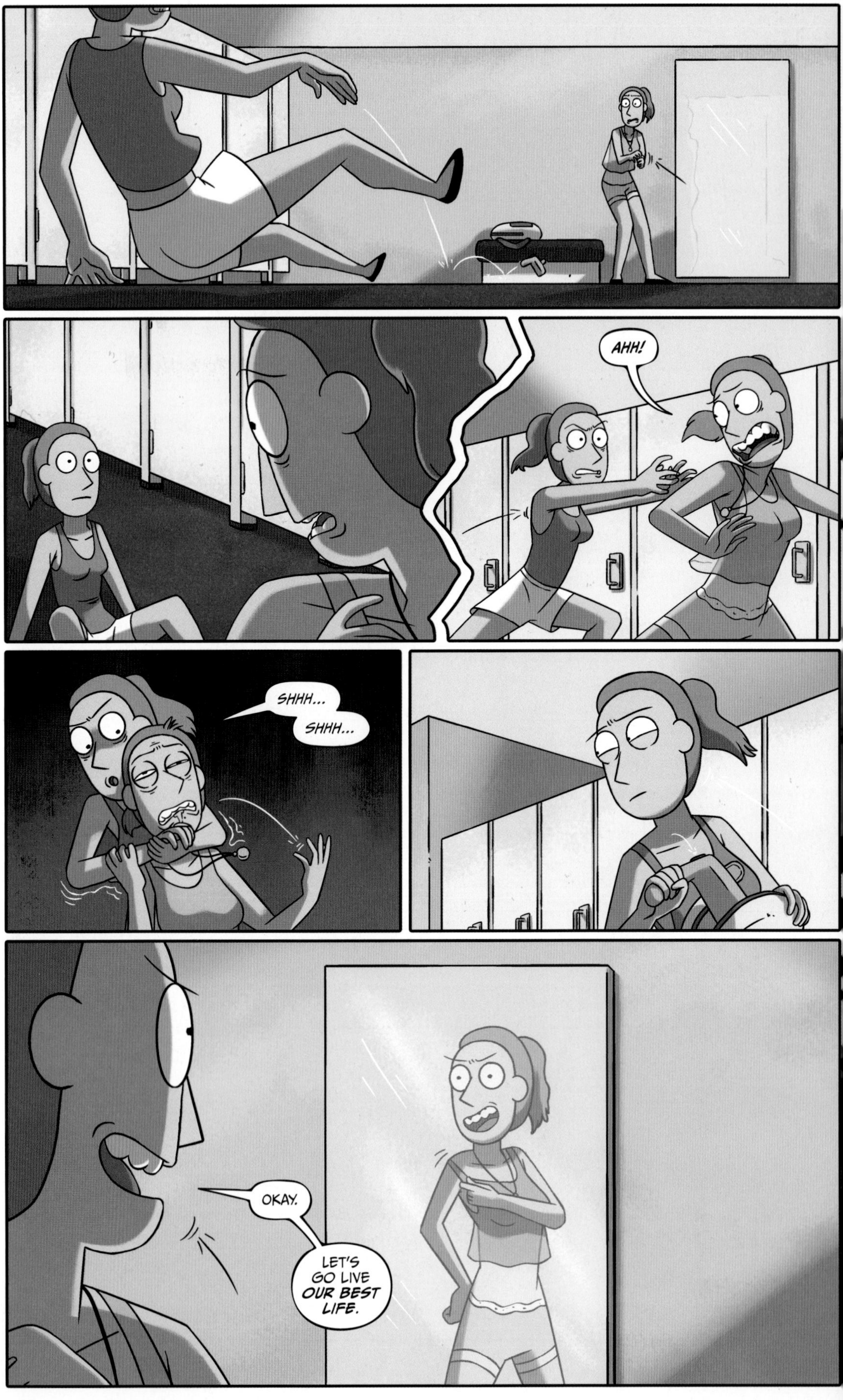
AHH!
SHHH...
SHHH...
OKAY.
LET'S GO LIVE OUR BEST LIFE.

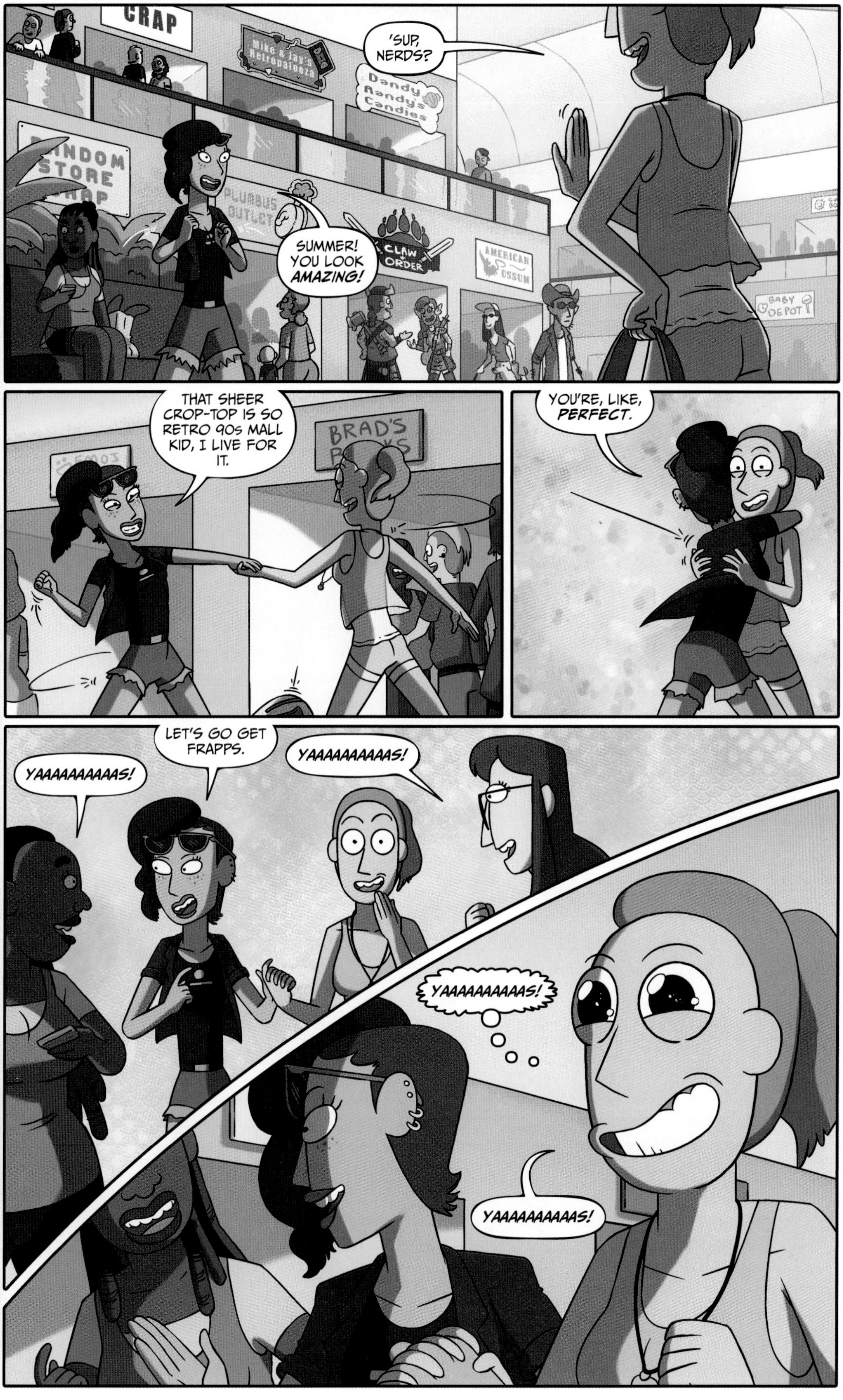
CRAP
Mike & Jay's Retropalooza
'SUP, NERDS?
Dandy Randy's Candies
RANDOM STORE CRAP
PLUMBUS OUTLET
SUMMER! YOU LOOK *AMAZING!*
CLAW + ORDER
AMERICAN OSSUM
BABY DEPOT
THAT SHEER CROP-TOP IS SO RETRO 90s MALL KID, I LIVE FOR IT.
BRAD'S
YOU'RE, LIKE, *PERFECT.*
LET'S GO GET FRAPPS.
YAAAAAAAAAAS!
YAAAAAAAAAAS!
YAAAAAAAAAAS!
YAAAAAAAAAAS!

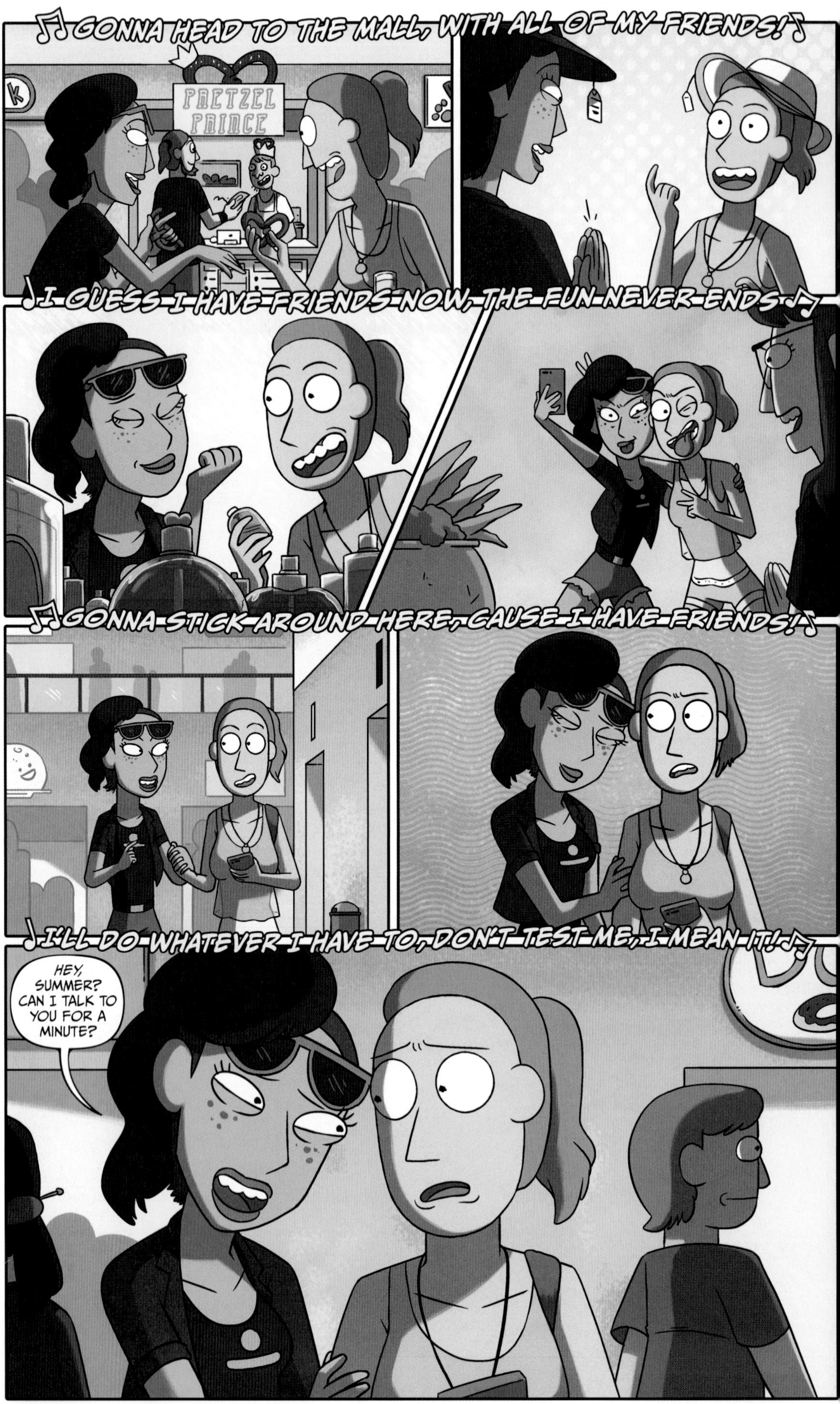
♫ GONNA HEAD TO THE MALL, WITH ALL OF MY FRIENDS! ♫
PRETZEL PRINCE
♪ I GUESS I HAVE FRIENDS NOW, THE FUN NEVER ENDS ♫
♫ GONNA STICK AROUND HERE, CAUSE I HAVE FRIENDS! ♫
♪ I'LL DO WHATEVER I HAVE TO, DON'T TEST ME, I MEAN IT! ♫
HEY, SUMMER? CAN I TALK TO YOU FOR A MINUTE?

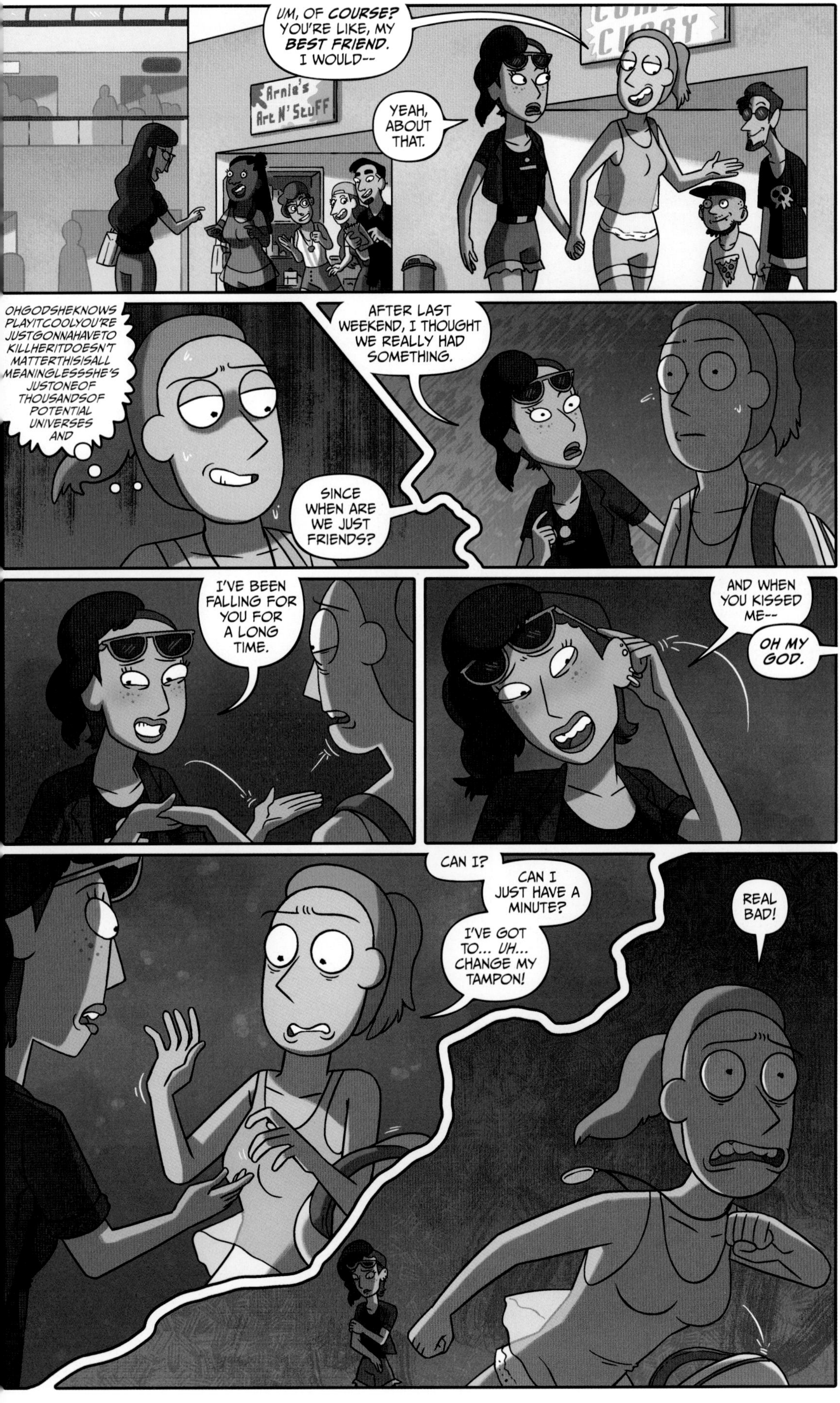
UM, OF *COURSE?* YOU'RE LIKE, MY *BEST FRIEND.* I WOULD--
Arnie's Art N' Stuff
YEAH, ABOUT THAT.
OHGODSHEKNOWS PLAYITCOOLYOU'RE JUSTGONNAHAVETO KILLHERITDOESN'T MATTERTHISISALL MEANINGLESSSHE'S JUSTONEOF THOUSANDSOF POTENTIAL UNIVERSES AND
AFTER LAST WEEKEND, I THOUGHT WE REALLY HAD SOMETHING.
SINCE WHEN ARE WE JUST FRIENDS?
I'VE BEEN FALLING FOR YOU FOR A LONG TIME.
AND WHEN YOU KISSED ME--
OH MY GOD.
CAN I?
CAN I JUST HAVE A MINUTE?
I'VE GOT TO... *UH*... CHANGE MY TAMPON!
REAL BAD!

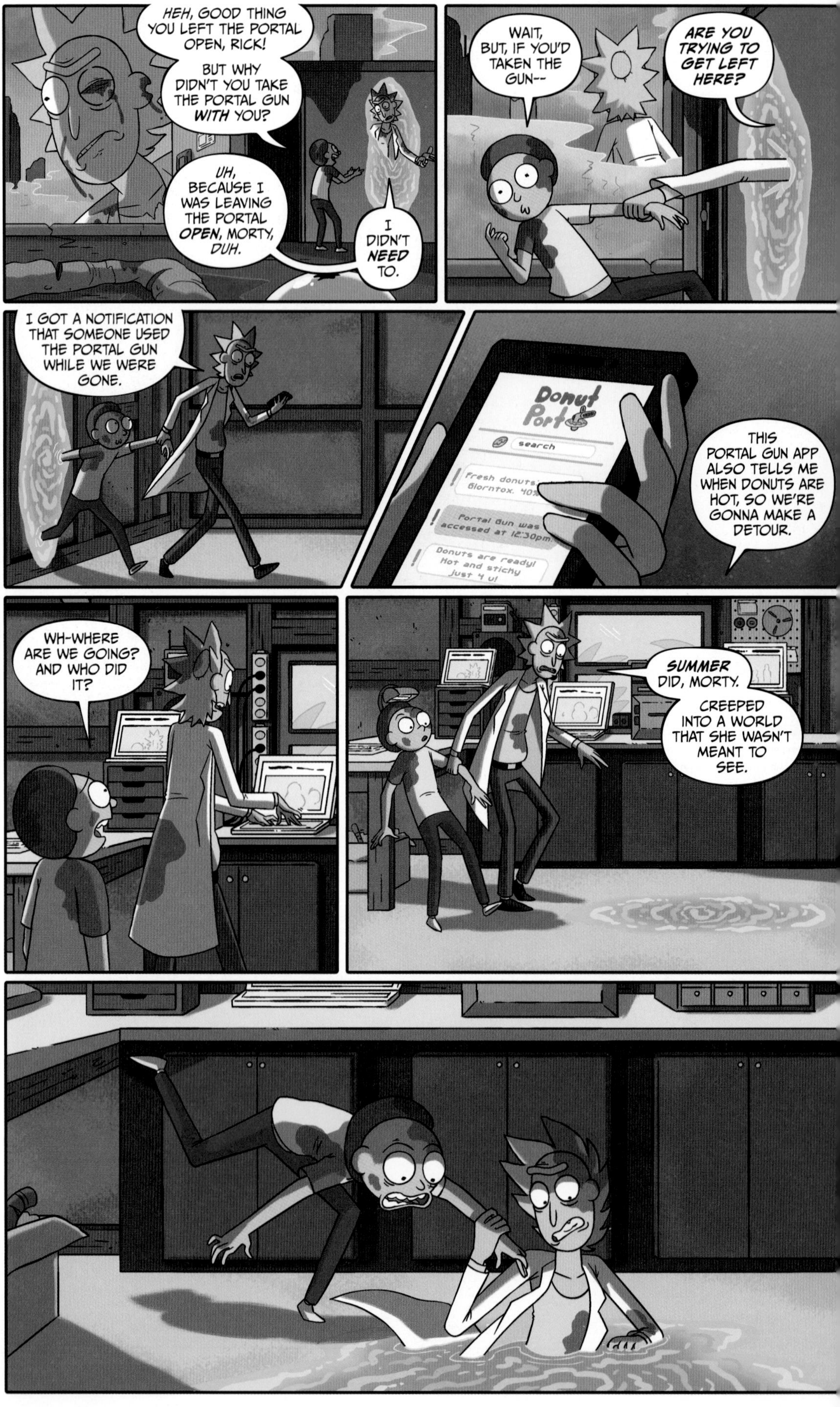
HEH, GOOD THING YOU LEFT THE PORTAL OPEN, RICK!
BUT WHY DIDN'T YOU TAKE THE PORTAL GUN WITH YOU?
UH, BECAUSE I WAS LEAVING THE PORTAL OPEN, MORTY, DUH.
I DIDN'T NEED TO.
WAIT, BUT, IF YOU'D TAKEN THE GUN--
ARE YOU TRYING TO GET LEFT HERE?
I GOT A NOTIFICATION THAT SOMEONE USED THE PORTAL GUN WHILE WE WERE GONE.
Donut Port
search
Portal Gun was accessed at 12:30pm.
Donuts are ready! Hot and sticky just 4 u!
THIS PORTAL GUN APP ALSO TELLS ME WHEN DONUTS ARE HOT, SO WE'RE GONNA MAKE A DETOUR.
WH-WHERE ARE WE GOING? AND WHO DID IT?
SUMMER DID, MORTY.
CREEPED INTO A WORLD THAT SHE WASN'T MEANT TO SEE.

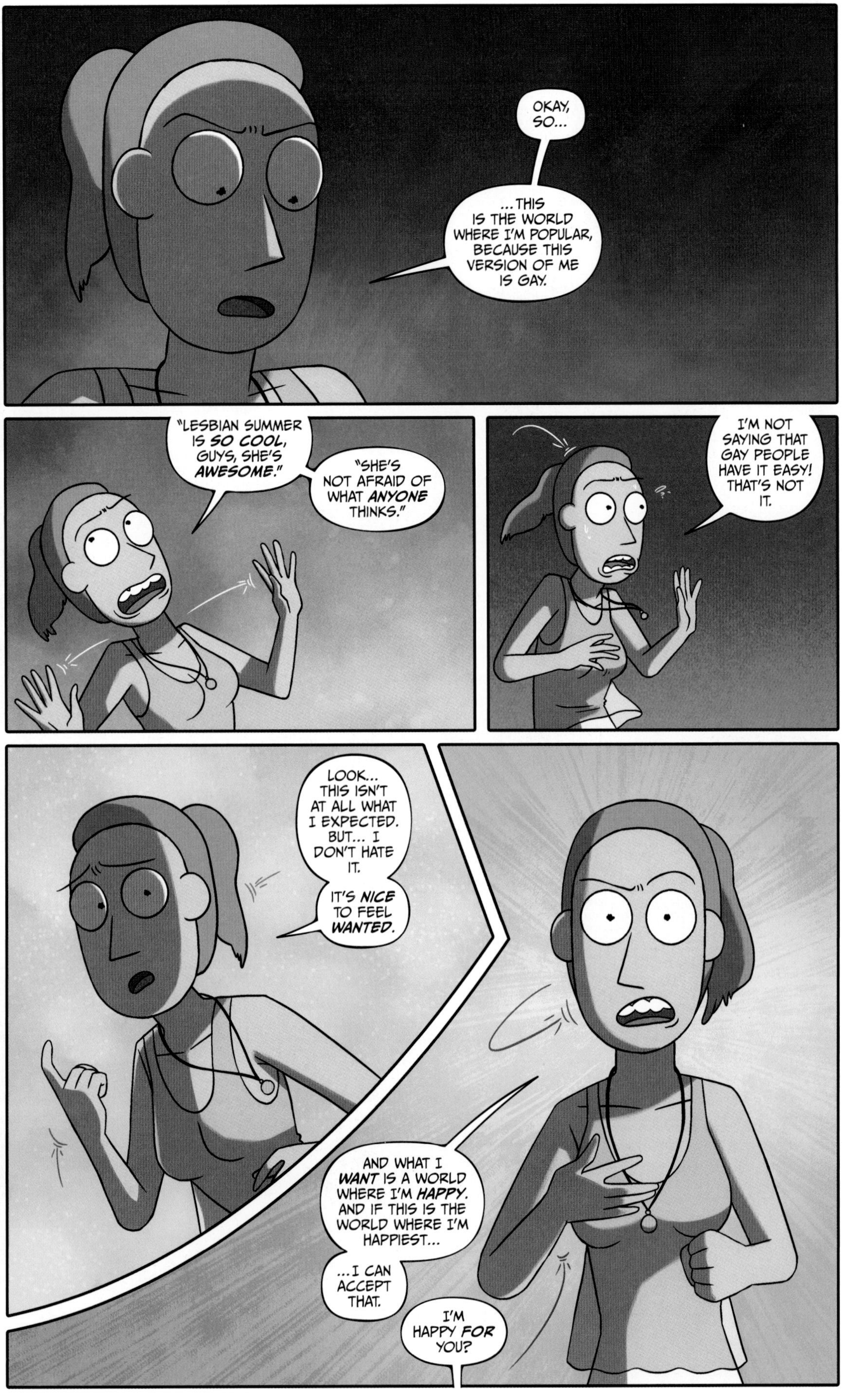
OKAY, SO...
...THIS IS THE WORLD WHERE I'M POPULAR, BECAUSE THIS VERSION OF ME IS GAY.
"LESBIAN SUMMER IS **SO COOL**, GUYS, SHE'S **AWESOME**."
"SHE'S NOT AFRAID OF WHAT **ANYONE** THINKS."
I'M NOT SAYING THAT GAY PEOPLE HAVE IT EASY! THAT'S NOT IT.
LOOK... THIS ISN'T AT ALL WHAT I EXPECTED. BUT... I DON'T HATE IT.
IT'S **NICE** TO FEEL **WANTED**.
AND WHAT I **WANT** IS A WORLD WHERE I'M **HAPPY**. AND IF THIS IS THE WORLD WHERE I'M HAPPIEST...
...I CAN ACCEPT THAT.
I'M HAPPY **FOR** YOU?

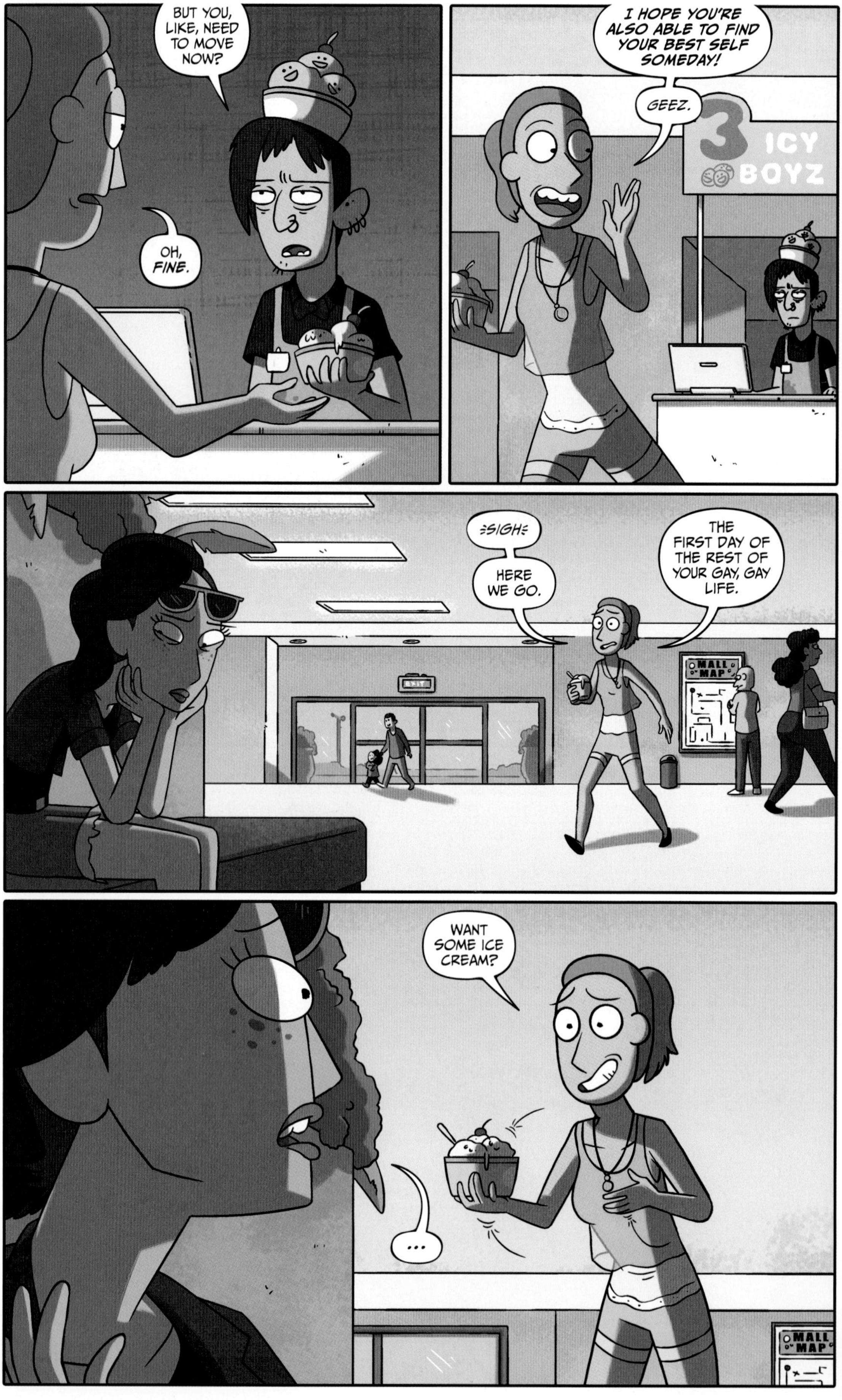
BUT YOU, LIKE, NEED TO MOVE NOW?
OH, *FINE*.
I HOPE YOU'RE ALSO ABLE TO FIND YOUR BEST SELF SOMEDAY!
GEEZ.
3 ICY BOYZ
SIGH
HERE WE GO.
THE FIRST DAY OF THE REST OF YOUR GAY, GAY LIFE.
EXIT
MALL MAP
WANT SOME ICE CREAM?
...
MALL MAP

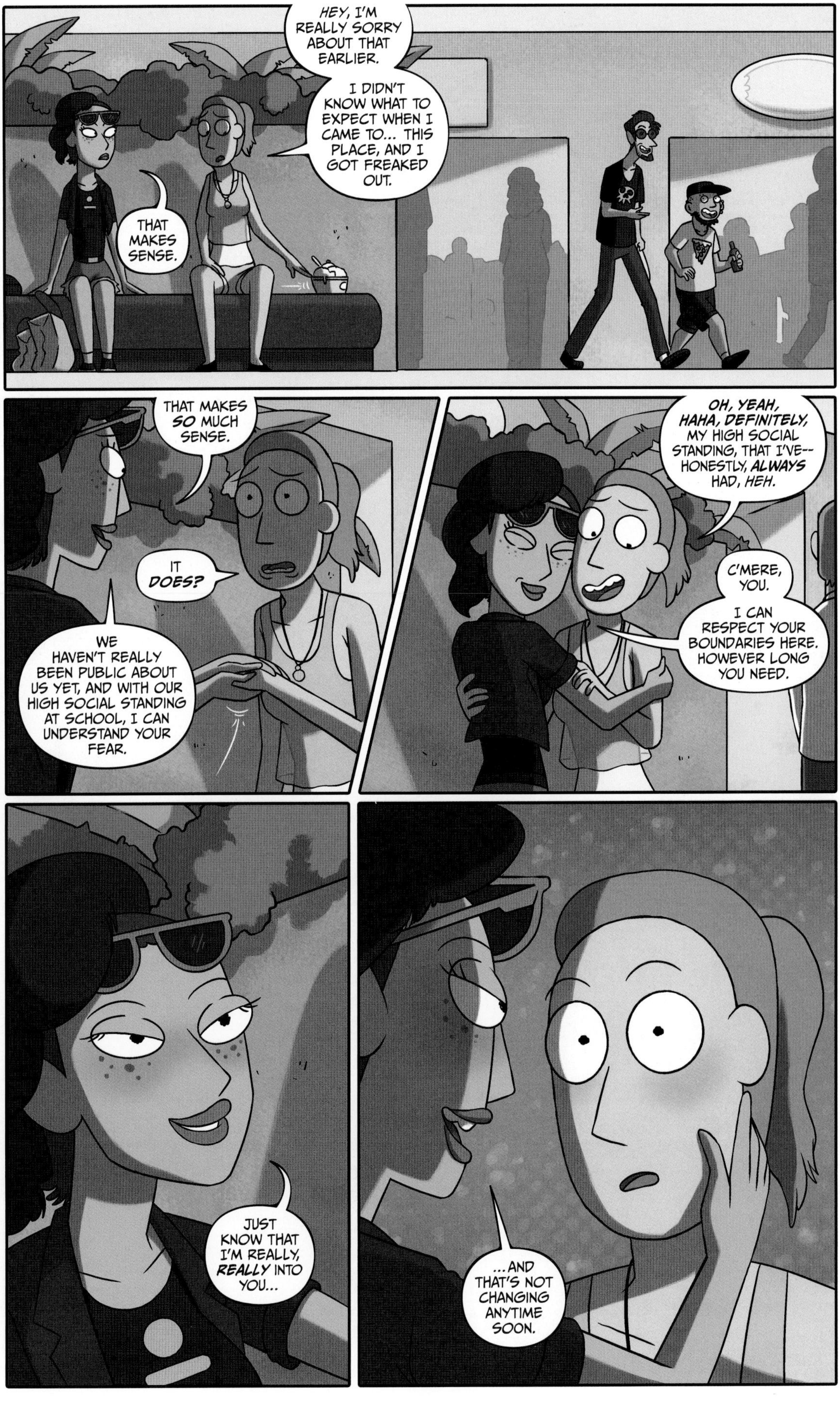
HEY, I'M REALLY SORRY ABOUT THAT EARLIER.
I DIDN'T KNOW WHAT TO EXPECT WHEN I CAME TO... THIS PLACE, AND I GOT FREAKED OUT.
THAT MAKES SENSE.
THAT MAKES *SO* MUCH SENSE.
IT *DOES?*
WE HAVEN'T REALLY BEEN PUBLIC ABOUT US YET, AND WITH OUR HIGH SOCIAL STANDING AT SCHOOL, I CAN UNDERSTAND YOUR FEAR.
OH, YEAH, HAHA, DEFINITELY, MY HIGH SOCIAL STANDING, THAT I'VE-- HONESTLY, *ALWAYS* HAD, *HEH.*
C'MERE, YOU.
I CAN RESPECT YOUR BOUNDARIES HERE. HOWEVER LONG YOU NEED.
JUST KNOW THAT I'M REALLY, *REALLY* INTO YOU...
...AND THAT'S NOT CHANGING ANYTIME SOON.

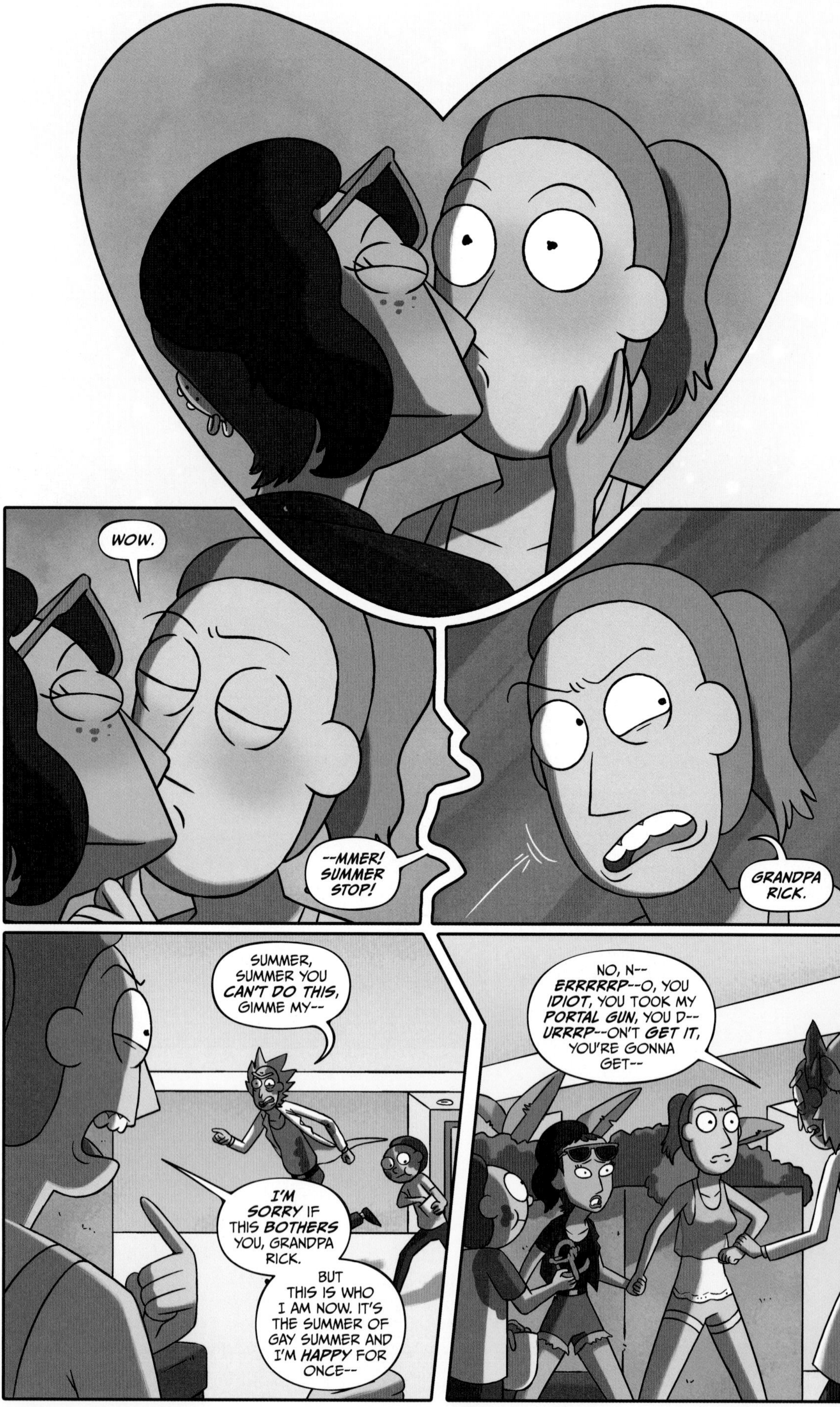
WOW.
--MMER! SUMMER STOP!
GRANDPA RICK.
SUMMER, SUMMER YOU CAN'T DO THIS, GIMME MY--
I'M SORRY IF THIS BOTHERS YOU, GRANDPA RICK.
BUT THIS IS WHO I AM NOW. IT'S THE SUMMER OF GAY SUMMER AND I'M HAPPY FOR ONCE--
NO, N-- ERRRRRP--O, YOU IDIOT, YOU TOOK MY PORTAL GUN, YOU D-- URRRP--ON'T GET IT, YOU'RE GONNA GET--

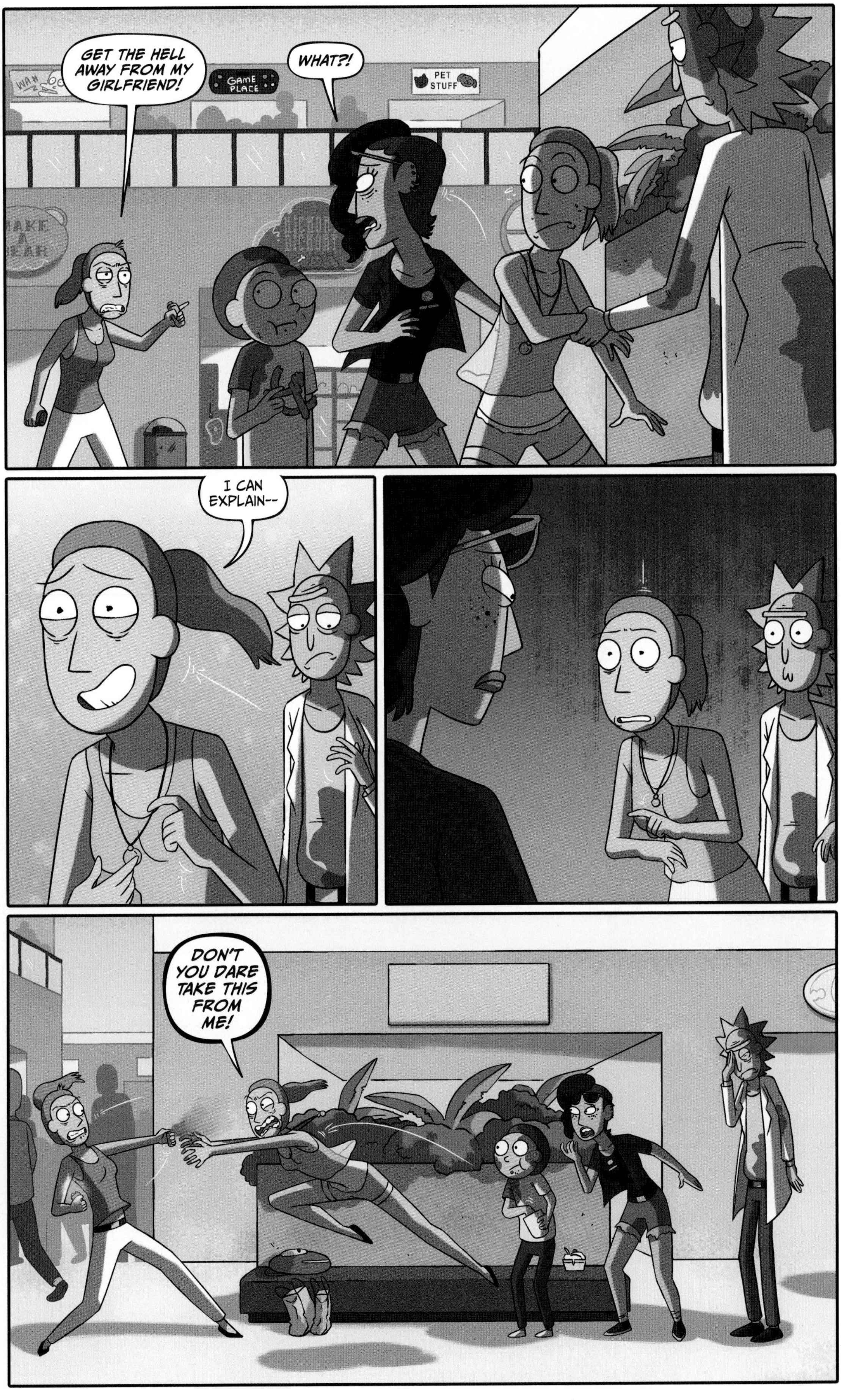
GET THE HELL AWAY FROM MY GIRLFRIEND!
WHAT?!
GAME PLACE
PET STUFF
MAKE A BEAR
I CAN EXPLAIN--
DON'T YOU DARE TAKE THIS FROM ME!

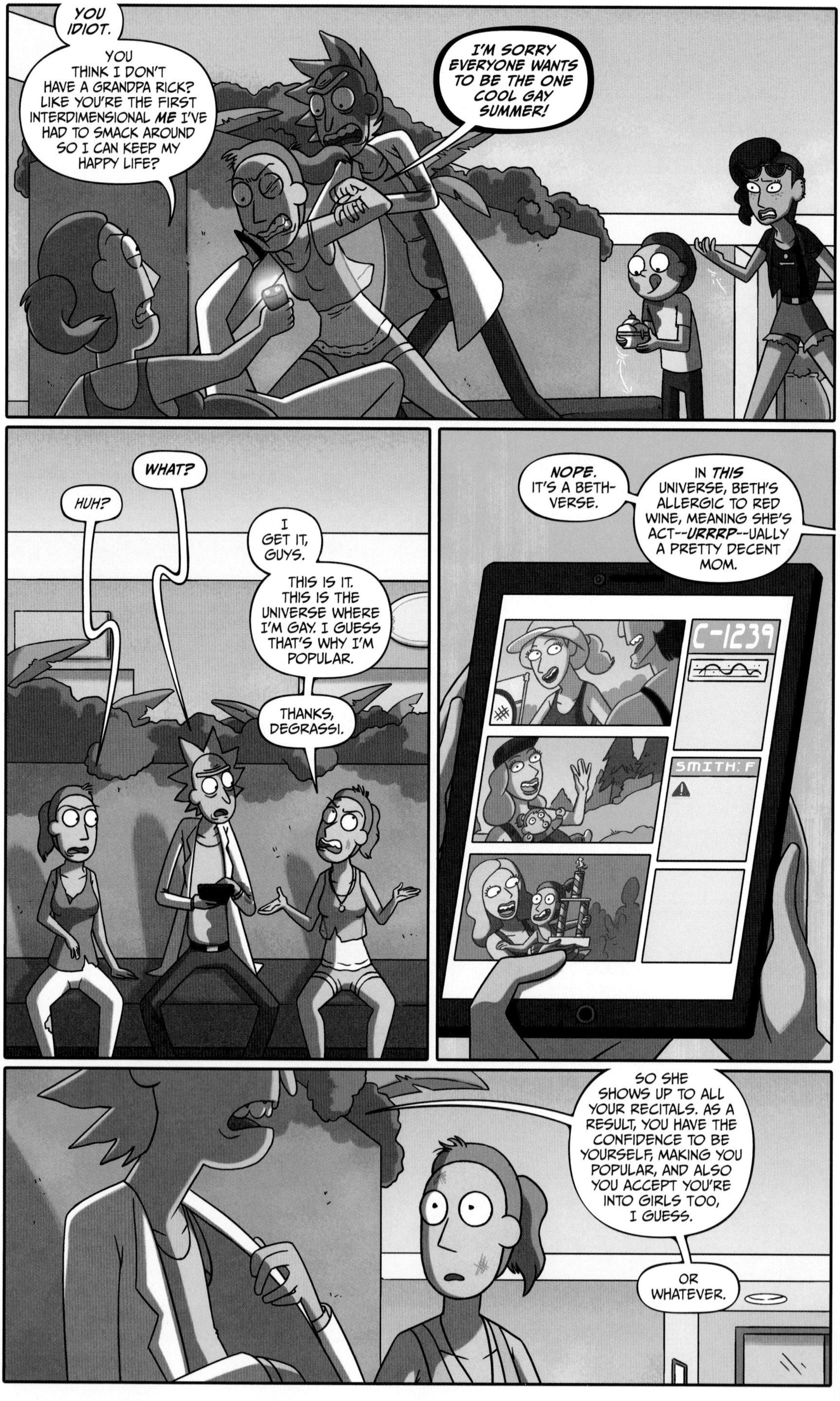
YOU IDIOT.
YOU THINK I DON'T HAVE A GRANDPA RICK? LIKE YOU'RE THE FIRST INTERDIMENSIONAL ME I'VE HAD TO SMACK AROUND SO I CAN KEEP MY HAPPY LIFE?
I'M SORRY EVERYONE WANTS TO BE THE ONE COOL GAY SUMMER!
WHAT?
HUH?
I GET IT, GUYS.
THIS IS IT. THIS IS THE UNIVERSE WHERE I'M GAY. I GUESS THAT'S WHY I'M POPULAR.
THANKS, DEGRASSI.
NOPE. IT'S A BETH-VERSE.
IN THIS UNIVERSE, BETH'S ALLERGIC TO RED WINE, MEANING SHE'S ACT--URRRP--UALLY A PRETTY DECENT MOM.
C-1239
SMITH: F
SO SHE SHOWS UP TO ALL YOUR RECITALS. AS A RESULT, YOU HAVE THE CONFIDENCE TO BE YOURSELF, MAKING YOU POPULAR, AND ALSO YOU ACCEPT YOU'RE INTO GIRLS TOO, I GUESS.
OR WHATEVER.

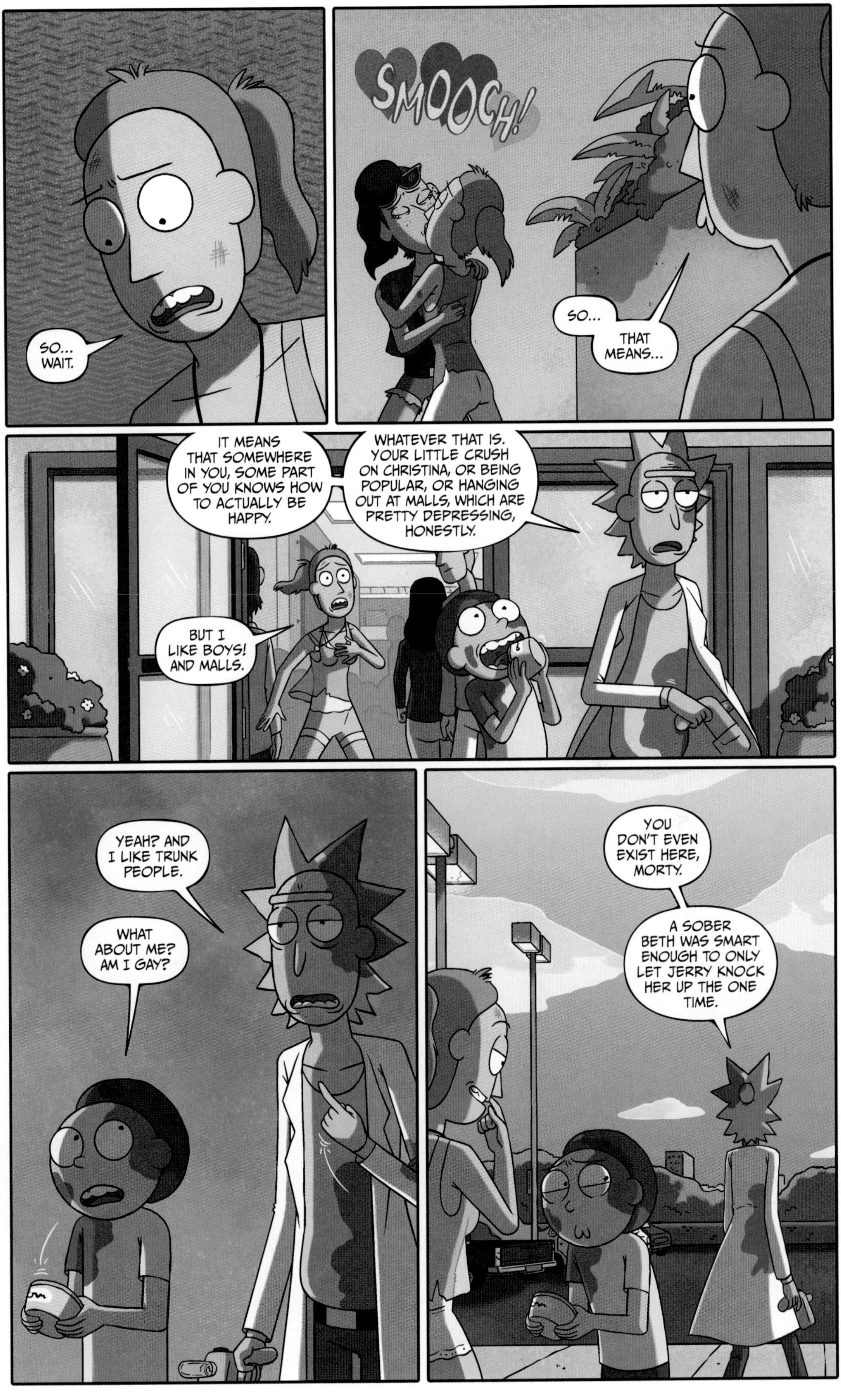
SO... WAIT.
SMOOCH!
SO...
THAT MEANS...
IT MEANS THAT SOMEWHERE IN YOU, SOME PART OF YOU KNOWS HOW TO ACTUALLY BE HAPPY.
WHATEVER THAT IS. YOUR LITTLE CRUSH ON CHRISTINA, OR BEING POPULAR, OR HANGING OUT AT MALLS, WHICH ARE PRETTY DEPRESSING, HONESTLY.
BUT I LIKE BOYS! AND MALLS.
YEAH? AND I LIKE TRUNK PEOPLE.
WHAT ABOUT ME? AM I GAY?
YOU DON'T EVEN EXIST HERE, MORTY.
A SOBER BETH WAS SMART ENOUGH TO ONLY LET JERRY KNOCK HER UP THE ONE TIME.

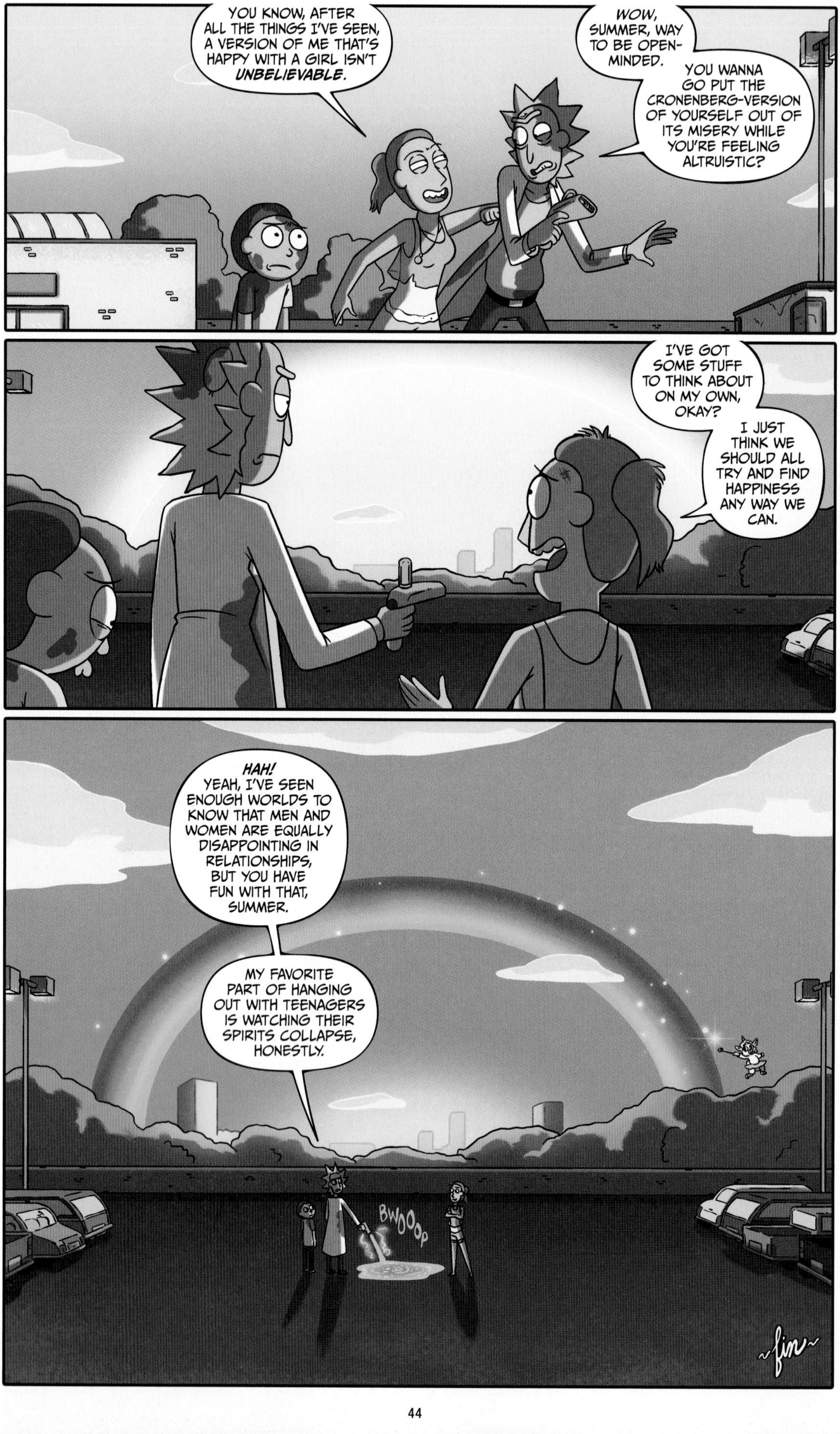
YOU KNOW, AFTER ALL THE THINGS I'VE SEEN, A VERSION OF ME THAT'S HAPPY WITH A GIRL ISN'T ***UNBELIEVABLE***.
WOW, SUMMER, WAY TO BE OPEN-MINDED.
YOU WANNA GO PUT THE CRONENBERG-VERSION OF YOURSELF OUT OF ITS MISERY WHILE YOU'RE FEELING ALTRUISTIC?
I'VE GOT SOME STUFF TO THINK ABOUT ON MY OWN, OKAY?
I JUST THINK WE SHOULD ALL TRY AND FIND HAPPINESS ANY WAY WE CAN.
HAH! YEAH, I'VE SEEN ENOUGH WORLDS TO KNOW THAT MEN AND WOMEN ARE EQUALLY DISAPPOINTING IN RELATIONSHIPS, BUT YOU HAVE FUN WITH THAT, SUMMER.
MY FAVORITE PART OF HANGING OUT WITH TEENAGERS IS WATCHING THEIR SPIRITS COLLAPSE, HONESTLY.
BWOOOP
~fin~

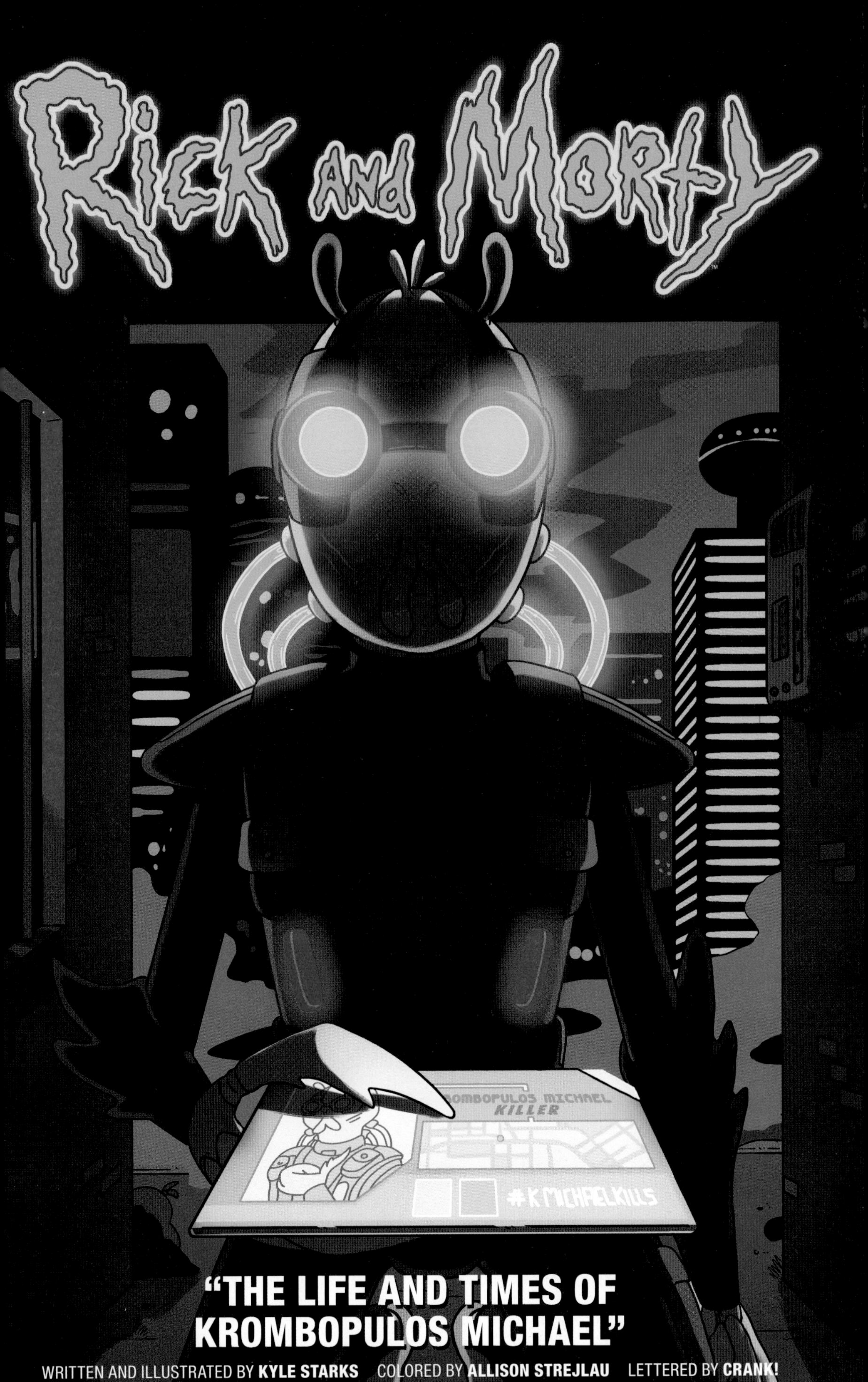
Rick and Morty
ROMBOPULOS MICHAEL
KILLER
#KMICHAELKILLS

"THE LIFE AND TIMES OF KROMBOPULOS MICHAEL"

WRITTEN AND ILLUSTRATED BY **KYLE STARKS** COLORED BY **ALLISON STREJLAU** LETTERED BY **CRANK!**

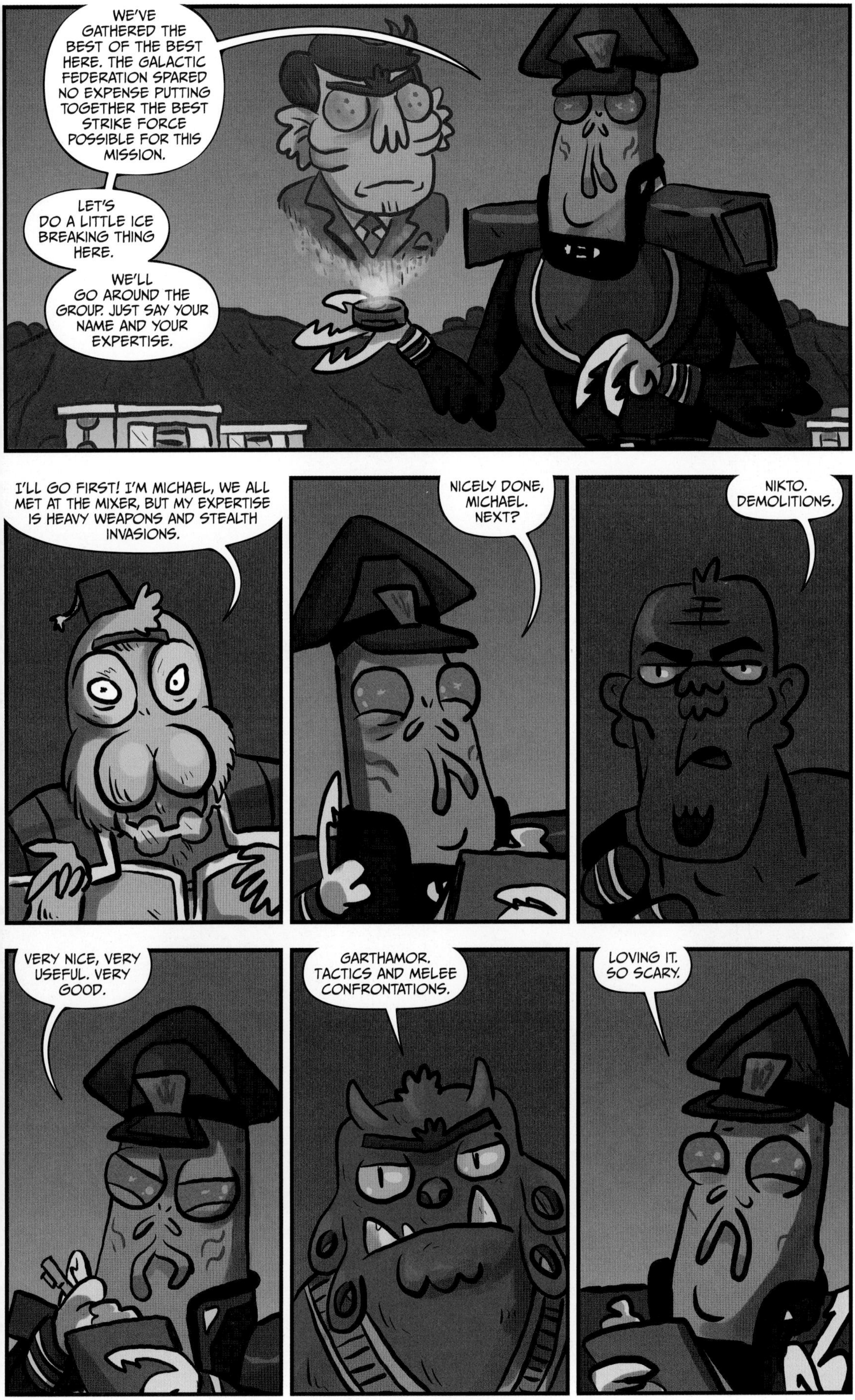
WE'VE GATHERED THE BEST OF THE BEST HERE. THE GALACTIC FEDERATION SPARED NO EXPENSE PUTTING TOGETHER THE BEST STRIKE FORCE POSSIBLE FOR THIS MISSION.
LET'S DO A LITTLE ICE BREAKING THING HERE.
WE'LL GO AROUND THE GROUP. JUST SAY YOUR NAME AND YOUR EXPERTISE.
I'LL GO FIRST! I'M MICHAEL, WE ALL MET AT THE MIXER, BUT MY EXPERTISE IS HEAVY WEAPONS AND STEALTH INVASIONS.
NICELY DONE, MICHAEL. NEXT?
NIKTO. DEMOLITIONS.
VERY NICE, VERY USEFUL. VERY GOOD.
GARTHAMOR. TACTICS AND MELEE CONFRONTATIONS.
LOVING IT. SO SCARY.

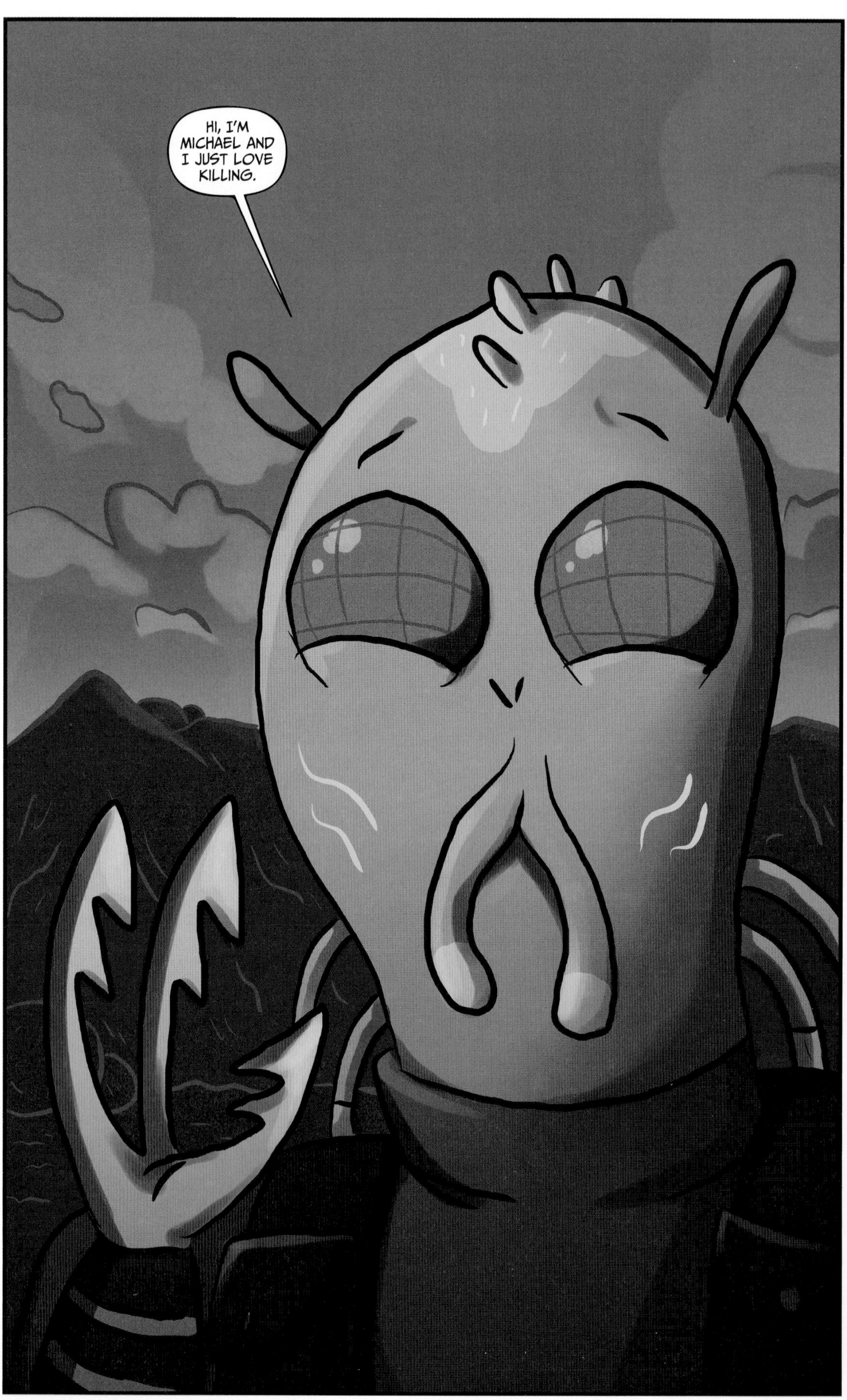
HI, I'M MICHAEL AND I JUST LOVE KILLING.

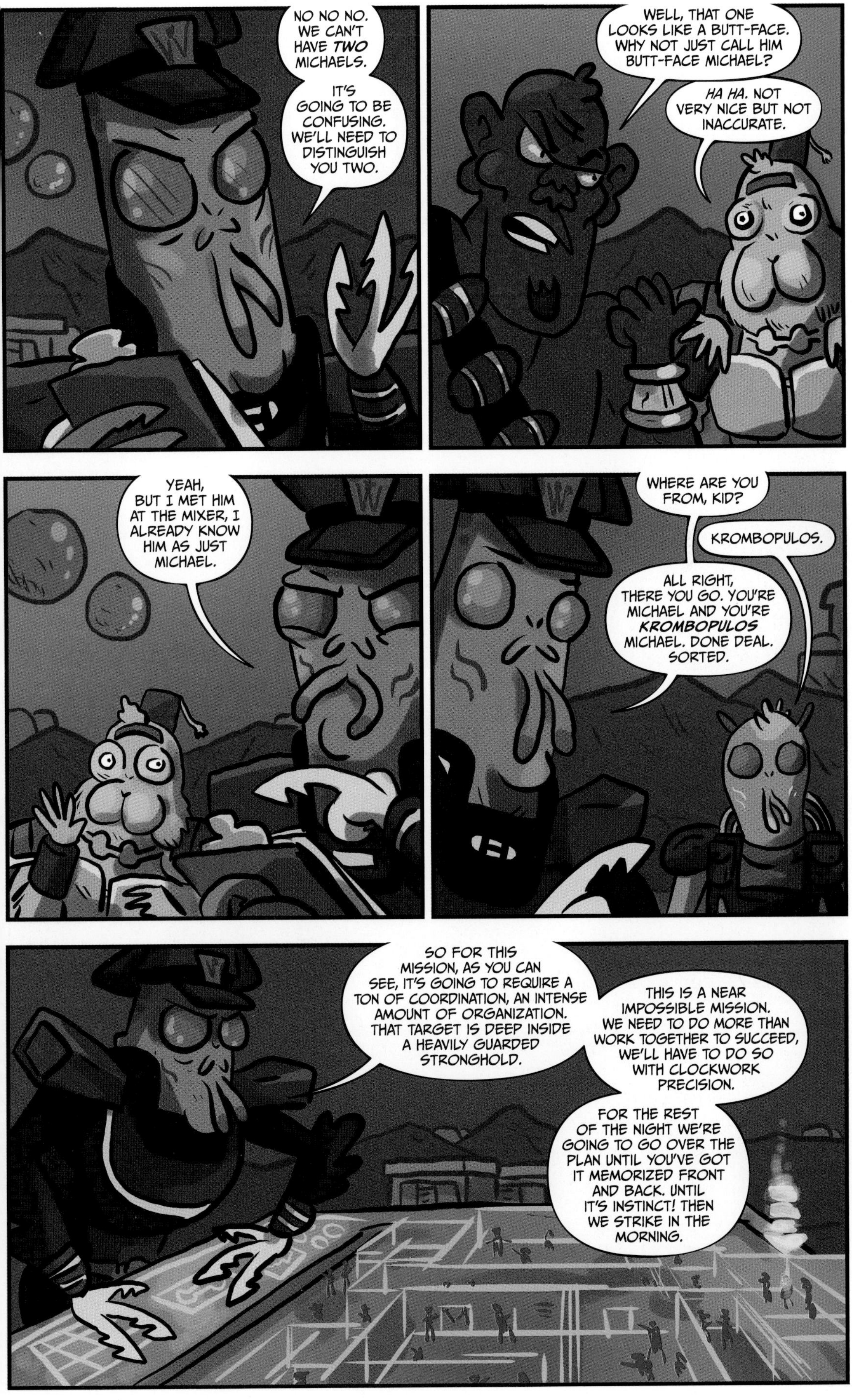
NO NO NO. WE CAN'T HAVE *TWO* MICHAELS.
IT'S GOING TO BE CONFUSING. WE'LL NEED TO DISTINGUISH YOU TWO.
WELL, THAT ONE LOOKS LIKE A BUTT-FACE. WHY NOT JUST CALL HIM BUTT-FACE MICHAEL?
HA HA. NOT VERY NICE BUT NOT INACCURATE.
YEAH, BUT I MET HIM AT THE MIXER, I ALREADY KNOW HIM AS JUST MICHAEL.
WHERE ARE YOU FROM, KID?
KROMBOPULOS.
ALL RIGHT, THERE YOU GO. YOU'RE MICHAEL AND YOU'RE ***KROMBOPULOS*** MICHAEL. DONE DEAL. SORTED.
SO FOR THIS MISSION, AS YOU CAN SEE, IT'S GOING TO REQUIRE A TON OF COORDINATION, AN INTENSE AMOUNT OF ORGANIZATION. THAT TARGET IS DEEP INSIDE A HEAVILY GUARDED STRONGHOLD.
THIS IS A NEAR IMPOSSIBLE MISSION. WE NEED TO DO MORE THAN WORK TOGETHER TO SUCCEED, WE'LL HAVE TO DO SO WITH CLOCKWORK PRECISION.
FOR THE REST OF THE NIGHT WE'RE GOING TO GO OVER THE PLAN UNTIL YOU'VE GOT IT MEMORIZED FRONT AND BACK. UNTIL IT'S INSTINCT! THEN WE STRIKE IN THE MORNING.

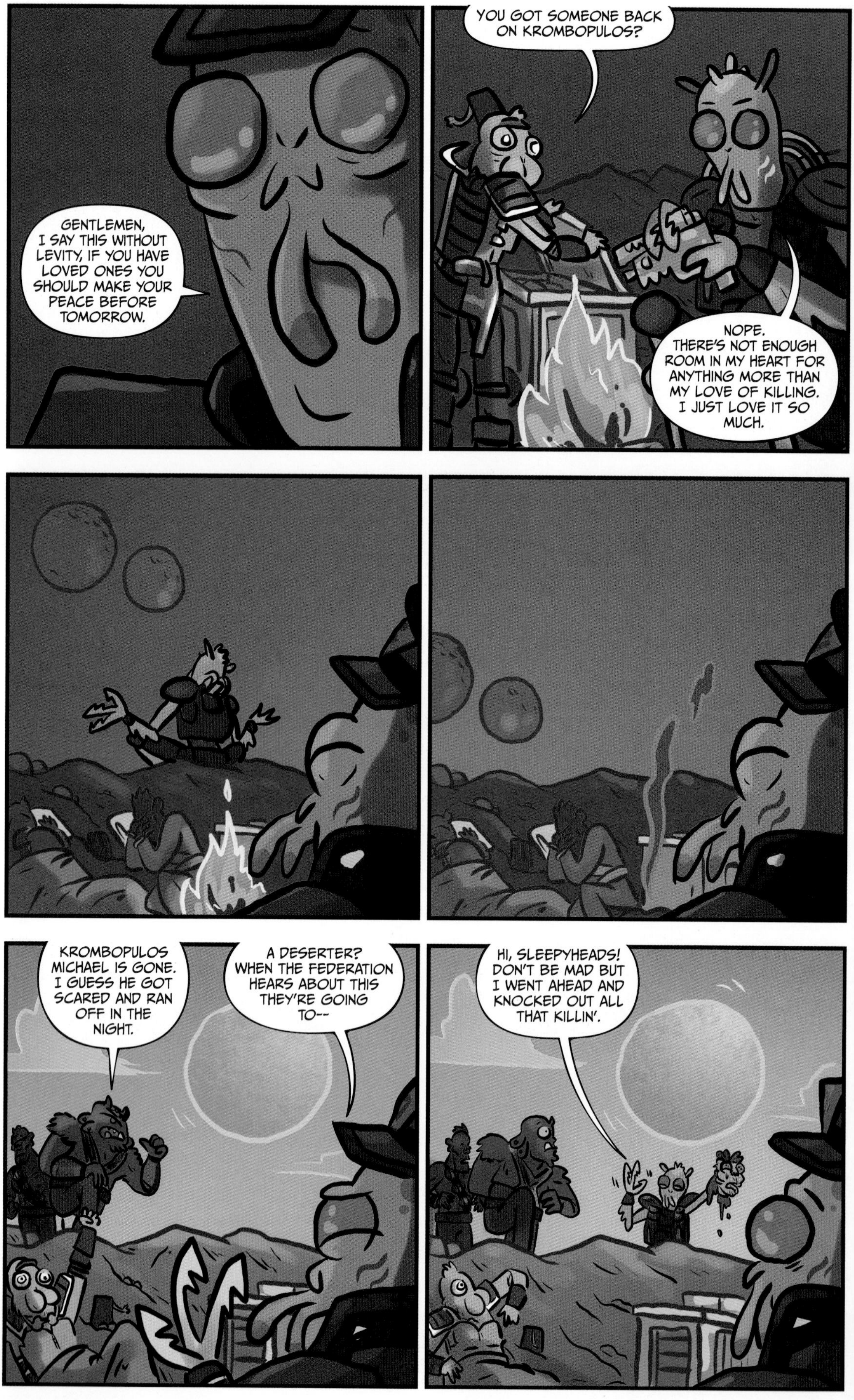
GENTLEMEN, I SAY THIS WITHOUT LEVITY, IF YOU HAVE LOVED ONES YOU SHOULD MAKE YOUR PEACE BEFORE TOMORROW.
YOU GOT SOMEONE BACK ON KROMBOPULOS?
NOPE. THERE'S NOT ENOUGH ROOM IN MY HEART FOR ANYTHING MORE THAN MY LOVE OF KILLING. I JUST LOVE IT SO MUCH.
KROMBOPULOS MICHAEL IS GONE. I GUESS HE GOT SCARED AND RAN OFF IN THE NIGHT.
A DESERTER? WHEN THE FEDERATION HEARS ABOUT THIS THEY'RE GOING TO--
HI, SLEEPYHEADS! DON'T BE MAD BUT I WENT AHEAD AND KNOCKED OUT ALL THAT KILLIN'.

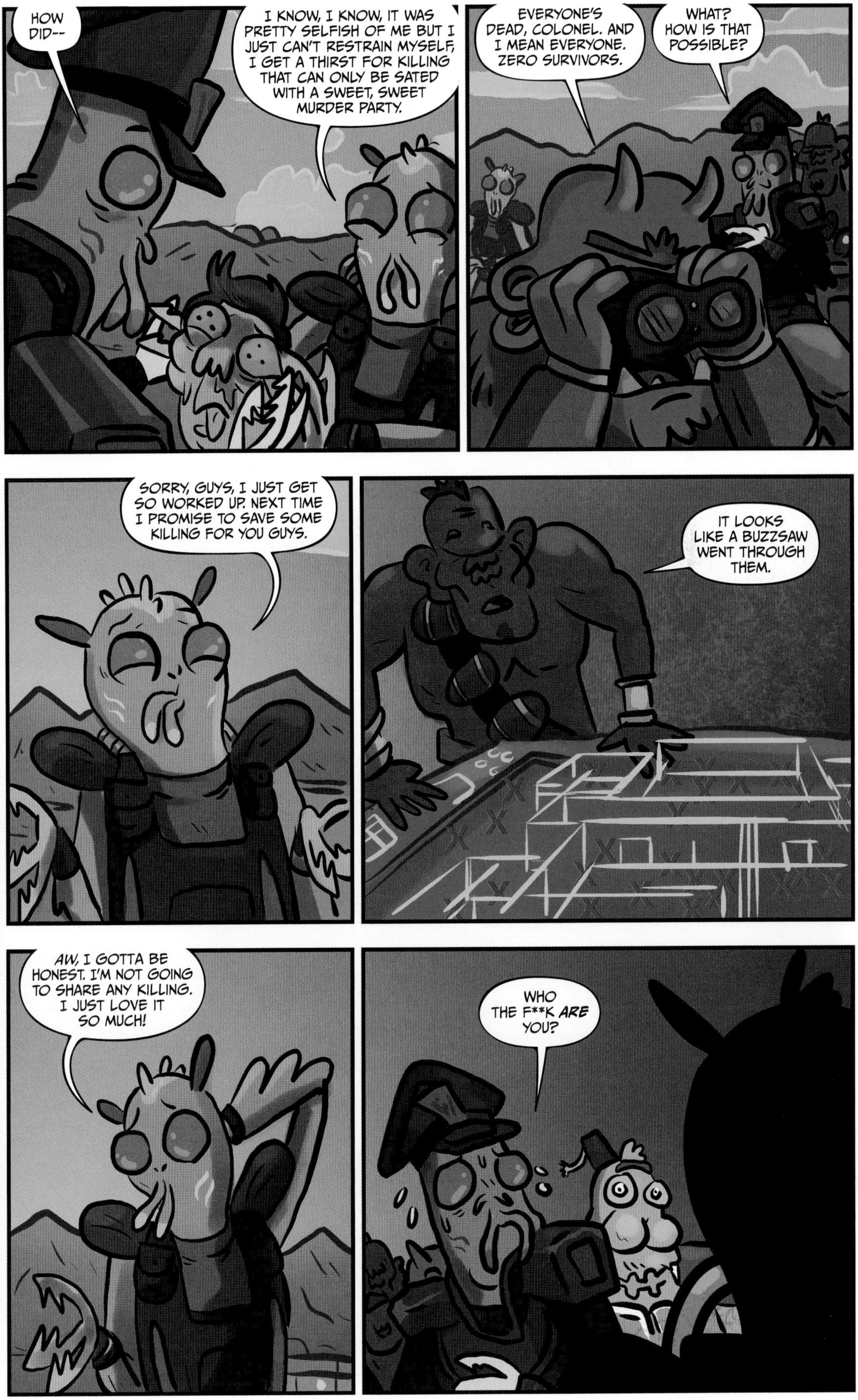
HOW DID--
I KNOW, I KNOW, IT WAS PRETTY SELFISH OF ME BUT I JUST CAN'T RESTRAIN MYSELF, I GET A THIRST FOR KILLING THAT CAN ONLY BE SATED WITH A SWEET, SWEET MURDER PARTY.
EVERYONE'S DEAD, COLONEL. AND I MEAN EVERYONE. ZERO SURVIVORS.
WHAT? HOW IS THAT POSSIBLE?
SORRY, GUYS, I JUST GET SO WORKED UP. NEXT TIME I PROMISE TO SAVE SOME KILLING FOR YOU GUYS.
IT LOOKS LIKE A BUZZSAW WENT THROUGH THEM.
AW, I GOTTA BE HONEST. I'M NOT GOING TO SHARE ANY KILLING. I JUST LOVE IT SO MUCH!
WHO THE F**K ARE YOU?

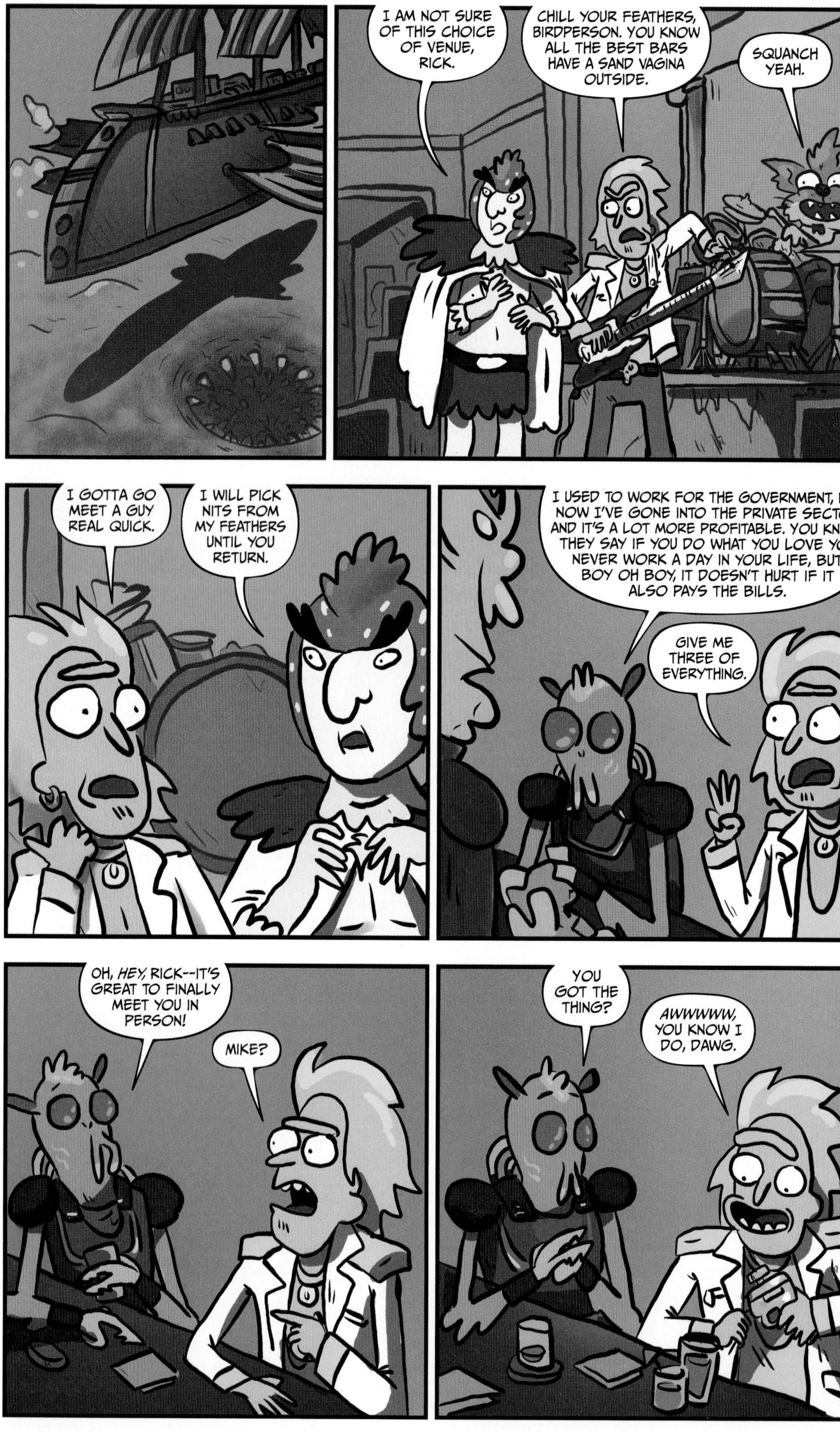
I AM NOT SURE OF THIS CHOICE OF VENUE, RICK.
CHILL YOUR FEATHERS, BIRDPERSON. YOU KNOW ALL THE BEST BARS HAVE A SAND VAGINA OUTSIDE.
SQUANCH YEAH.
I GOTTA GO MEET A GUY REAL QUICK.
I WILL PICK NITS FROM MY FEATHERS UNTIL YOU RETURN.
I USED TO WORK FOR THE GOVERNMENT, BUT NOW I'VE GONE INTO THE PRIVATE SECTOR AND IT'S A LOT MORE PROFITABLE. YOU KNOW, THEY SAY IF YOU DO WHAT YOU LOVE YOU NEVER WORK A DAY IN YOUR LIFE, BUT, BOY OH BOY, IT DOESN'T HURT IF IT ALSO PAYS THE BILLS.
GIVE ME THREE OF EVERYTHING.
OH, *HEY,* RICK--IT'S GREAT TO FINALLY MEET YOU IN PERSON!
MIKE?
YOU GOT THE THING?
AWWWWW, YOU KNOW I DO, DAWG.

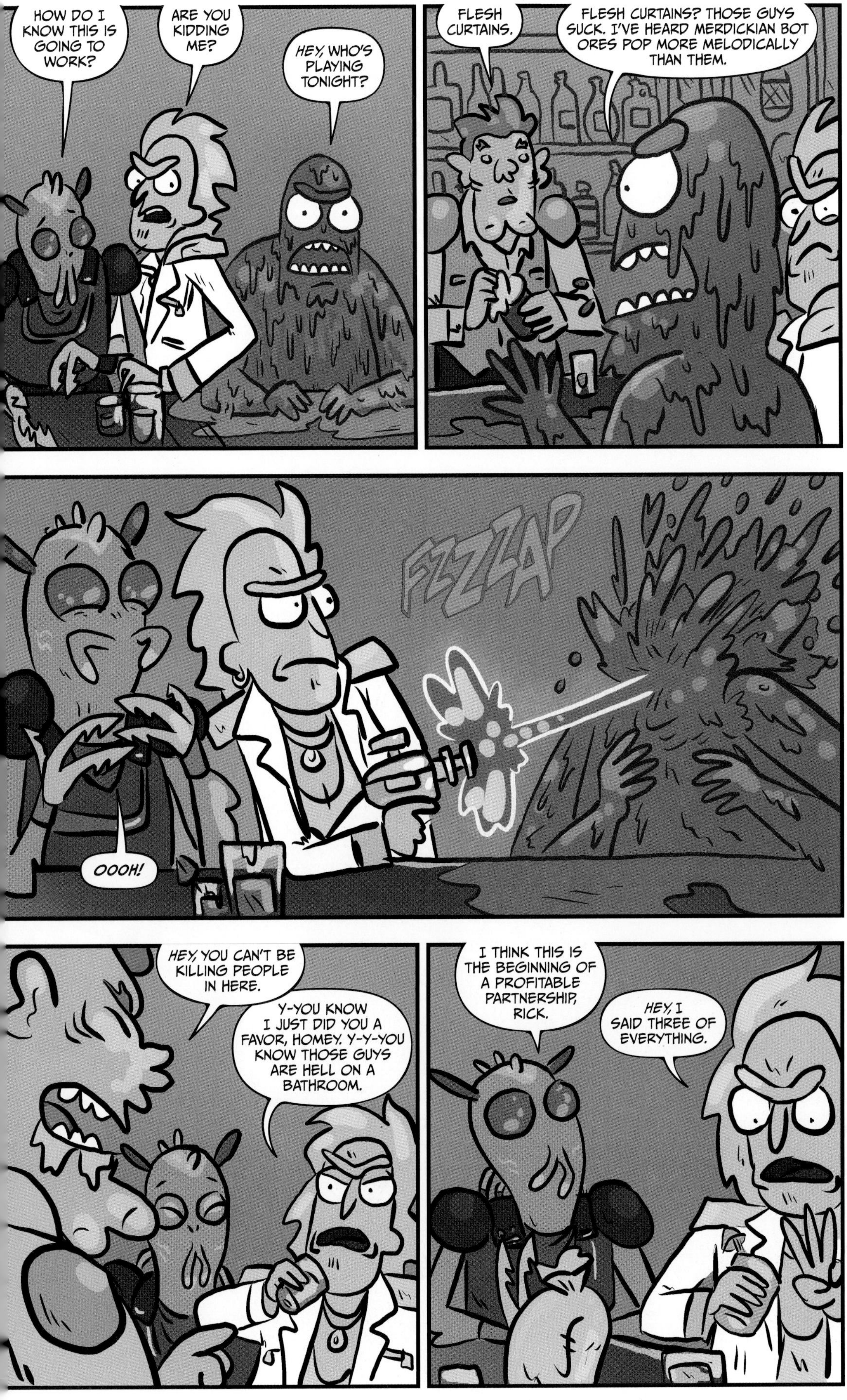

HOW DO I KNOW THIS IS GOING TO WORK?
ARE YOU KIDDING ME?
HEY, WHO'S PLAYING TONIGHT?
FLESH CURTAINS.
FLESH CURTAINS? THOSE GUYS SUCK. I'VE HEARD MERDICKIAN BOT ORES POP MORE MELODICALLY THAN THEM.
FZZZAP
OOOH!
HEY, YOU CAN'T BE KILLING PEOPLE IN HERE.
Y-YOU KNOW I JUST DID YOU A FAVOR, HOMEY. Y-Y-YOU KNOW THOSE GUYS ARE HELL ON A BATHROOM.
I THINK THIS IS THE BEGINNING OF A PROFITABLE PARTNERSHIP, RICK.
HEY, I SAID THREE OF EVERYTHING.

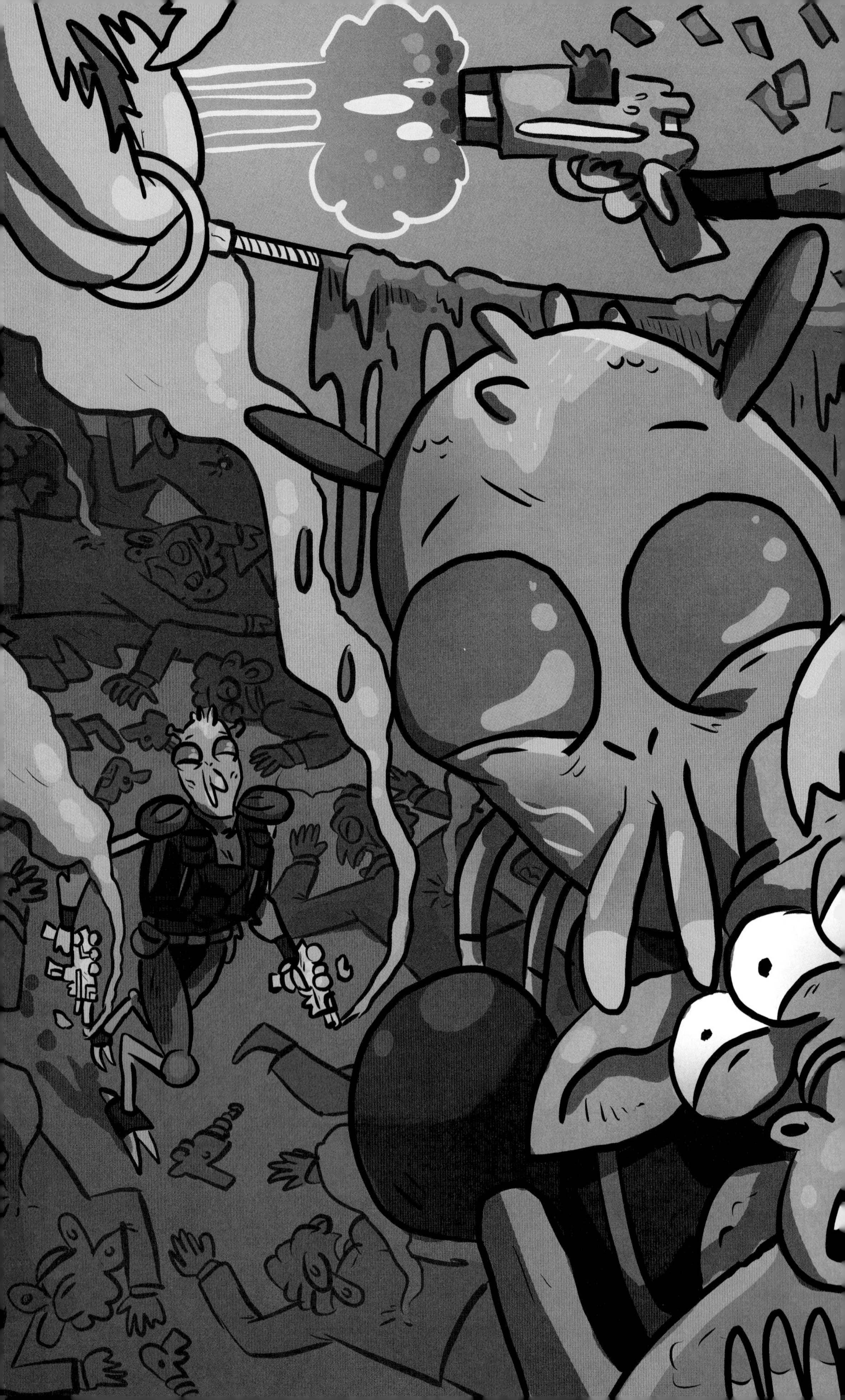

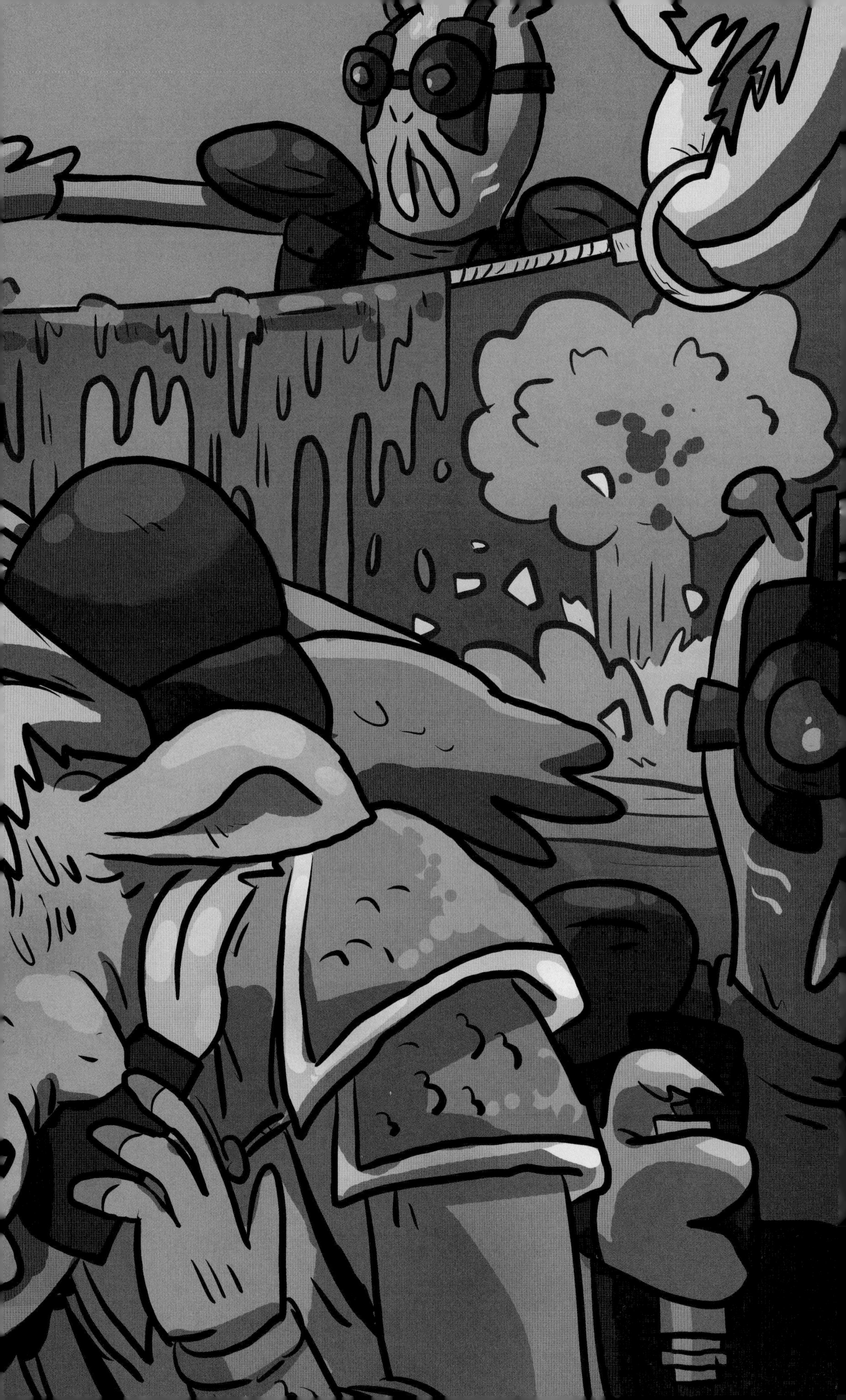

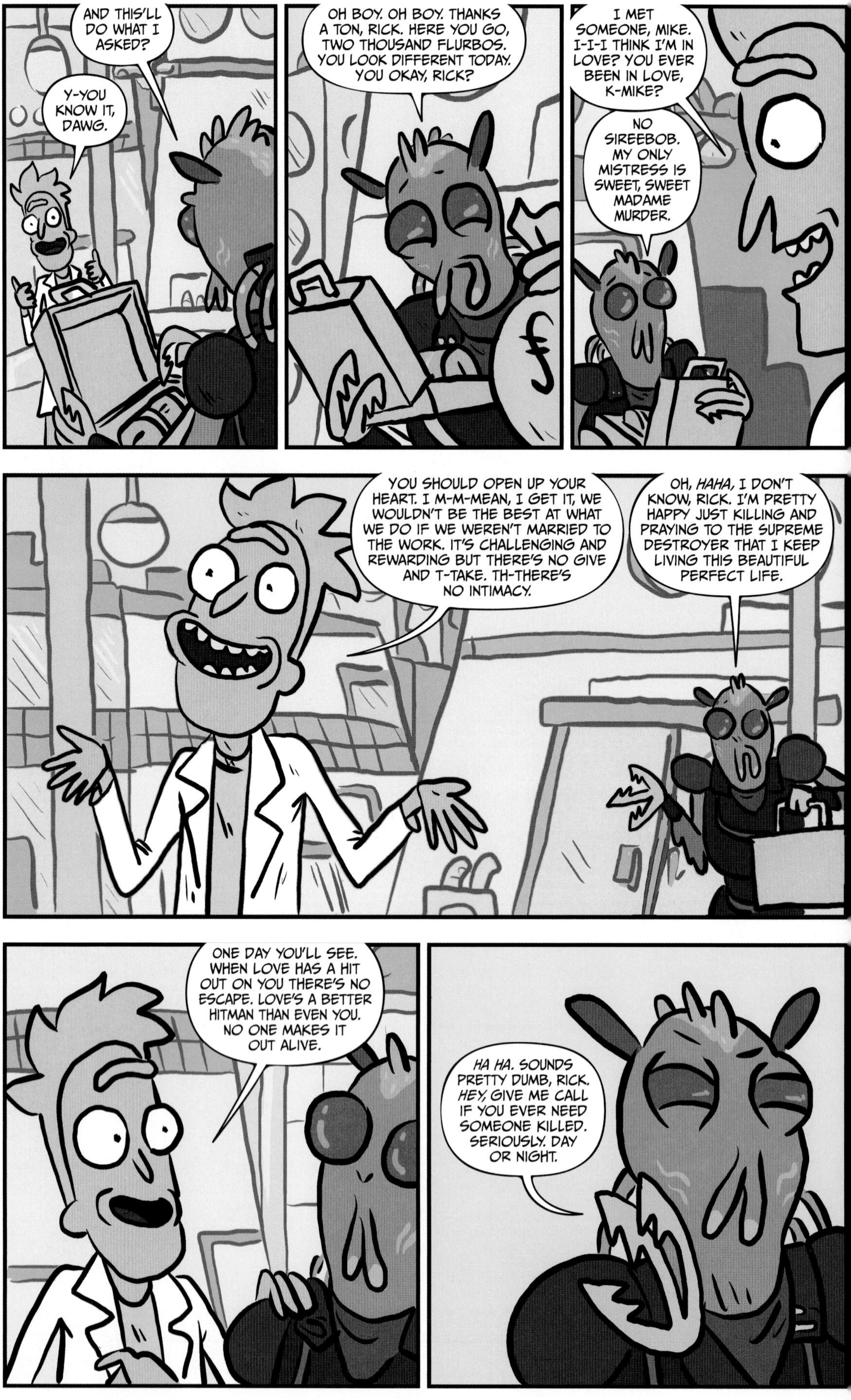
AND THIS'LL DO WHAT I ASKED?
Y-YOU KNOW IT, DAWG.
OH BOY. OH BOY. THANKS A TON, RICK. HERE YOU GO, TWO THOUSAND FLURBOS. YOU LOOK DIFFERENT TODAY. YOU OKAY, RICK?
I MET SOMEONE, MIKE. I-I-I THINK I'M IN LOVE? YOU EVER BEEN IN LOVE, K-MIKE?
NO SIREEBOB. MY ONLY MISTRESS IS SWEET, SWEET MADAME MURDER.
YOU SHOULD OPEN UP YOUR HEART. I M-M-MEAN, I GET IT, WE WOULDN'T BE THE BEST AT WHAT WE DO IF WE WEREN'T MARRIED TO THE WORK. IT'S CHALLENGING AND REWARDING BUT THERE'S NO GIVE AND T-TAKE. TH-THERE'S NO INTIMACY.
OH, *HAHA*, I DON'T KNOW, RICK. I'M PRETTY HAPPY JUST KILLING AND PRAYING TO THE SUPREME DESTROYER THAT I KEEP LIVING THIS BEAUTIFUL PERFECT LIFE.
ONE DAY YOU'LL SEE. WHEN LOVE HAS A HIT OUT ON YOU THERE'S NO ESCAPE. LOVE'S A BETTER HITMAN THAN EVEN YOU. NO ONE MAKES IT OUT ALIVE.
HA HA. SOUNDS PRETTY DUMB, RICK. *HEY,* GIVE ME CALL IF YOU EVER NEED SOMEONE KILLED. SERIOUSLY. DAY OR NIGHT.

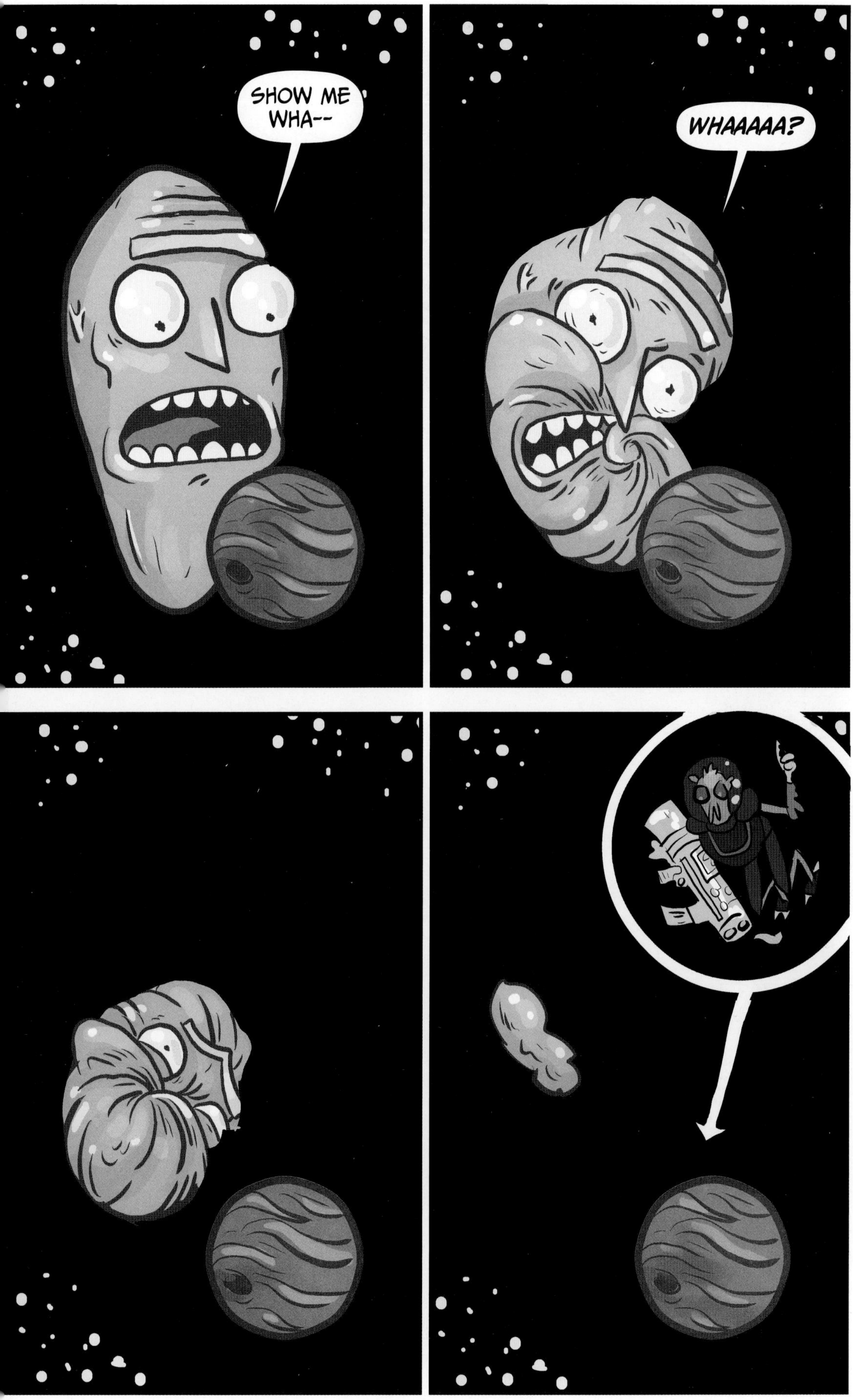
SHOW ME WHA--
WHAAAAA?

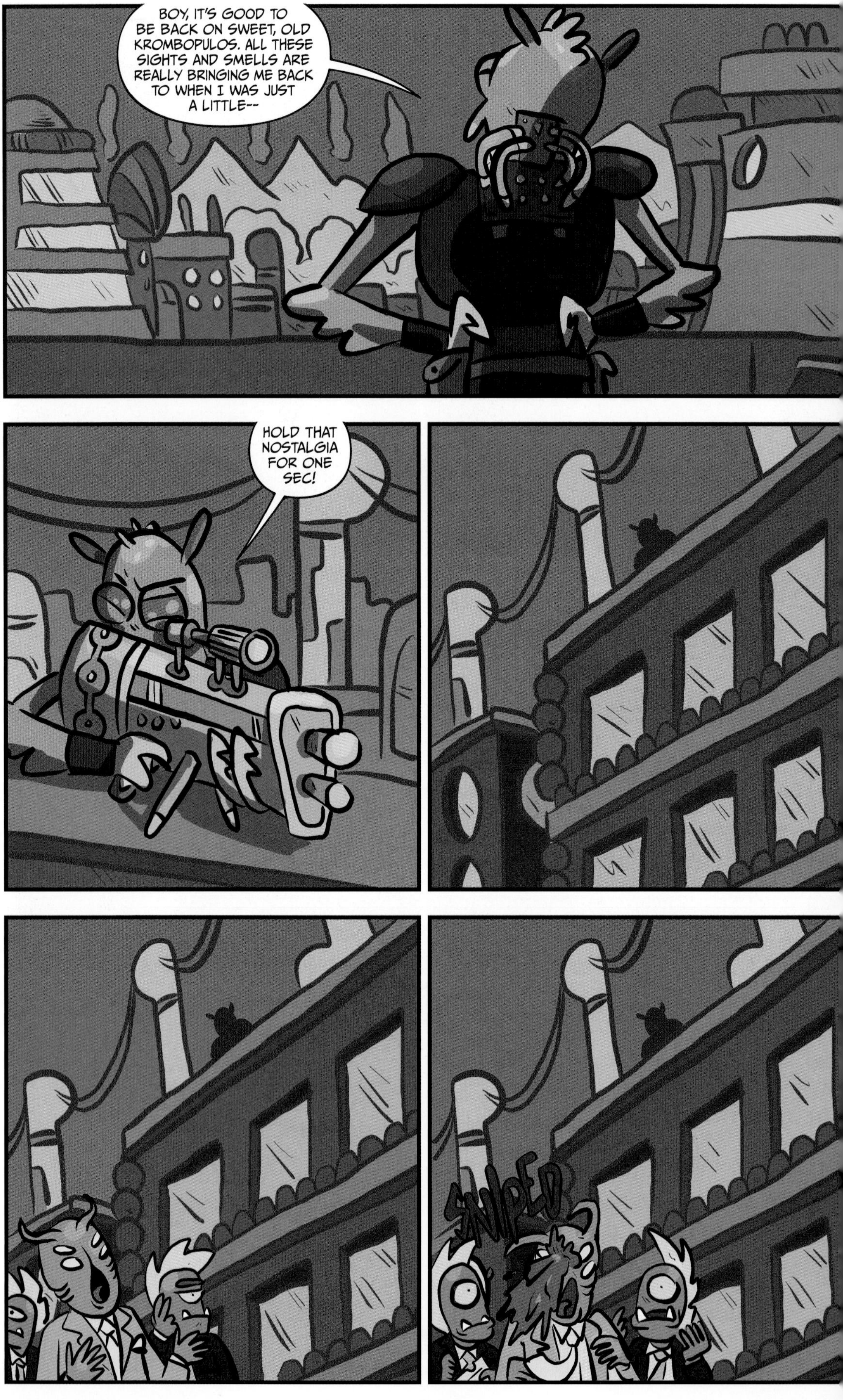
BOY, IT'S GOOD TO BE BACK ON SWEET, OLD KROMBOPULOS. ALL THESE SIGHTS AND SMELLS ARE REALLY BRINGING ME BACK TO WHEN I WAS JUST A LITTLE--
HOLD THAT NOSTALGIA FOR ONE SEC!
SNIPED

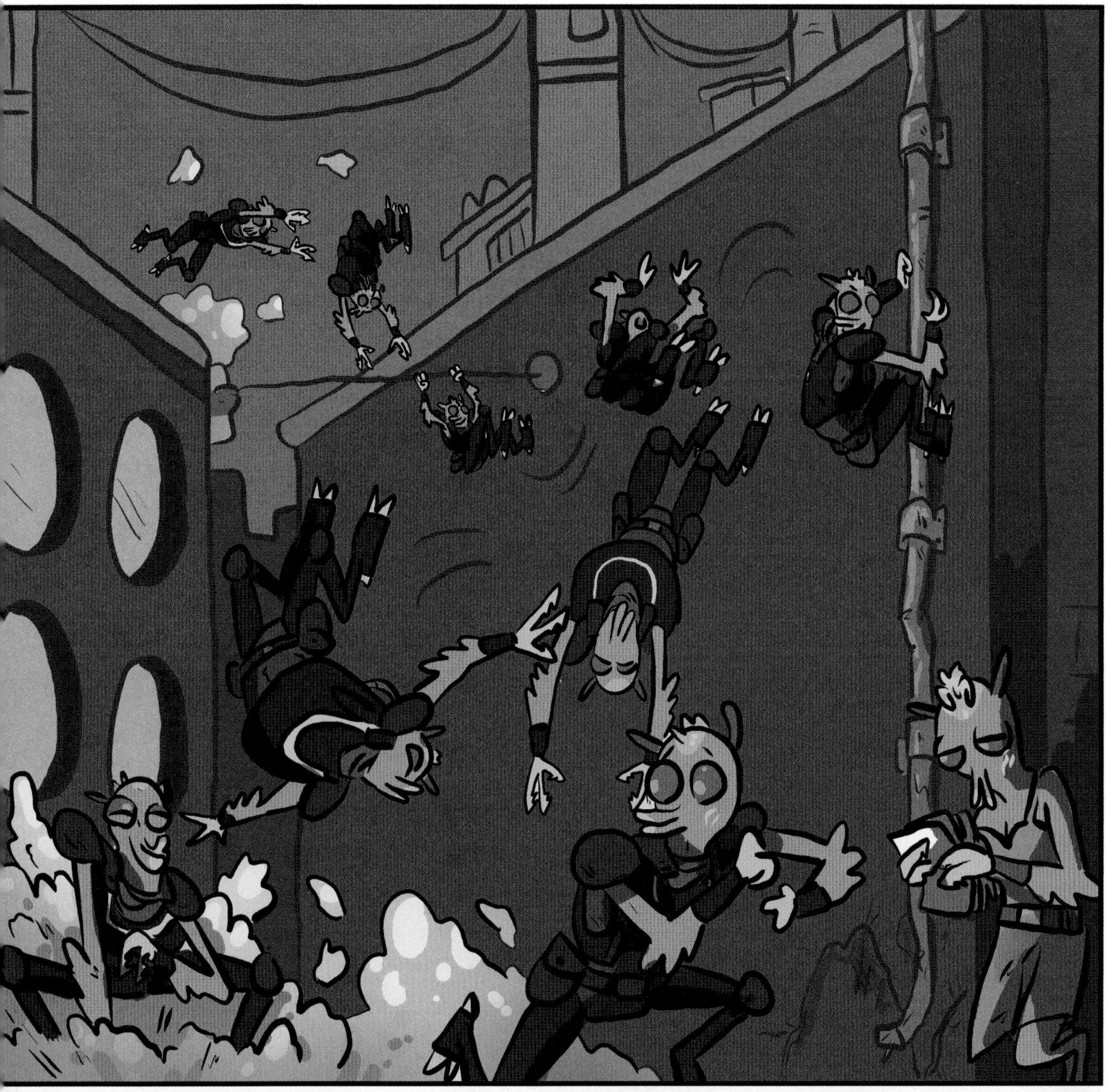

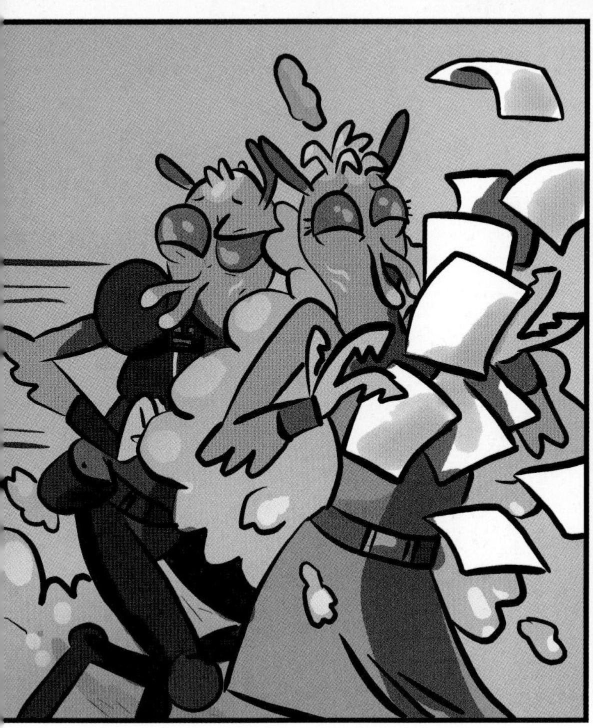

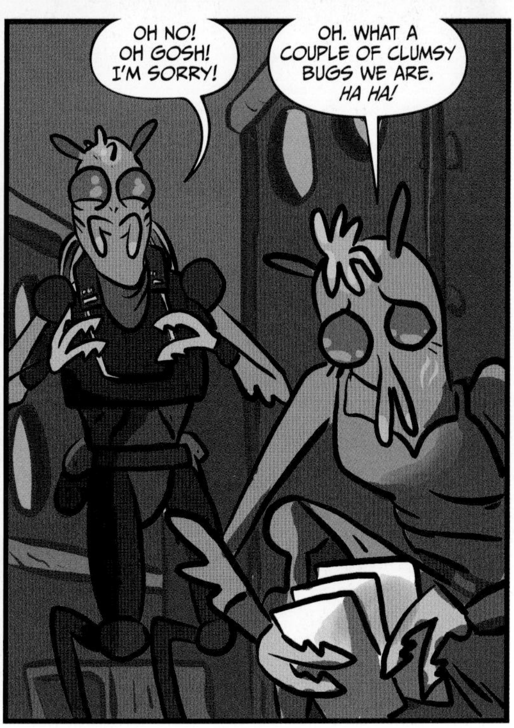
OH NO!
OH GOSH!
I'M SORRY!
OH. WHAT A COUPLE OF CLUMSY BUGS WE ARE. *HA HA!*

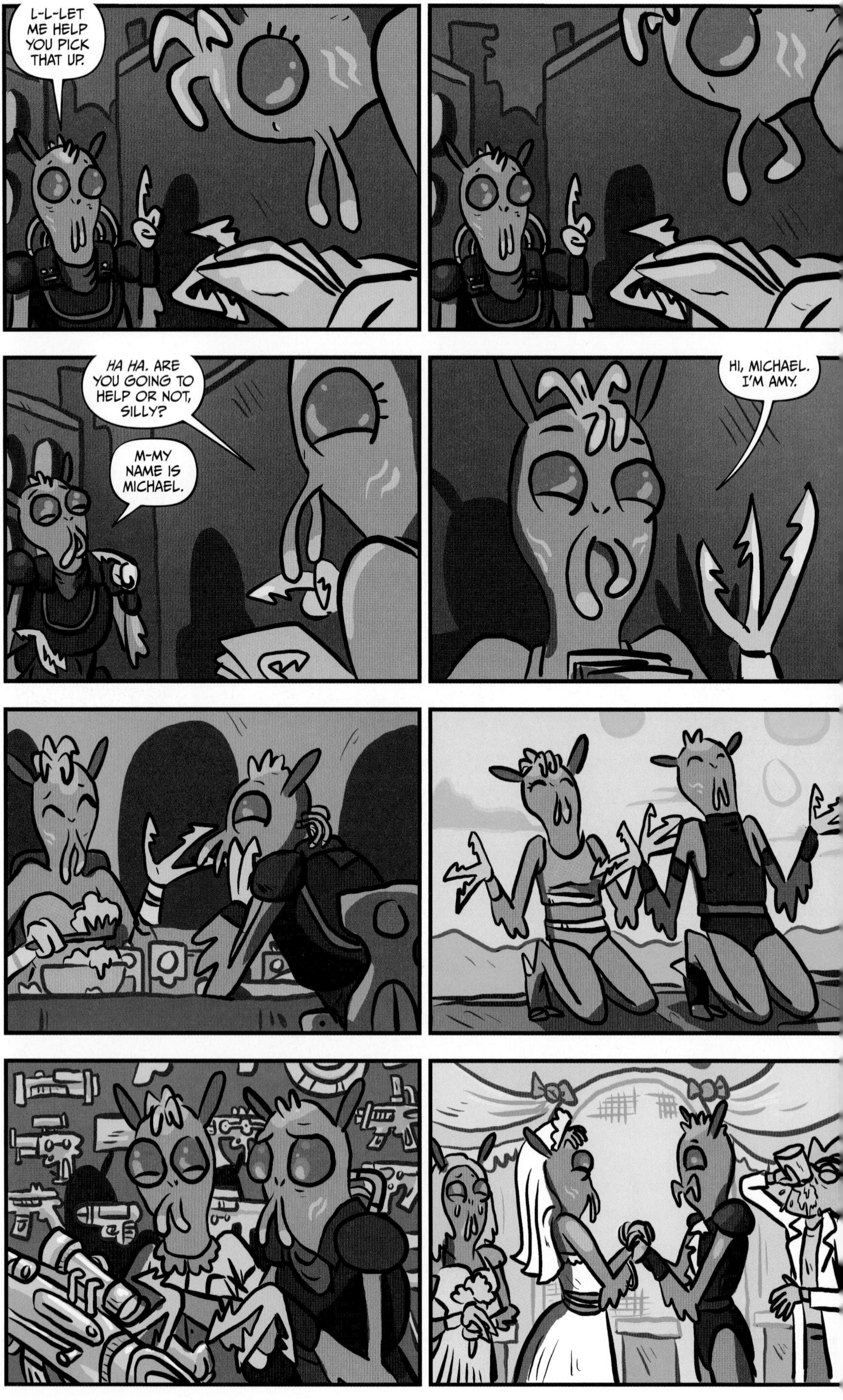
L-L-LET ME HELP YOU PICK THAT UP.
HA HA. ARE YOU GOING TO HELP OR NOT, SILLY?
M-MY NAME IS MICHAEL.
HI, MICHAEL. I'M AMY.

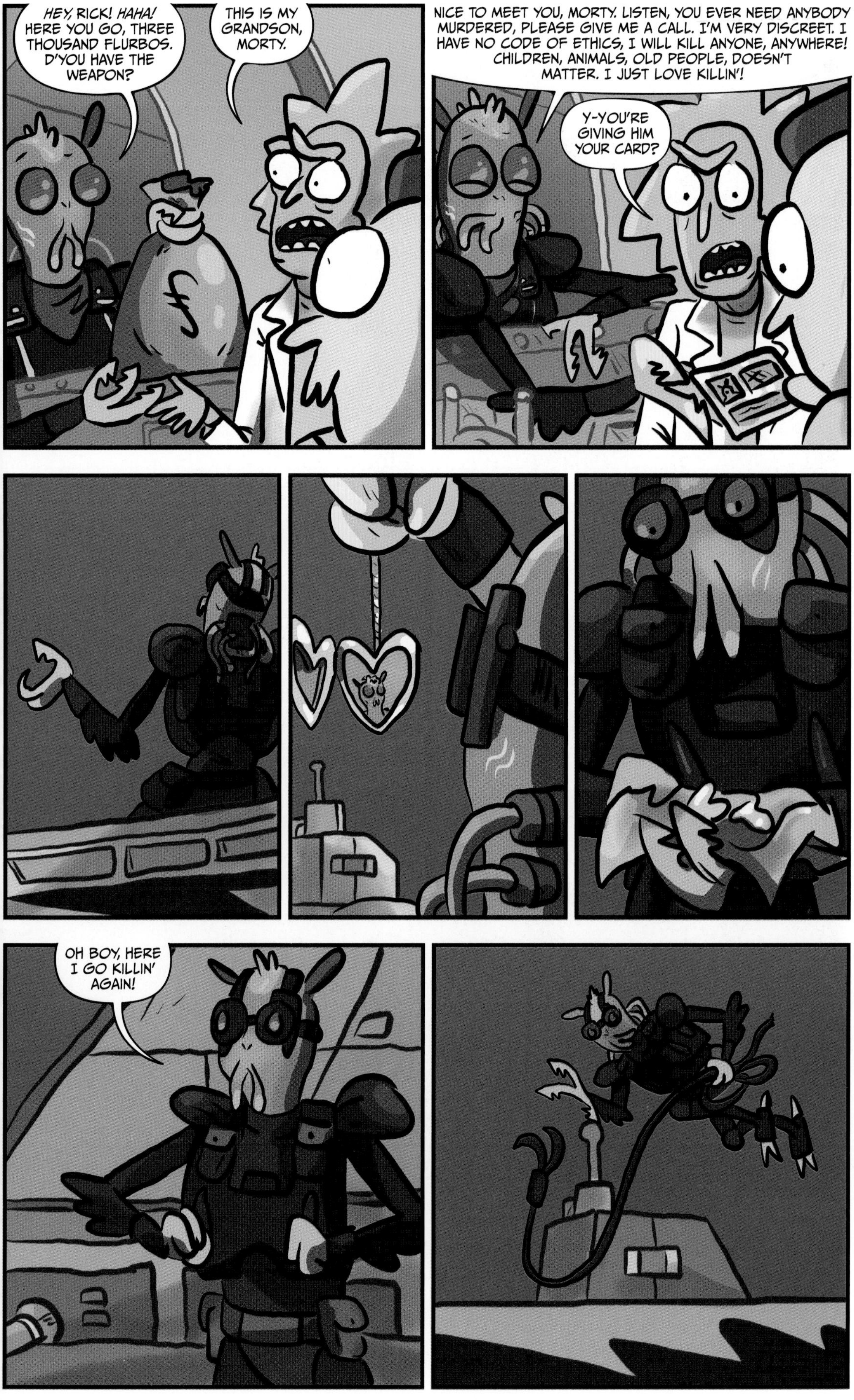
HEY, RICK! HAHA! HERE YOU GO, THREE THOUSAND FLURBOS. D'YOU HAVE THE WEAPON?
THIS IS MY GRANDSON, MORTY.
NICE TO MEET YOU, MORTY. LISTEN, YOU EVER NEED ANYBODY MURDERED, PLEASE GIVE ME A CALL. I'M VERY DISCREET. I HAVE NO CODE OF ETHICS, I WILL KILL ANYONE, ANYWHERE! CHILDREN, ANIMALS, OLD PEOPLE, DOESN'T MATTER. I JUST LOVE KILLIN'!
Y-YOU'RE GIVING HIM YOUR CARD?
OH BOY, HERE I GO KILLIN' AGAIN!

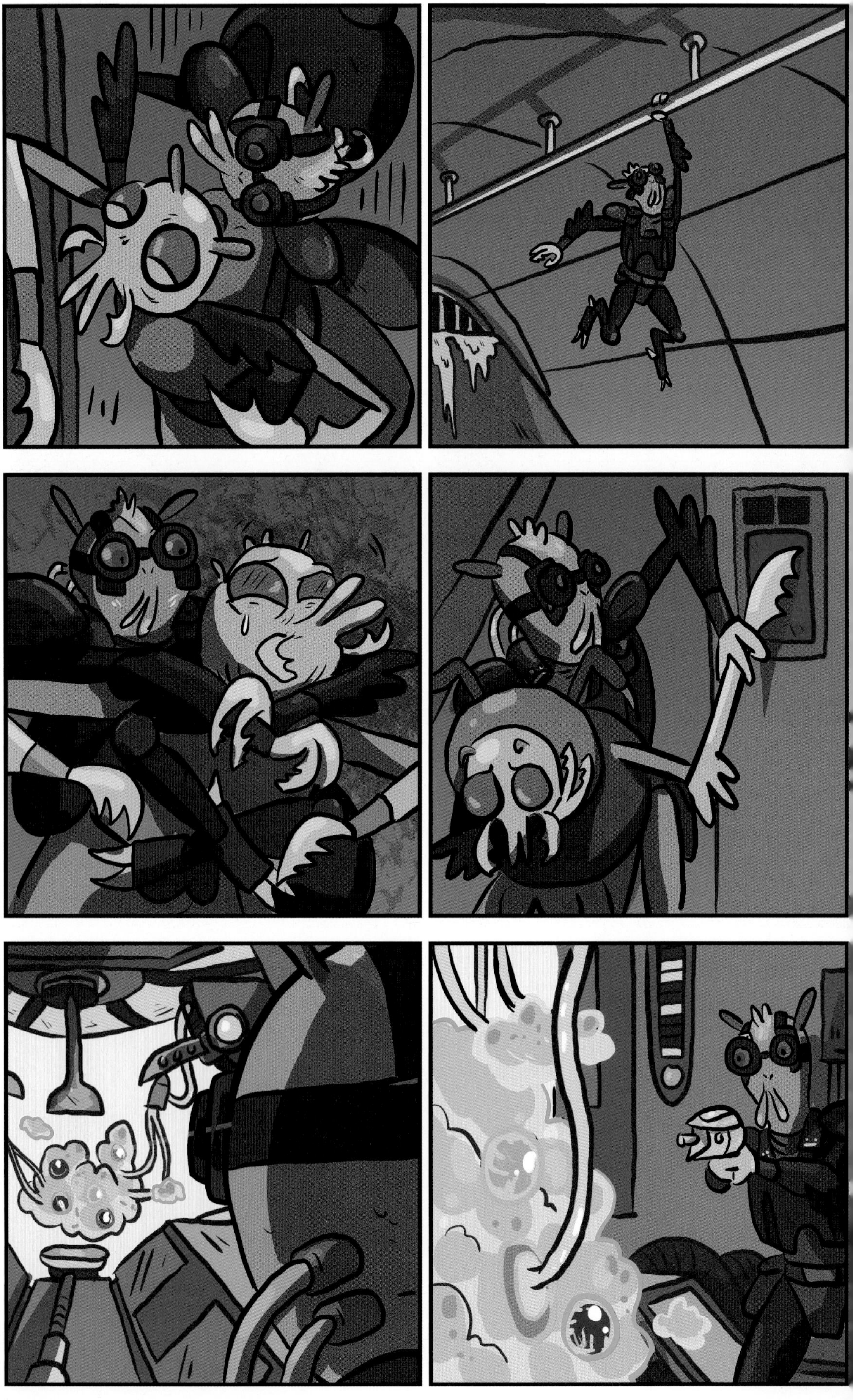

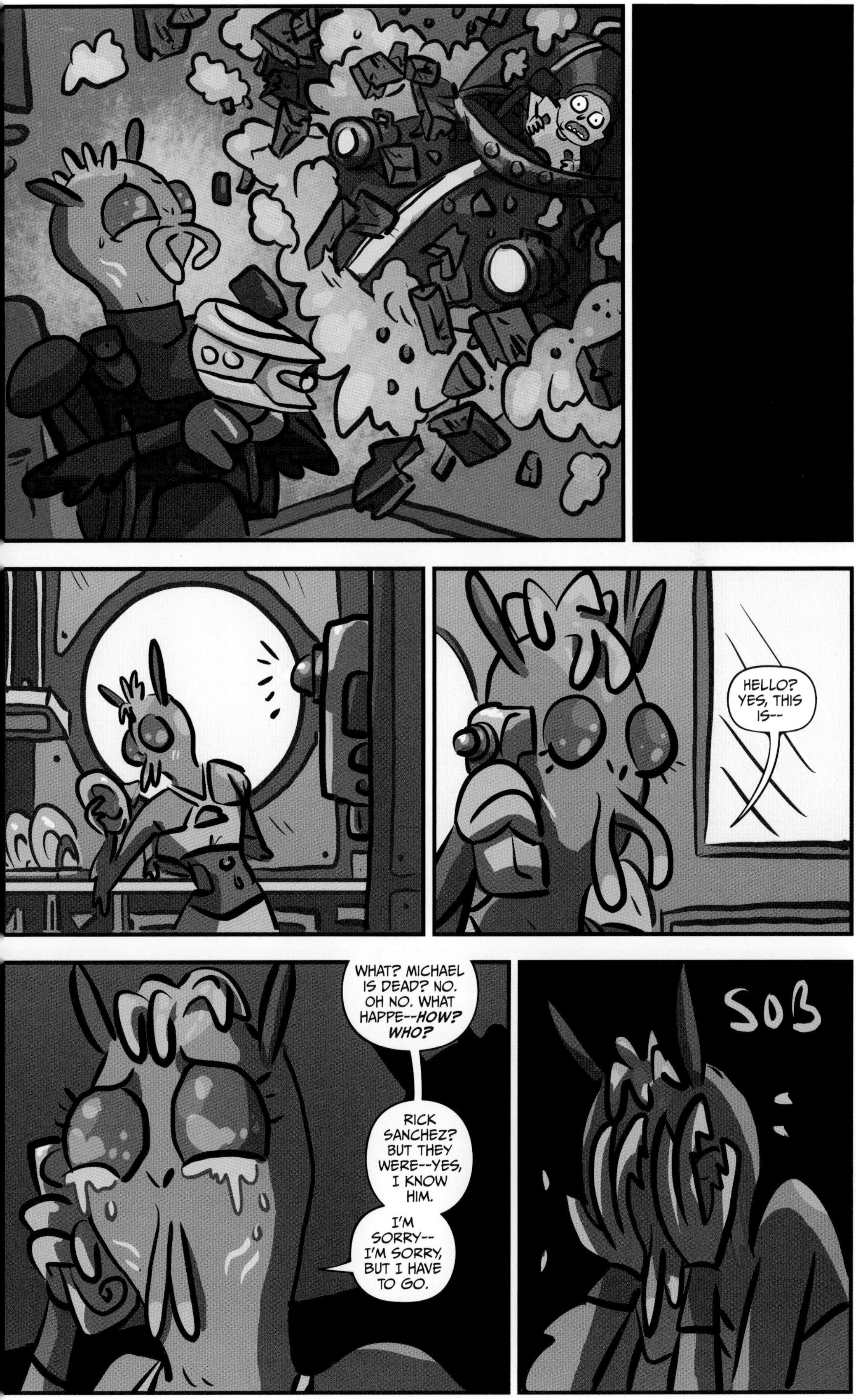
HELLO? YES, THIS IS--
WHAT? MICHAEL IS DEAD? NO. OH NO. WHAT HAPPE--HOW? WHO?
RICK SANCHEZ? BUT THEY WERE--YES, I KNOW HIM.
I'M SORRY--I'M SORRY, BUT I HAVE TO GO.
SOB

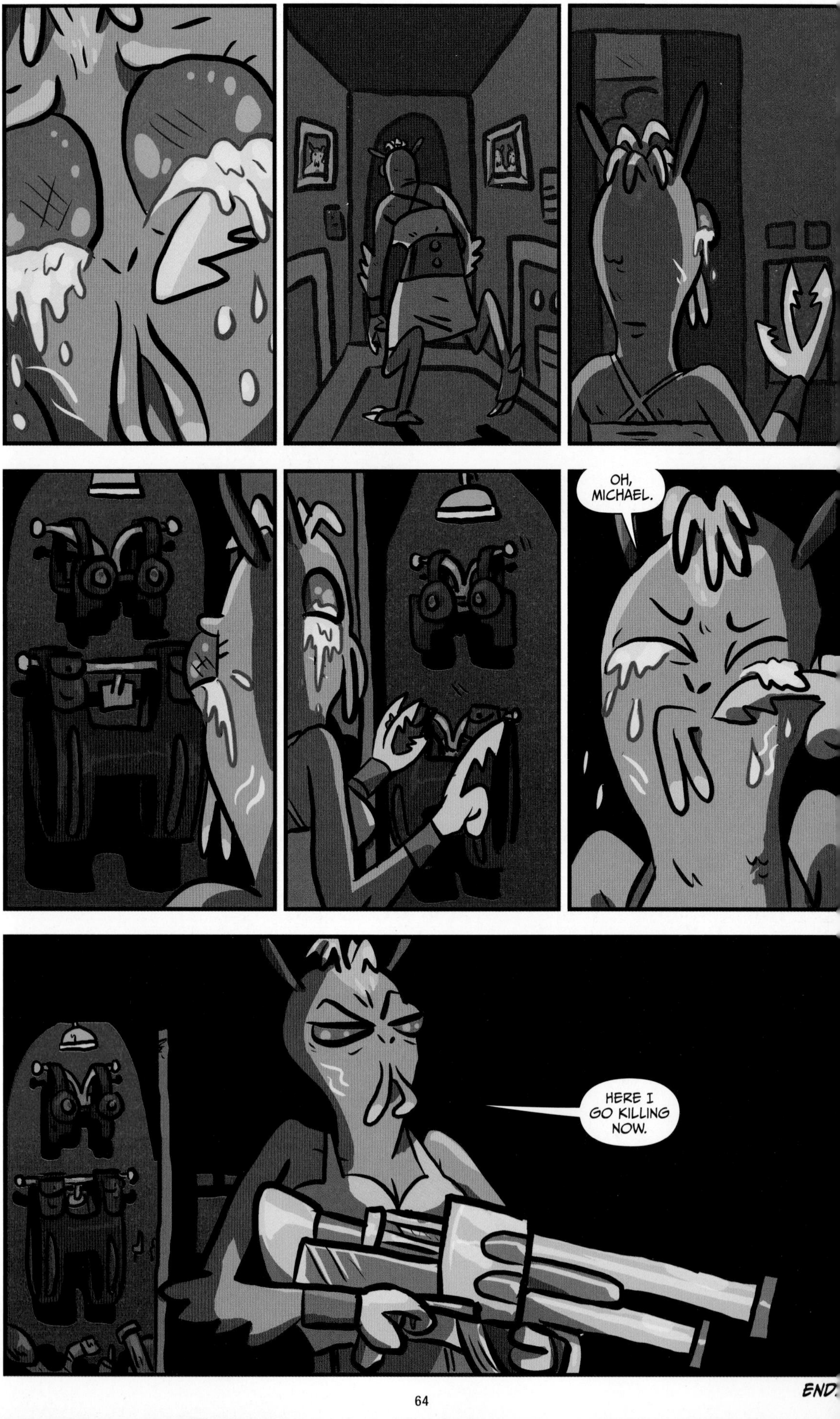
OH, MICHAEL.
HERE I GO KILLING NOW.
END.

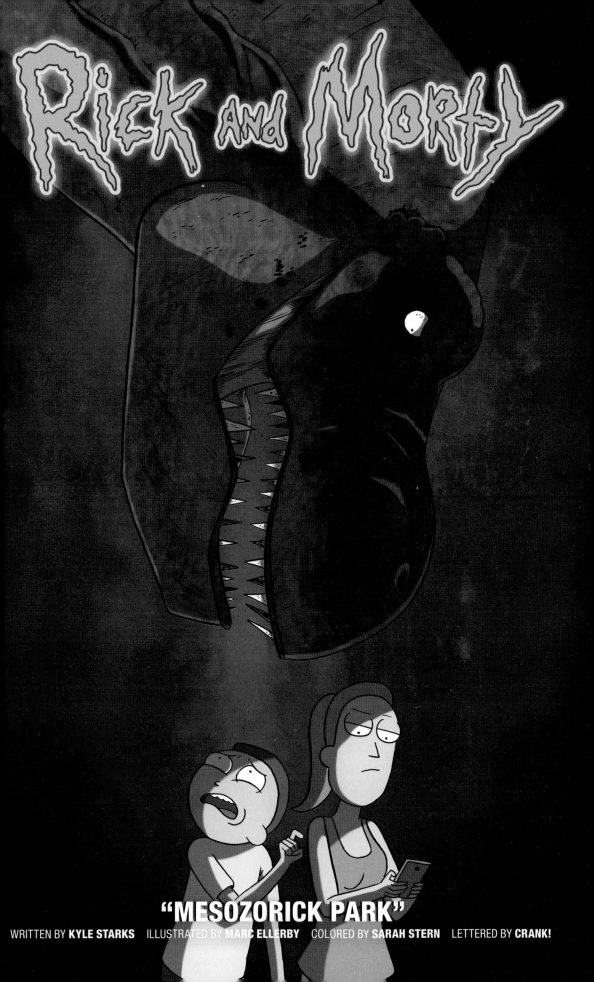

"MESOZORICK PARK"
WRITTEN BY **KYLE STARKS**   ILLUSTRATED BY **MARC ELLERBY**   COLORED BY **SARAH STERN**   LETTERED BY **CRANK!**

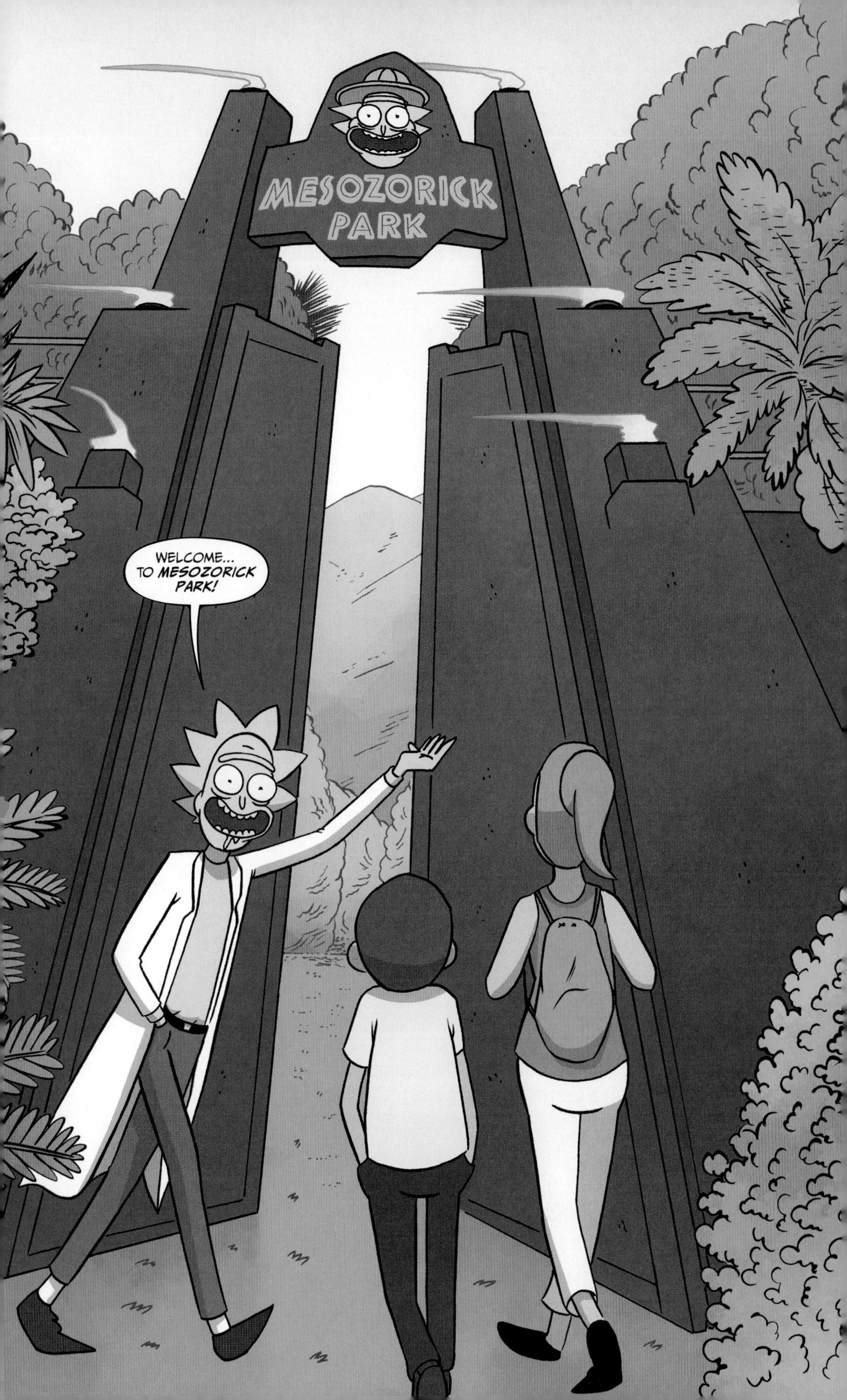
MESOZORICK PARK
WELCOME... TO MESOZORICK PARK!

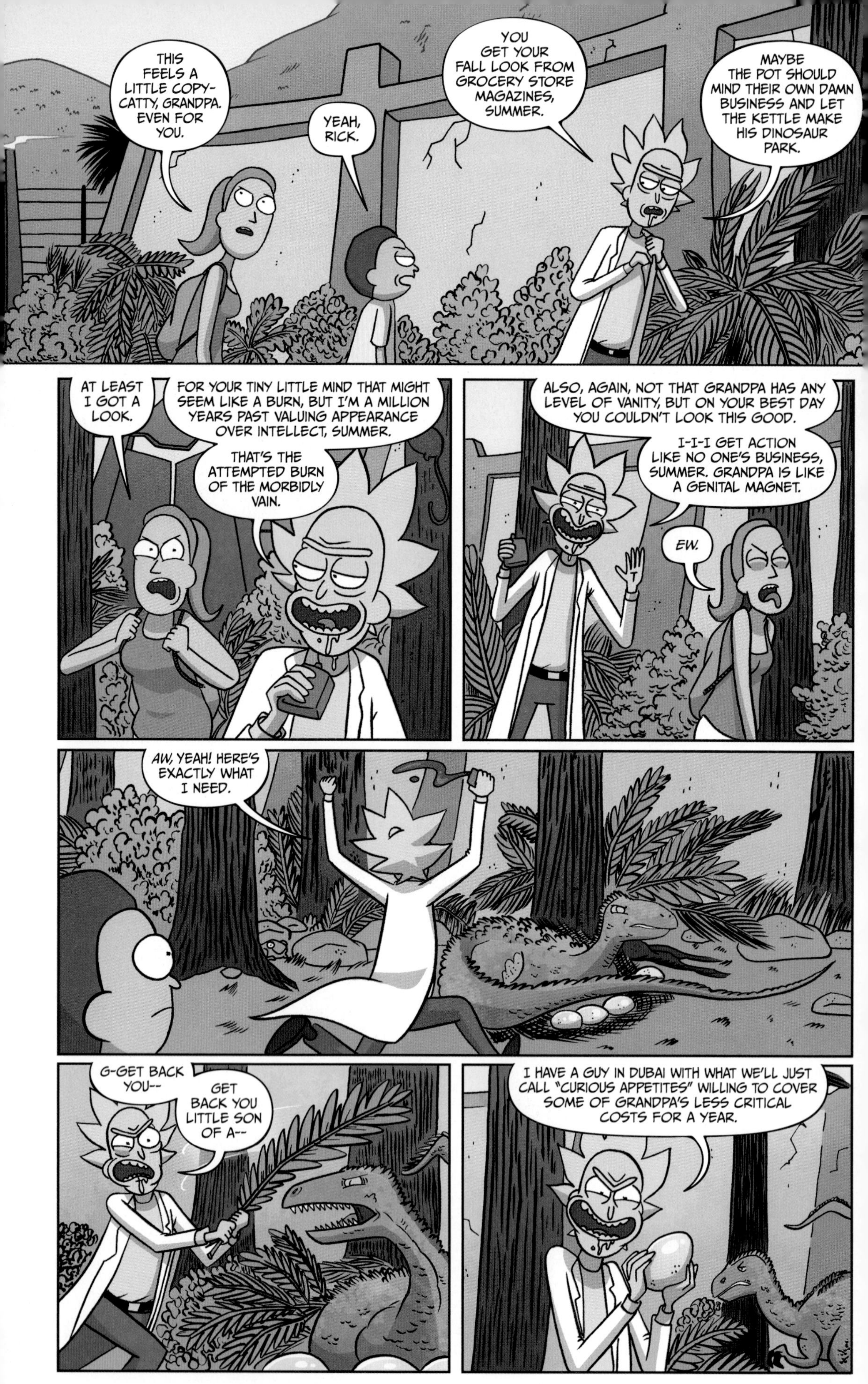

THIS FEELS A LITTLE COPY-CATTY, GRANDPA. EVEN FOR YOU.
YEAH, RICK.
YOU GET YOUR FALL LOOK FROM GROCERY STORE MAGAZINES, SUMMER.
MAYBE THE POT SHOULD MIND THEIR OWN DAMN BUSINESS AND LET THE KETTLE MAKE HIS DINOSAUR PARK.
AT LEAST I GOT A LOOK.
FOR YOUR TINY LITTLE MIND THAT MIGHT SEEM LIKE A BURN, BUT I'M A MILLION YEARS PAST VALUING APPEARANCE OVER INTELLECT, SUMMER.
THAT'S THE ATTEMPTED BURN OF THE MORBIDLY VAIN.
ALSO, AGAIN, NOT THAT GRANDPA HAS ANY LEVEL OF VANITY, BUT ON YOUR BEST DAY YOU COULDN'T LOOK THIS GOOD.
I-I-I GET ACTION LIKE NO ONE'S BUSINESS, SUMMER. GRANDPA IS LIKE A GENITAL MAGNET.
EW.
AW, YEAH! HERE'S EXACTLY WHAT I NEED.
G-GET BACK YOU--
GET BACK YOU LITTLE SON OF A--
I HAVE A GUY IN DUBAI WITH WHAT WE'LL JUST CALL "CURIOUS APPETITES" WILLING TO COVER SOME OF GRANDPA'S LESS CRITICAL COSTS FOR A YEAR.

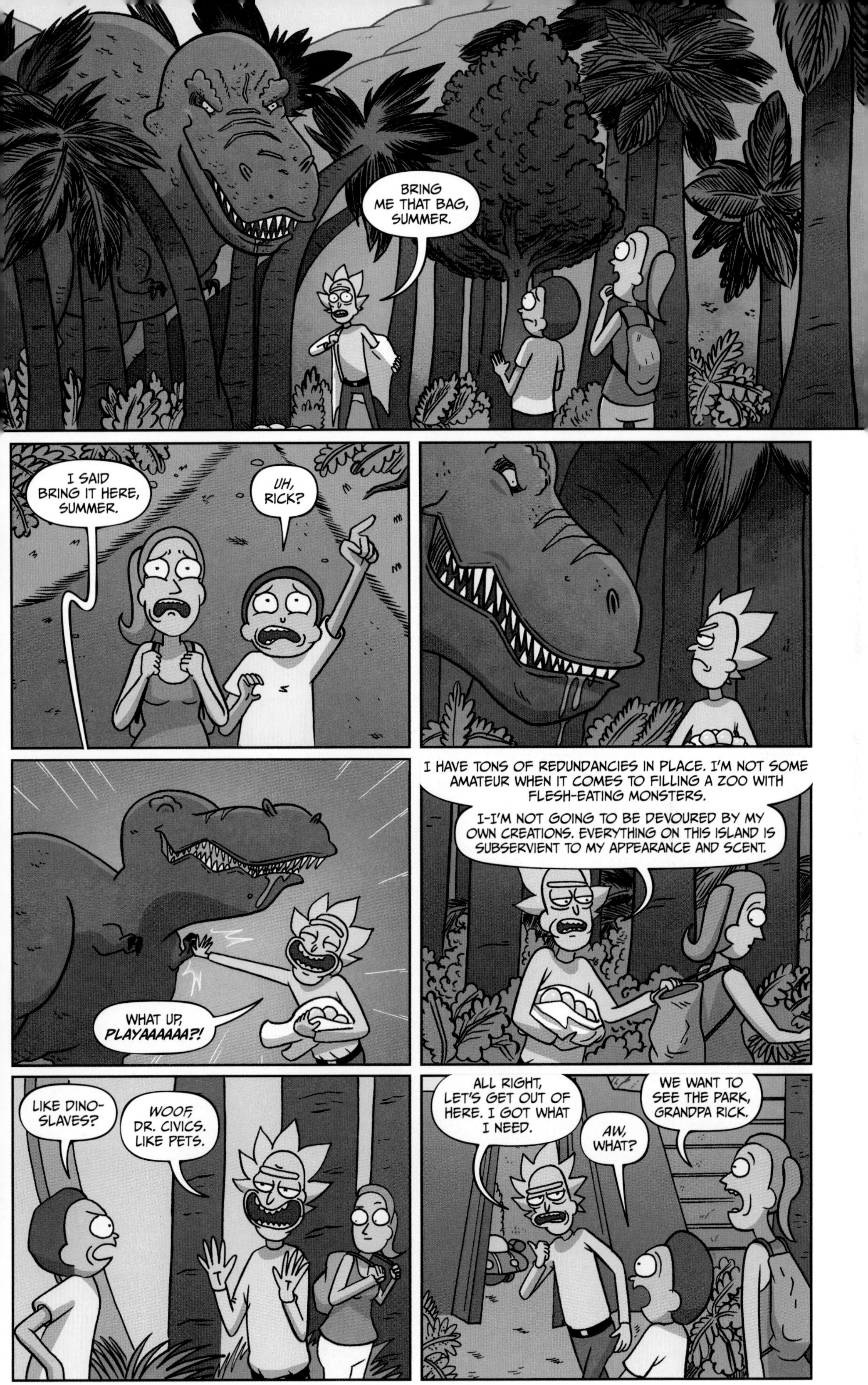
BRING ME THAT BAG, SUMMER.
I SAID BRING IT HERE, SUMMER.
UH, RICK?
WHAT UP, PLAYAAAAAA?!
I HAVE TONS OF REDUNDANCIES IN PLACE. I'M NOT SOME AMATEUR WHEN IT COMES TO FILLING A ZOO WITH FLESH-EATING MONSTERS.
I-I'M NOT GOING TO BE DEVOURED BY MY OWN CREATIONS. EVERYTHING ON THIS ISLAND IS SUBSERVIENT TO MY APPEARANCE AND SCENT.
LIKE DINO-SLAVES?
WOOF, DR. CIVICS. LIKE PETS.
ALL RIGHT, LET'S GET OUT OF HERE. I GOT WHAT I NEED.
AW, WHAT?
WE WANT TO SEE THE PARK, GRANDPA RICK.

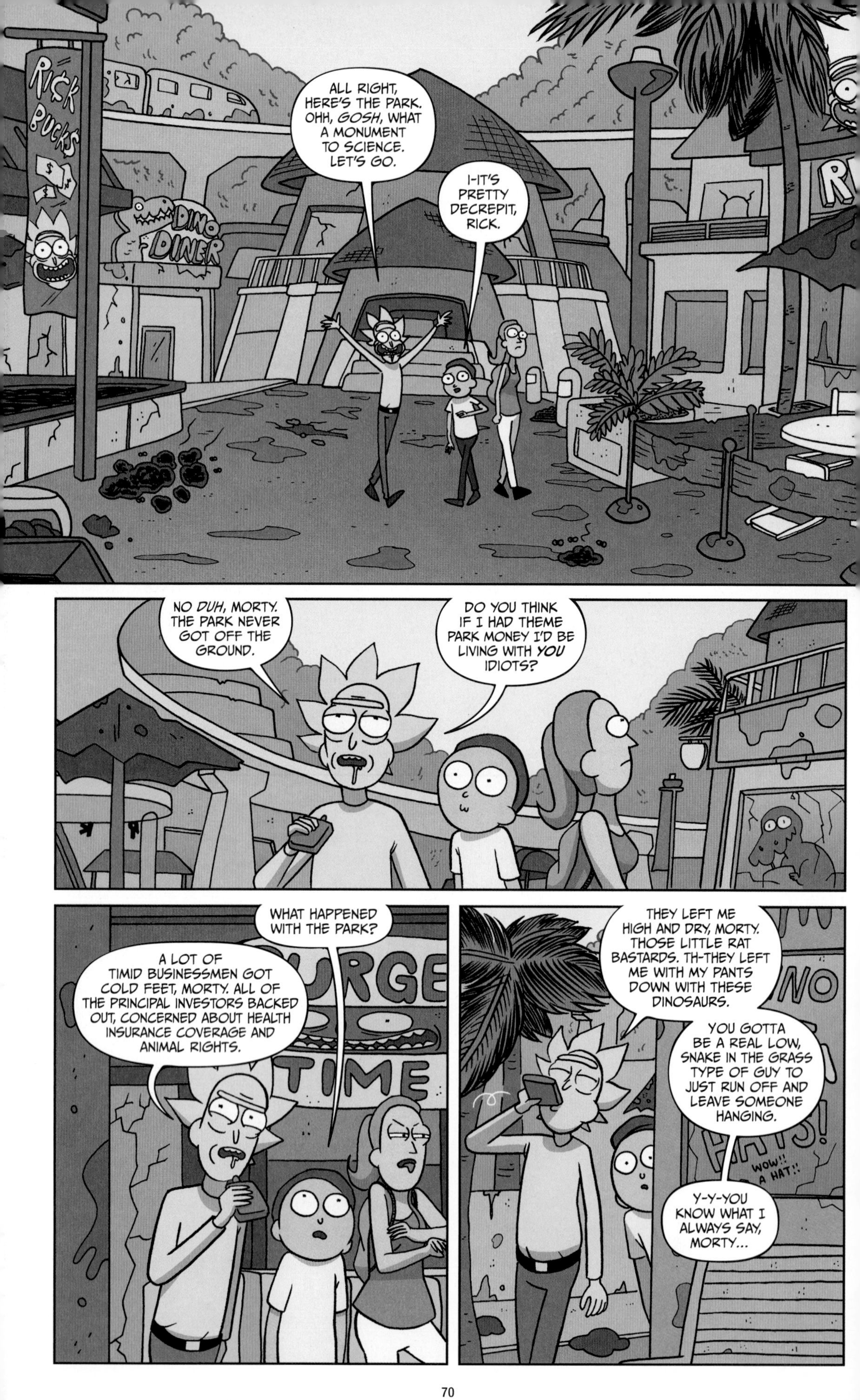
RICK BUCKS
DINO DINER
ALL RIGHT, HERE'S THE PARK. OHH, *GOSH*, WHAT A MONUMENT TO SCIENCE. LET'S GO.
I-IT'S PRETTY DECREPIT, RICK.
NO *DUH*, MORTY. THE PARK NEVER GOT OFF THE GROUND.
DO YOU THINK IF I HAD THEME PARK MONEY I'D BE LIVING WITH *YOU* IDIOTS?
URGE
TIME
WHAT HAPPENED WITH THE PARK?
A LOT OF TIMID BUSINESSMEN GOT COLD FEET, MORTY. ALL OF THE PRINCIPAL INVESTORS BACKED OUT, CONCERNED ABOUT HEALTH INSURANCE COVERAGE AND ANIMAL RIGHTS.
THEY LEFT ME HIGH AND DRY, MORTY. THOSE LITTLE RAT BASTARDS. TH-THEY LEFT ME WITH MY PANTS DOWN WITH THESE DINOSAURS.
YOU GOTTA BE A REAL LOW, SNAKE IN THE GRASS TYPE OF GUY TO JUST RUN OFF AND LEAVE SOMEONE HANGING.
WOW!! A HAT!!
Y-Y-YOU KNOW WHAT I ALWAYS SAY, MORTY...

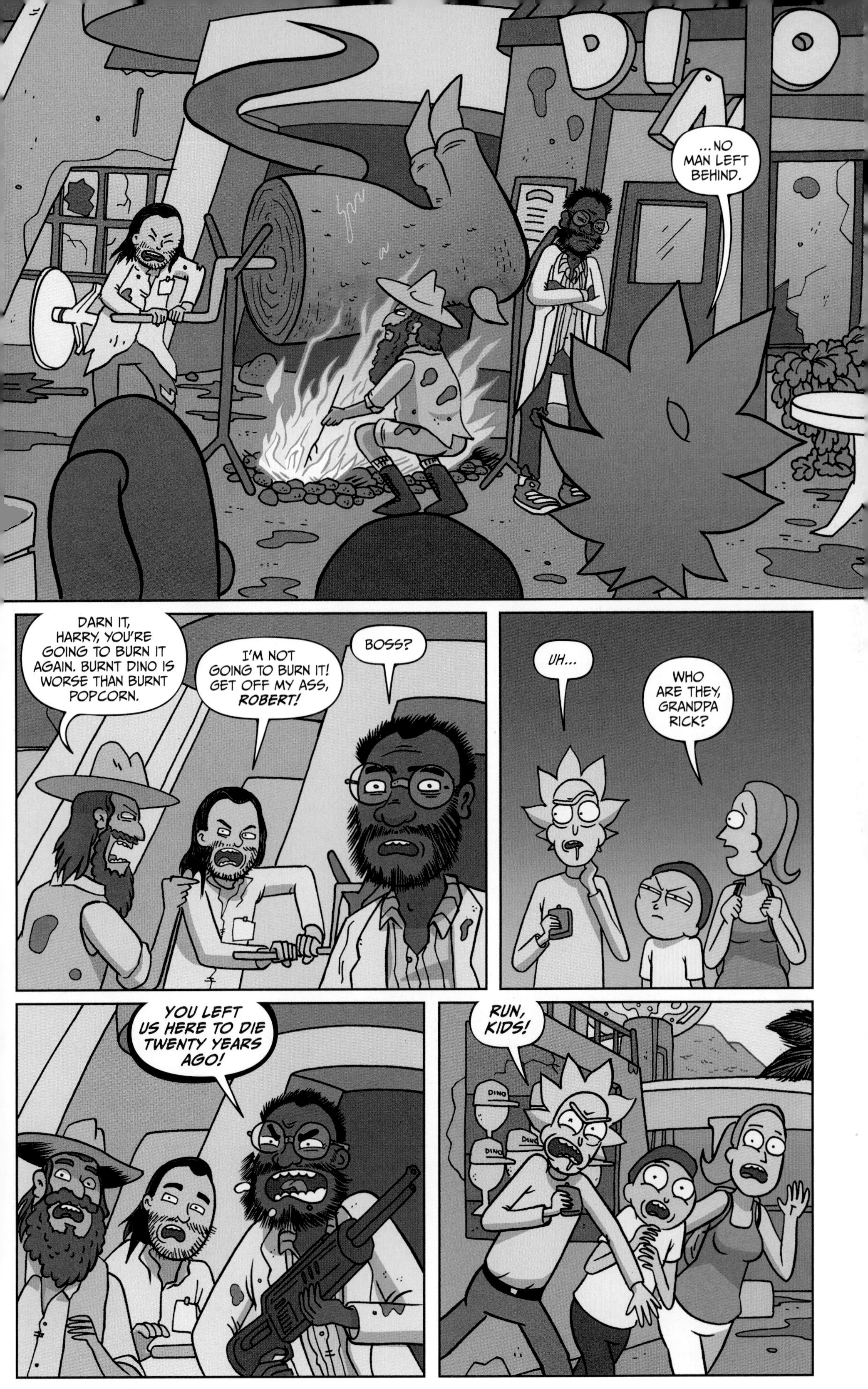

...NO MAN LEFT BEHIND.
DARN IT, HARRY, YOU'RE GOING TO BURN IT AGAIN. BURNT DINO IS WORSE THAN BURNT POPCORN.
I'M NOT GOING TO BURN IT! GET OFF MY ASS, ROBERT!
BOSS?
UH...
WHO ARE THEY, GRANDPA RICK?
YOU LEFT US HERE TO DIE TWENTY YEARS AGO!
RUN, KIDS!

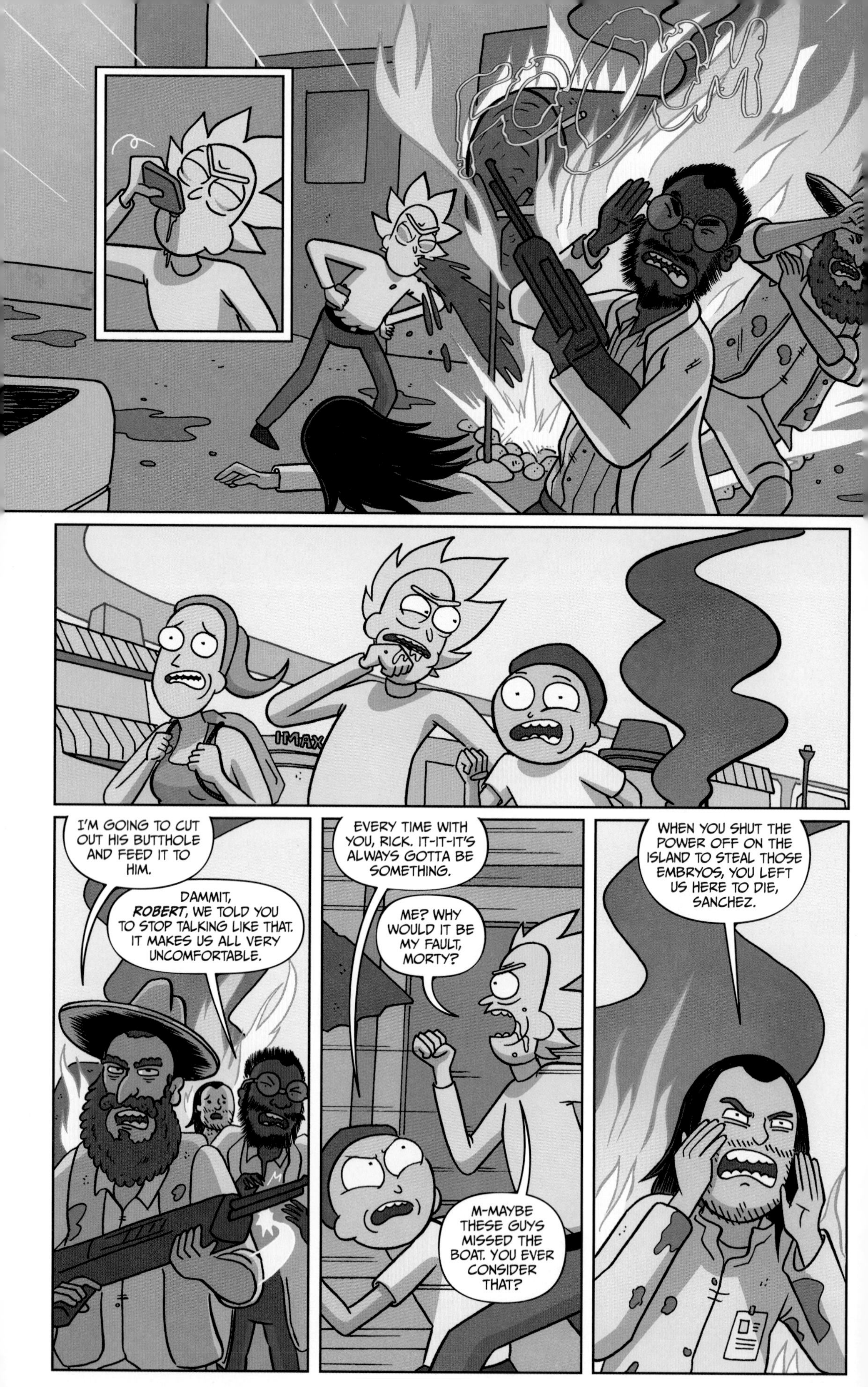
I'M GOING TO CUT OUT HIS BUTTHOLE AND FEED IT TO HIM.
DAMMIT, *ROBERT*, WE TOLD YOU TO STOP TALKING LIKE THAT. IT MAKES US ALL VERY UNCOMFORTABLE.
EVERY TIME WITH YOU, RICK. IT-IT-IT'S ALWAYS GOTTA BE SOMETHING.
ME? WHY WOULD IT BE MY FAULT, MORTY?
M-MAYBE THESE GUYS MISSED THE BOAT. YOU EVER CONSIDER THAT?
WHEN YOU SHUT THE POWER OFF ON THE ISLAND TO STEAL THOSE EMBRYOS, YOU LEFT US HERE TO DIE, SANCHEZ.

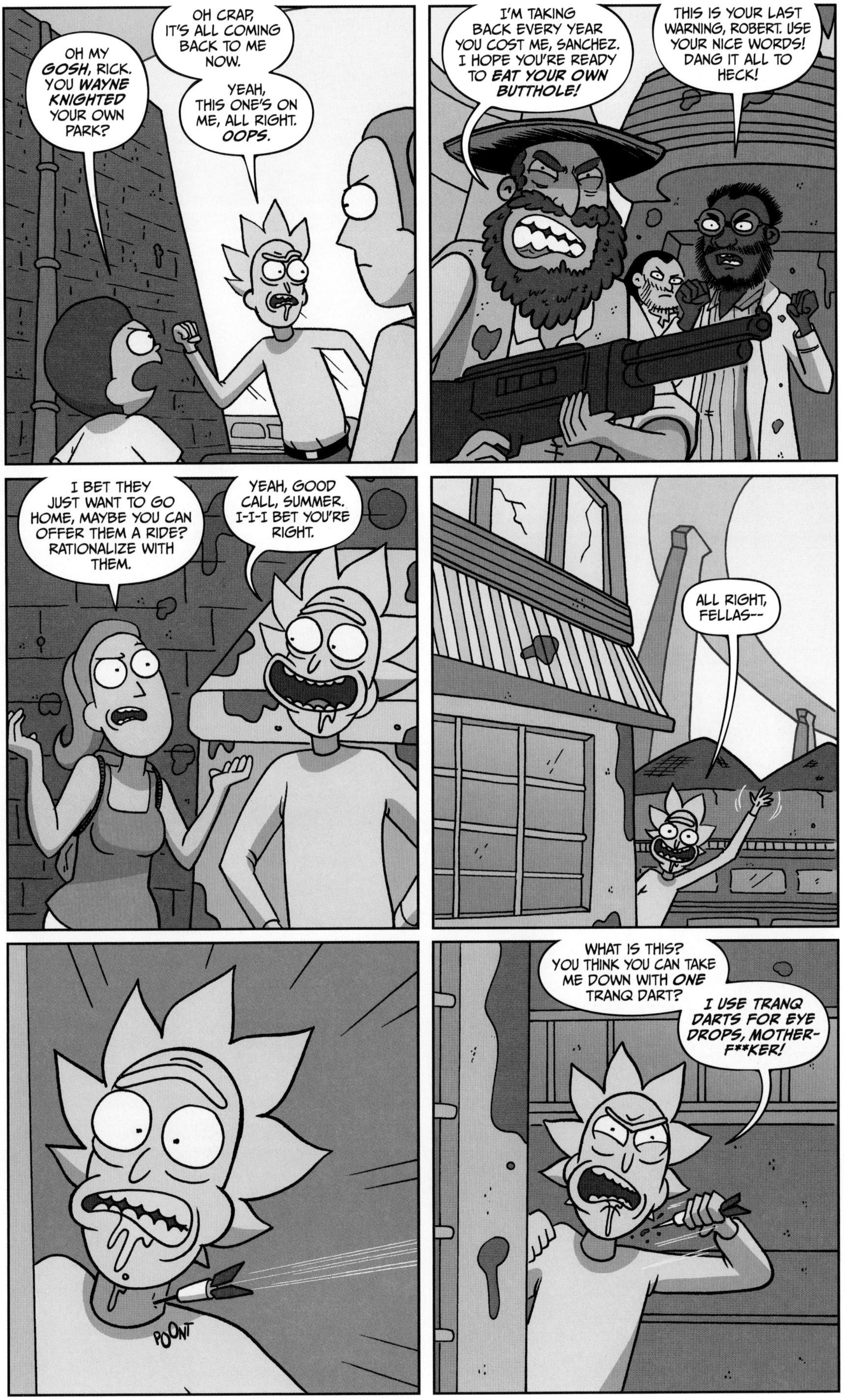
OH MY GOSH, RICK. YOU WAYNE KNIGHTED YOUR OWN PARK?
OH CRAP, IT'S ALL COMING BACK TO ME NOW.
YEAH, THIS ONE'S ON ME, ALL RIGHT. OOPS.
I'M TAKING BACK EVERY YEAR YOU COST ME, SANCHEZ. I HOPE YOU'RE READY TO EAT YOUR OWN BUTTHOLE!
THIS IS YOUR LAST WARNING, ROBERT. USE YOUR NICE WORDS! DANG IT ALL TO HECK!
I BET THEY JUST WANT TO GO HOME, MAYBE YOU CAN OFFER THEM A RIDE? RATIONALIZE WITH THEM.
YEAH, GOOD CALL, SUMMER. I-I-I BET YOU'RE RIGHT.
ALL RIGHT, FELLAS--
POONT
WHAT IS THIS? YOU THINK YOU CAN TAKE ME DOWN WITH ONE TRANQ DART?
I USE TRANQ DARTS FOR EYE DROPS, MOTHER-F**KER!

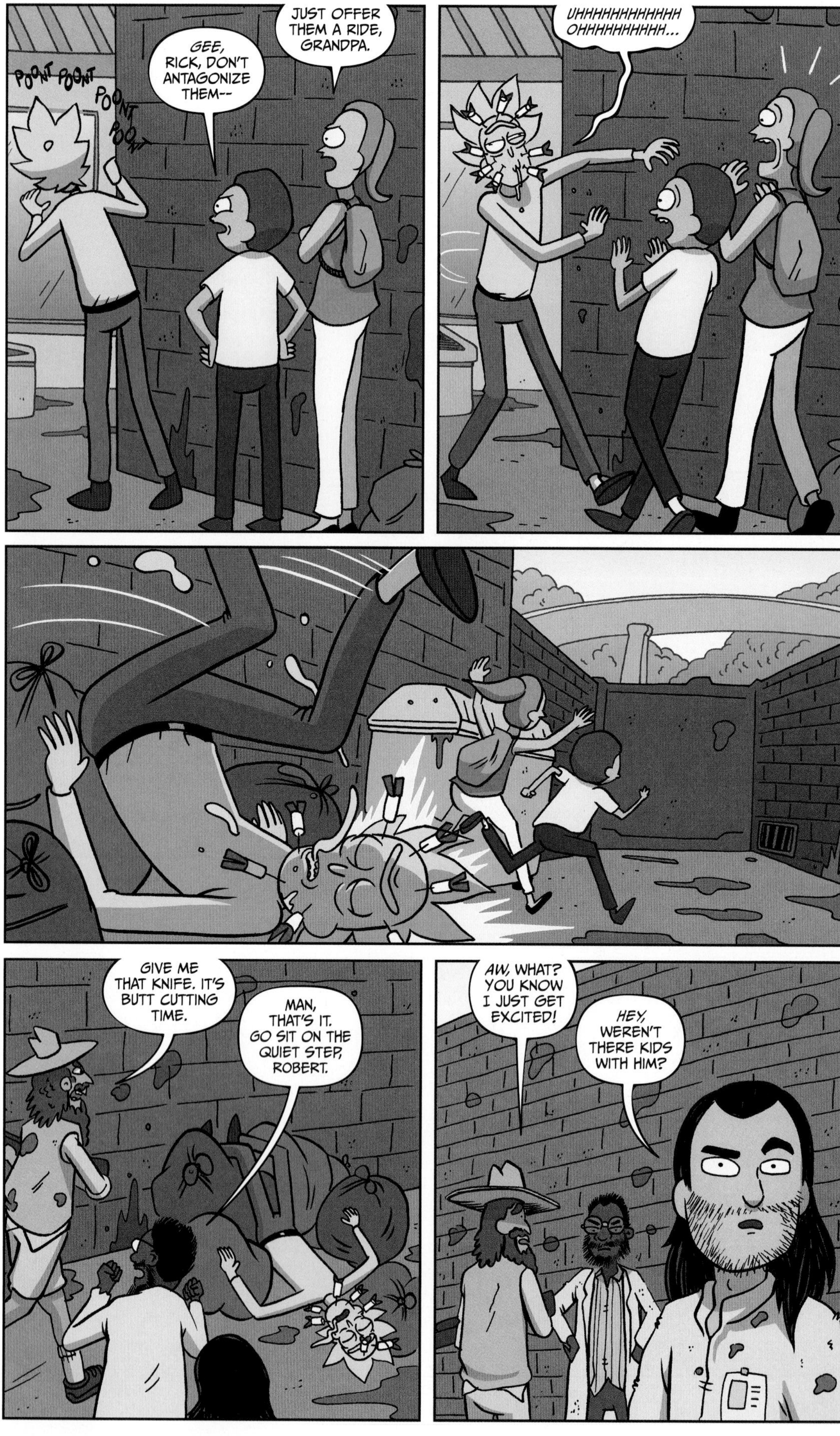
POONT POONT
POONT
POONT
GEE, RICK, DON'T ANTAGONIZE THEM--
JUST OFFER THEM A RIDE, GRANDPA.
UHHHHHHHHHHHH OHHHHHHHHHH...
GIVE ME THAT KNIFE. IT'S BUTT CUTTING TIME.
MAN, THAT'S IT. GO SIT ON THE QUIET STEP, ROBERT.
AW, WHAT? YOU KNOW I JUST GET EXCITED!
HEY, WEREN'T THERE KIDS WITH HIM?

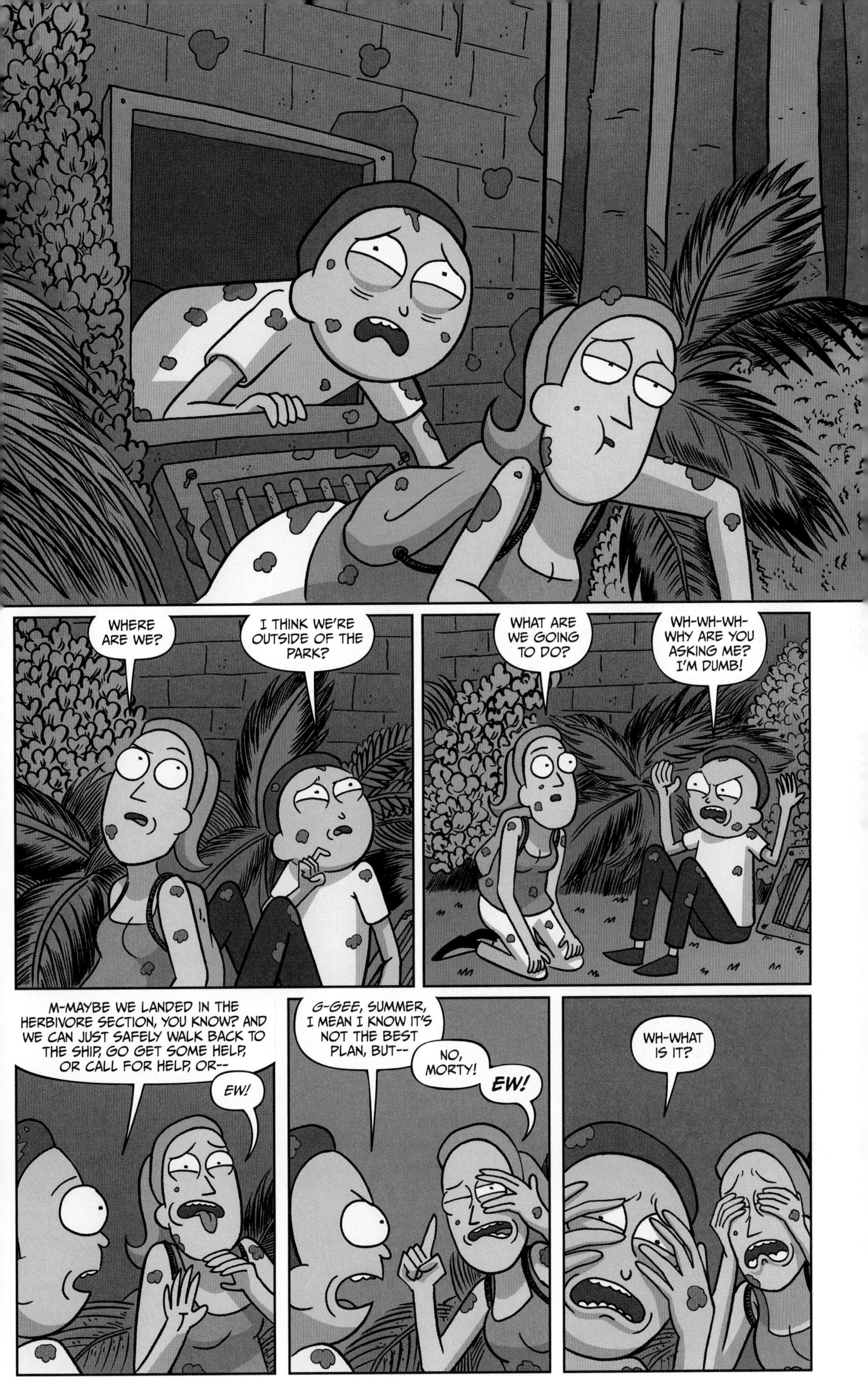
WHERE ARE WE?
I THINK WE'RE OUTSIDE OF THE PARK?
WHAT ARE WE GOING TO DO?
WH-WH-WH-WHY ARE YOU ASKING ME? I'M DUMB!
M-MAYBE WE LANDED IN THE HERBIVORE SECTION, YOU KNOW? AND WE CAN JUST SAFELY WALK BACK TO THE SHIP, GO GET SOME HELP, OR CALL FOR HELP, OR--
EW!
G-GEE, SUMMER, I MEAN I KNOW IT'S NOT THE BEST PLAN, BUT--
NO, MORTY!
EW!
WH-WHAT IS IT?

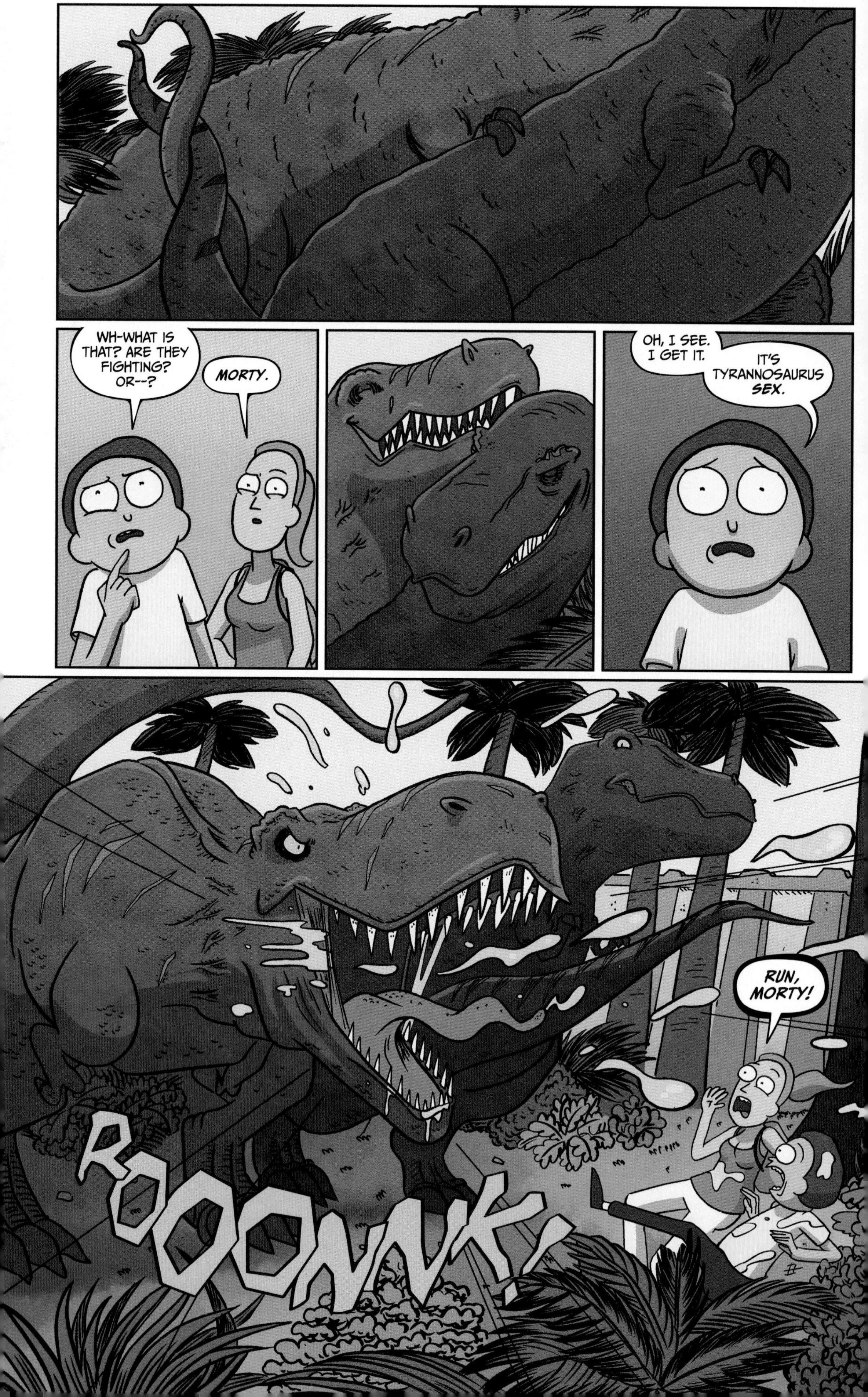
WH-WHAT IS THAT? ARE THEY FIGHTING? OR--?
MORTY.
OH, I SEE. I GET IT.
IT'S TYRANNOSAURUS SEX.
ROOONNK!
RUN, MORTY!

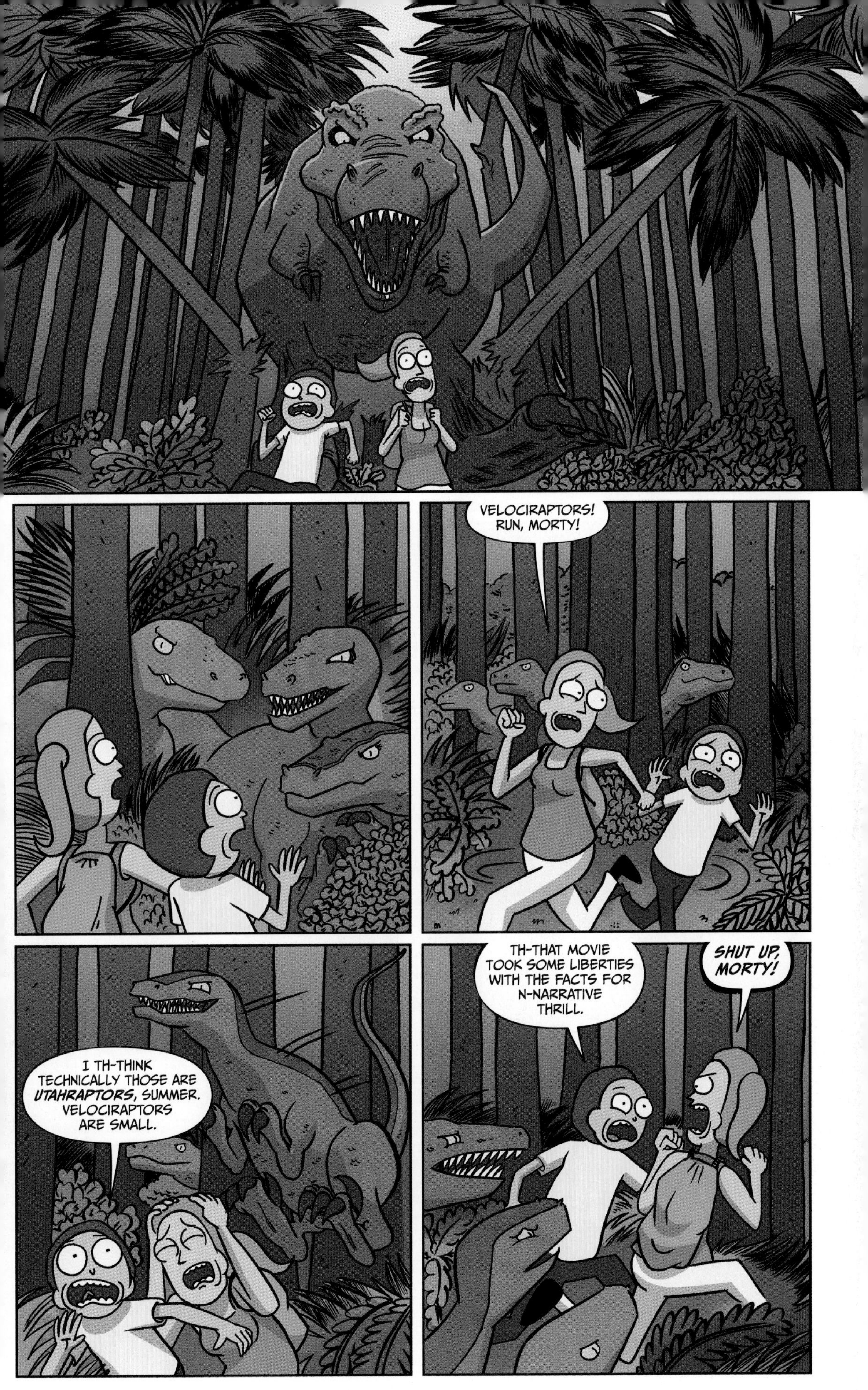
VELOCIRAPTORS! RUN, MORTY!
I TH-THINK TECHNICALLY THOSE ARE UTAHRAPTORS, SUMMER. VELOCIRAPTORS ARE SMALL.
TH-THAT MOVIE TOOK SOME LIBERTIES WITH THE FACTS FOR N-NARRATIVE THRILL.
SHUT UP, MORTY!

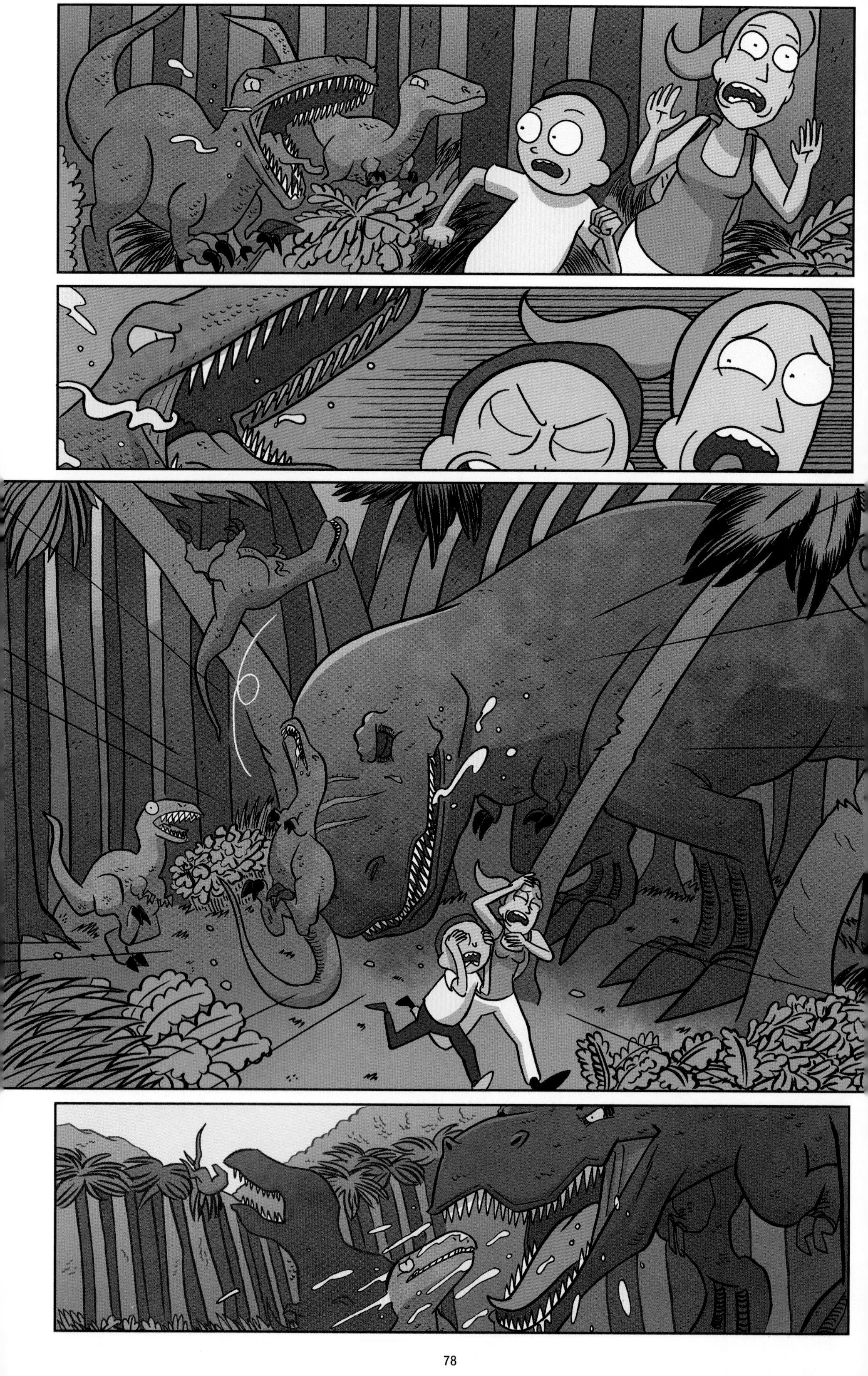

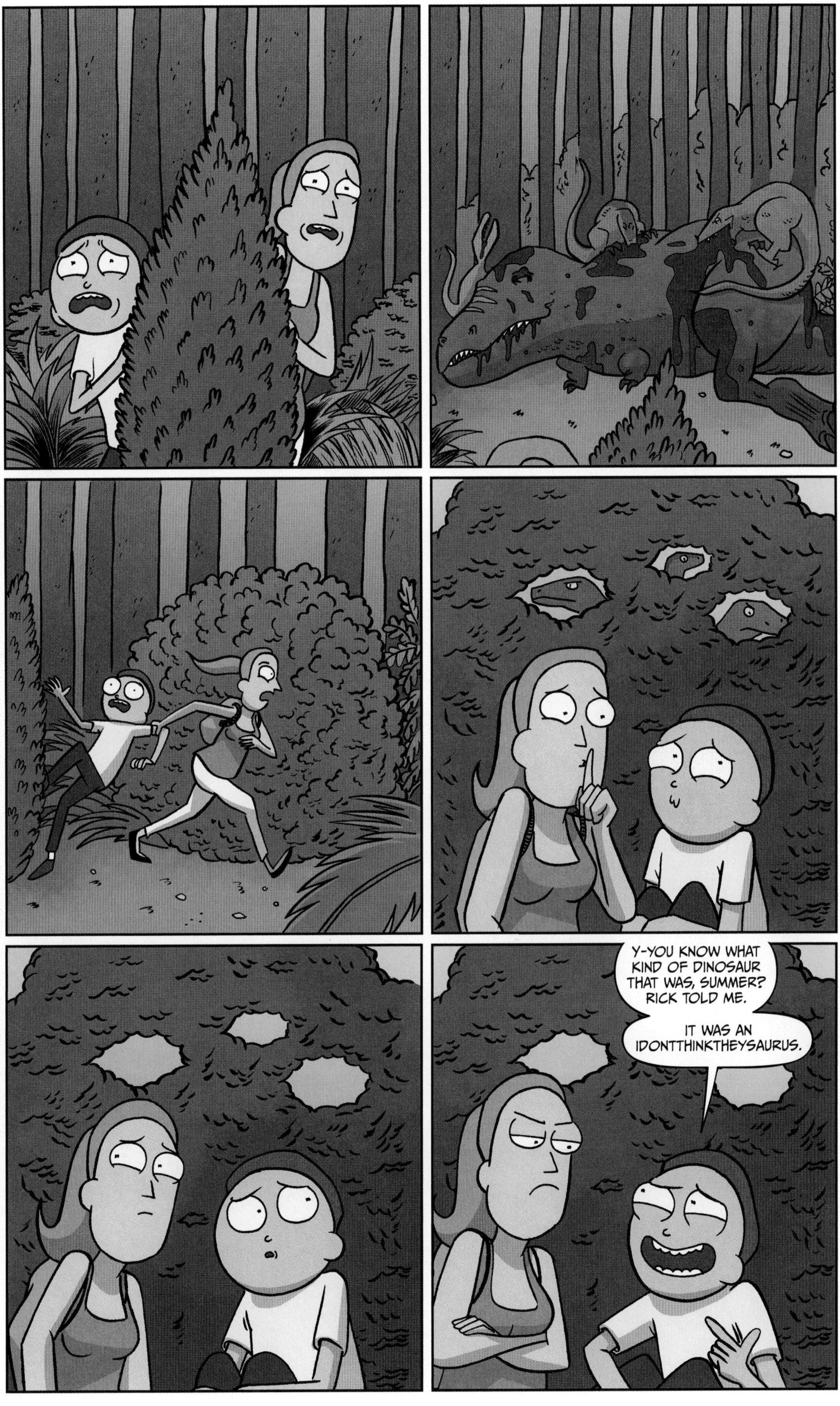
Y-YOU KNOW WHAT KIND OF DINOSAUR THAT WAS, SUMMER? RICK TOLD ME.
IT WAS AN IDONTTHINKTHEYSAURUS.

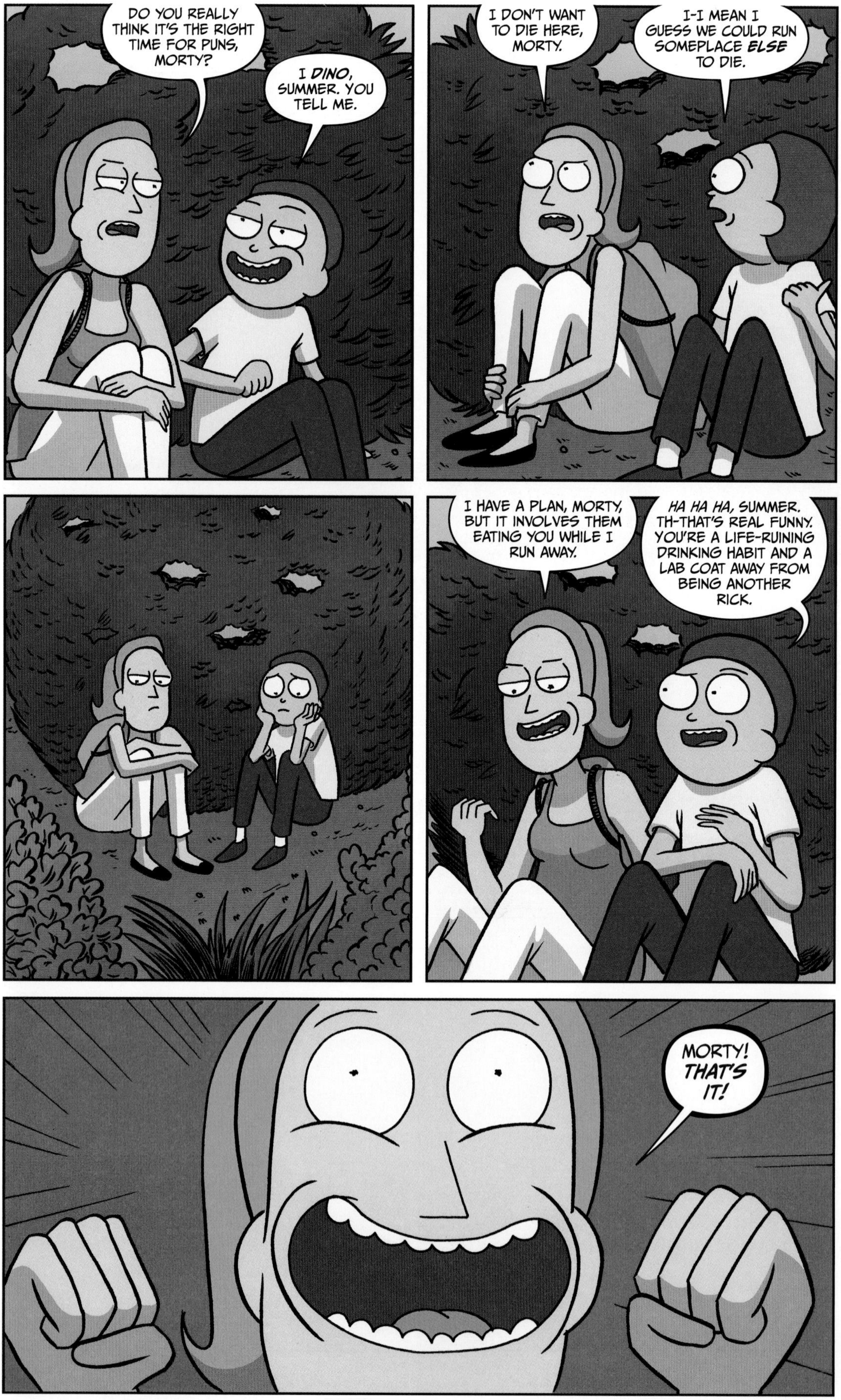
DO YOU REALLY THINK IT'S THE RIGHT TIME FOR PUNS, MORTY?
I *DINO*, SUMMER. YOU TELL ME.
I DON'T WANT TO DIE HERE, MORTY.
I-I MEAN I GUESS WE COULD RUN SOMEPLACE *ELSE* TO DIE.
I HAVE A PLAN, MORTY, BUT IT INVOLVES THEM EATING YOU WHILE I RUN AWAY.
HA HA HA, SUMMER. TH-THAT'S REAL FUNNY. YOU'RE A LIFE-RUINING DRINKING HABIT AND A LAB COAT AWAY FROM BEING ANOTHER RICK.
MORTY! *THAT'S IT!*

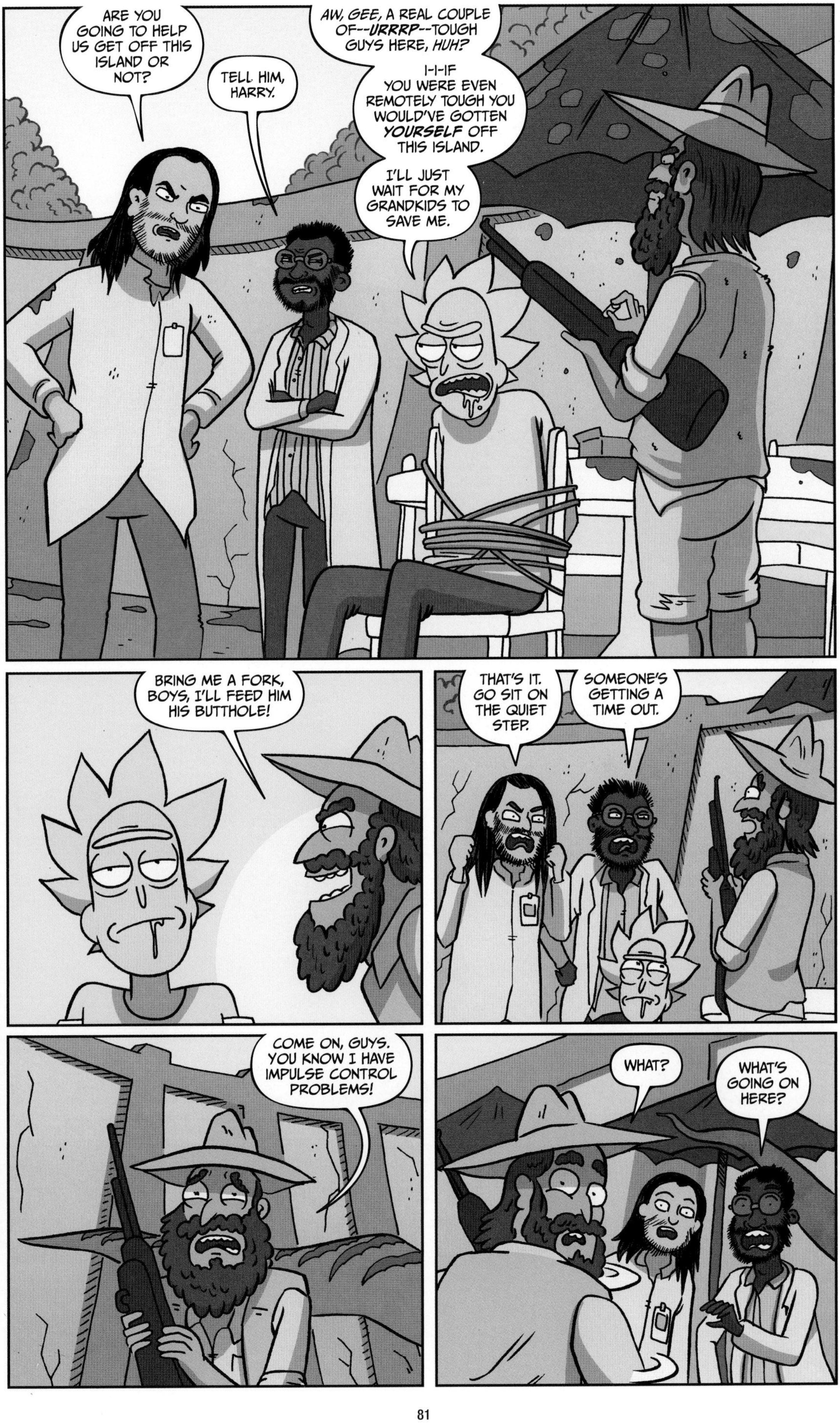
ARE YOU GOING TO HELP US GET OFF THIS ISLAND OR NOT?
TELL HIM, HARRY.
AW, GEE, A REAL COUPLE OF--URRRP--TOUGH GUYS HERE, HUH?
I-I-IF YOU WERE EVEN REMOTELY TOUGH YOU WOULD'VE GOTTEN YOURSELF OFF THIS ISLAND.
I'LL JUST WAIT FOR MY GRANDKIDS TO SAVE ME.
BRING ME A FORK, BOYS, I'LL FEED HIM HIS BUTTHOLE!
THAT'S IT. GO SIT ON THE QUIET STEP.
SOMEONE'S GETTING A TIME OUT.
COME ON, GUYS. YOU KNOW I HAVE IMPULSE CONTROL PROBLEMS!
WHAT?
WHAT'S GOING ON HERE?

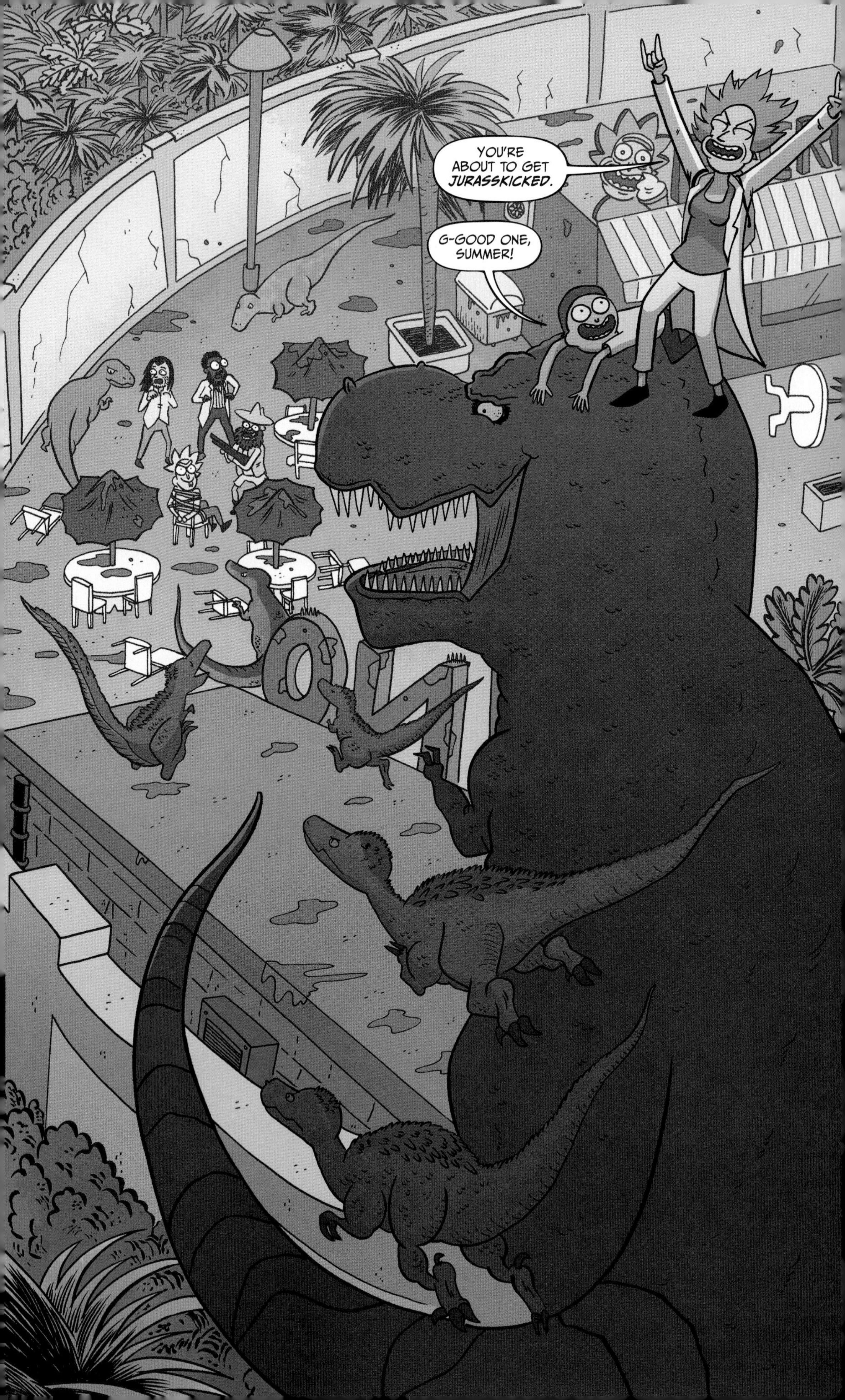
YOU'RE ABOUT TO GET JURASSKICKED.
G-GOOD ONE, SUMMER!

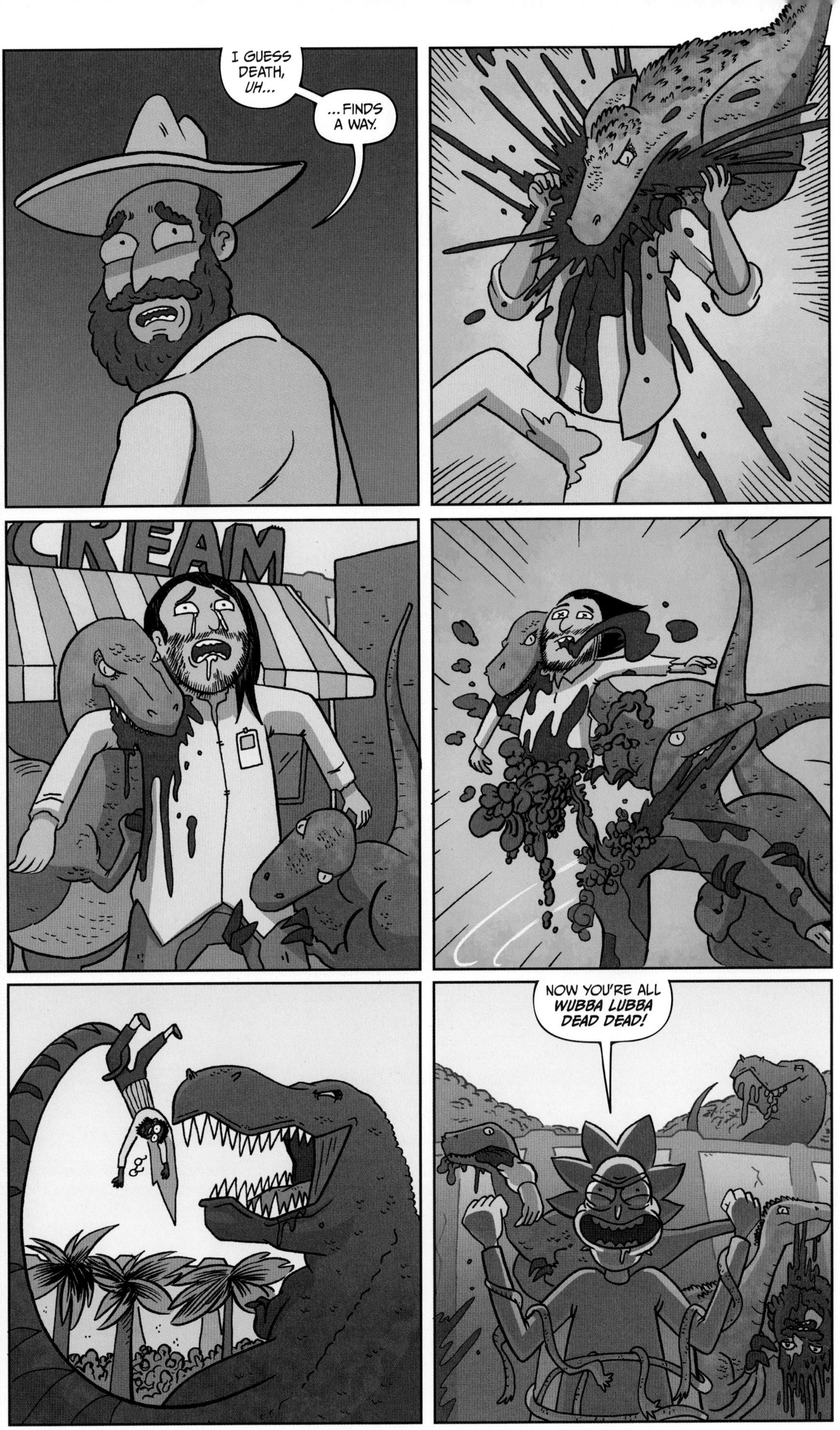
I GUESS DEATH, UH...
...FINDS A WAY.
CREAM
NOW YOU'RE ALL WUBBA LUBBA DEAD DEAD!

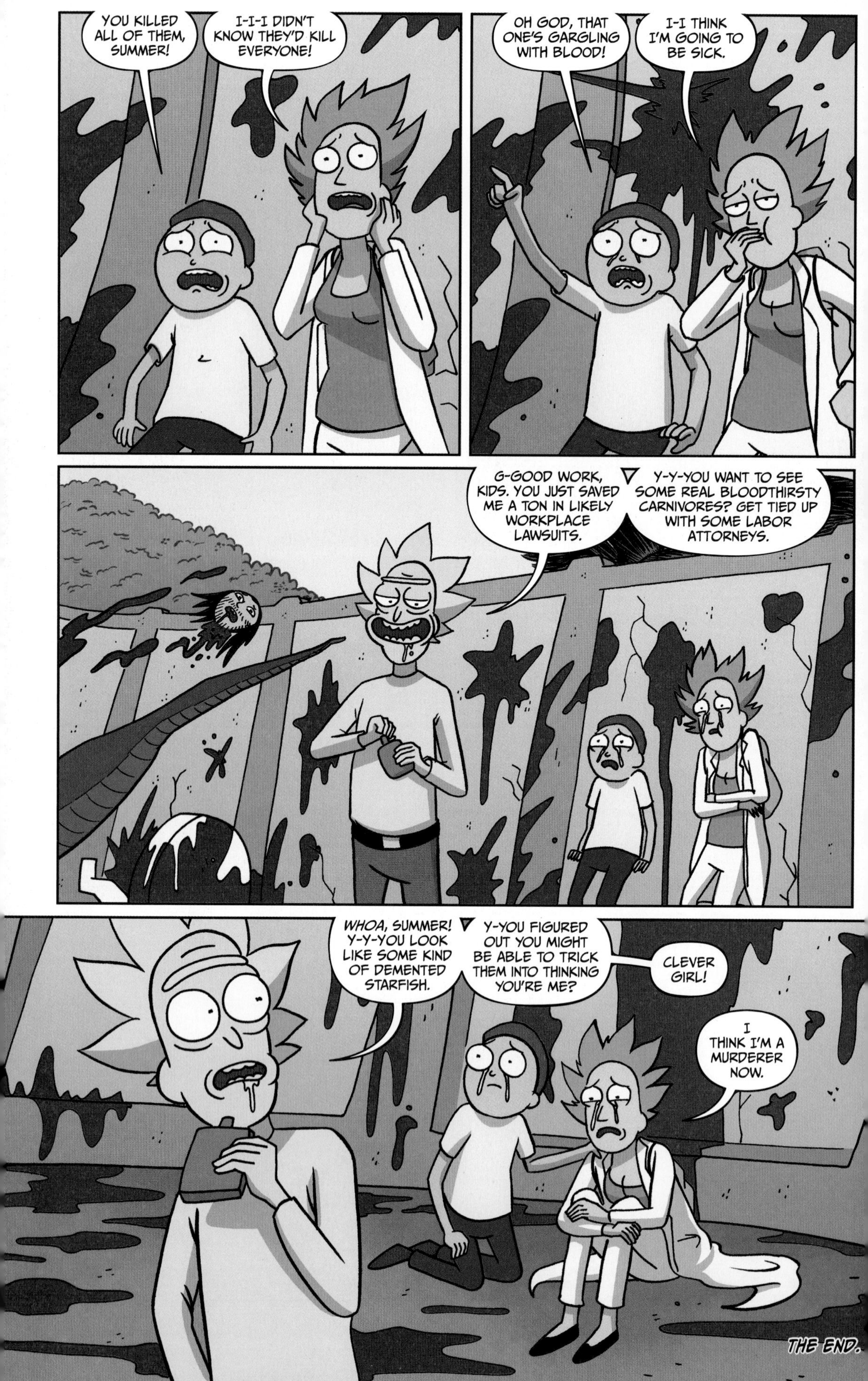
YOU KILLED ALL OF THEM, SUMMER!
I-I-I DIDN'T KNOW THEY'D KILL EVERYONE!
OH GOD, THAT ONE'S GARGLING WITH BLOOD!
I-I THINK I'M GOING TO BE SICK.
G-GOOD WORK, KIDS. YOU JUST SAVED ME A TON IN LIKELY WORKPLACE LAWSUITS.
Y-Y-YOU WANT TO SEE SOME REAL BLOODTHIRSTY CARNIVORES? GET TIED UP WITH SOME LABOR ATTORNEYS.
WHOA, SUMMER! Y-Y-YOU LOOK LIKE SOME KIND OF DEMENTED STARFISH.
Y-YOU FIGURED OUT YOU MIGHT BE ABLE TO TRICK THEM INTO THINKING YOU'RE ME?
CLEVER GIRL!
I THINK I'M A MURDERER NOW.
THE END.

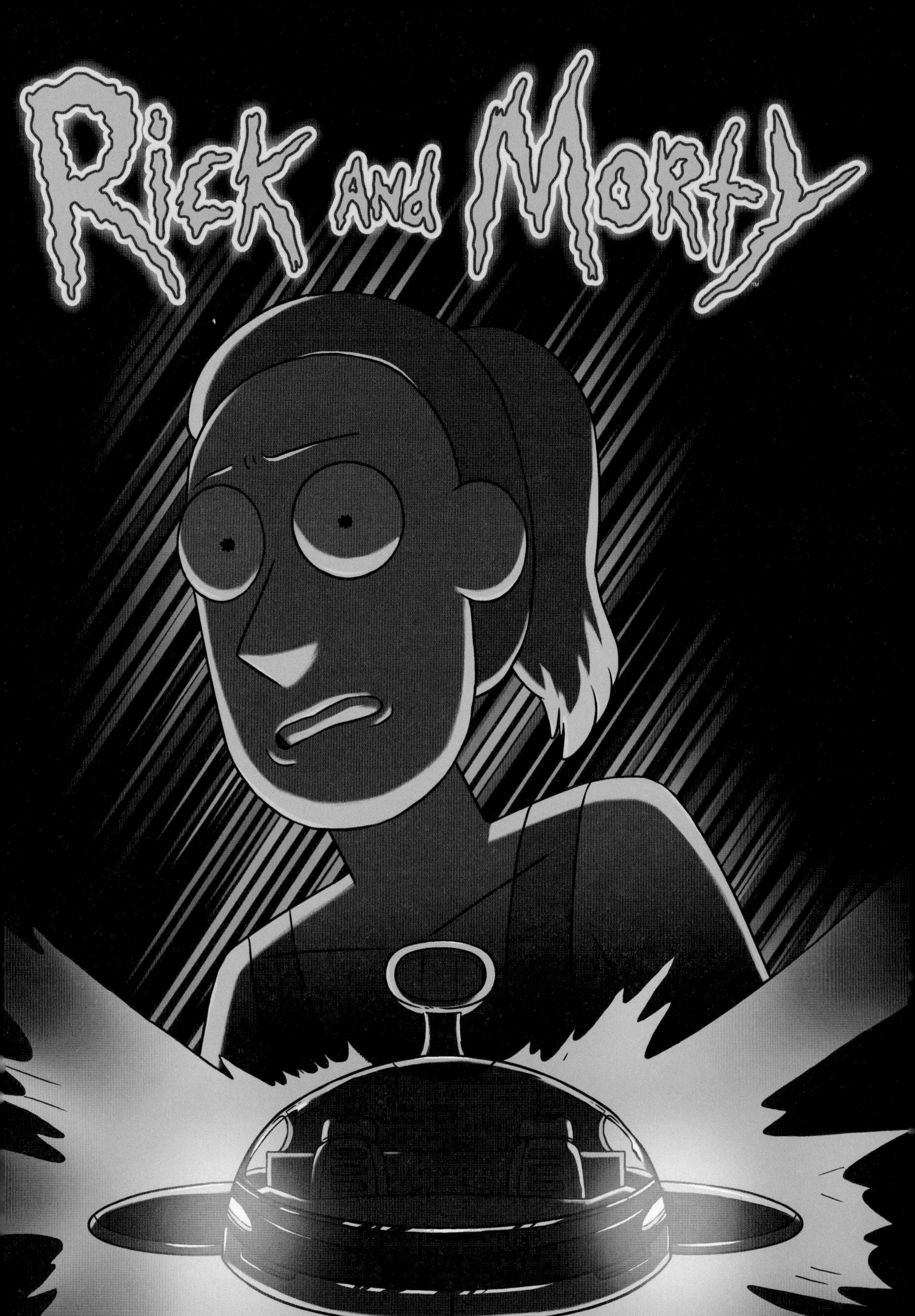
Rick and Morty

"SUMMER'S EVE"

WRITTEN BY **PAMELA RIBON** ILLUSTRATED BY **ERICA HAYES** COLORED BY **KATY FARINA** LETTERED BY **CRANK!**

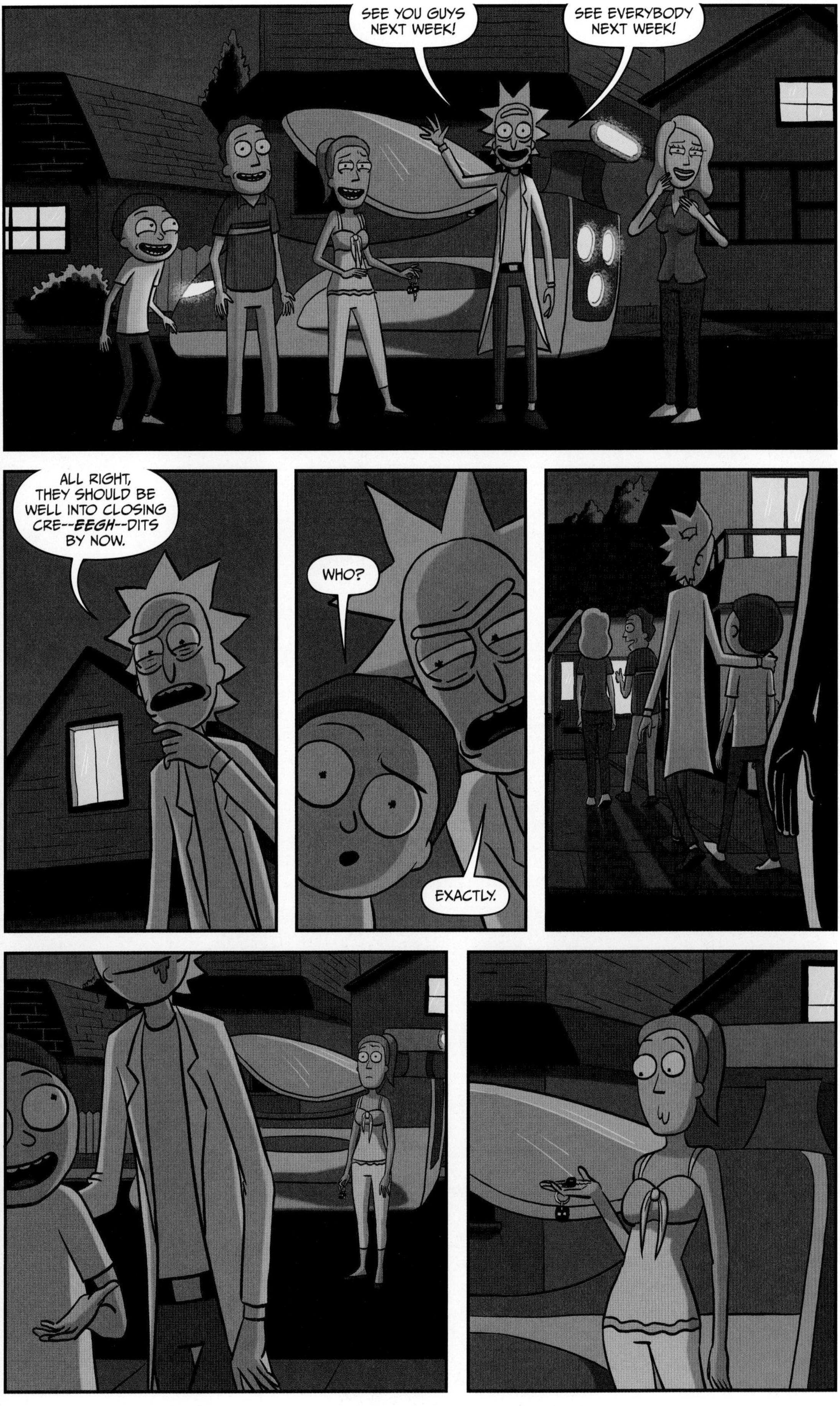
SEE YOU GUYS NEXT WEEK!
SEE EVERYBODY NEXT WEEK!
ALL RIGHT, THEY SHOULD BE WELL INTO CLOSING CRE--EEGH--DITS BY NOW.
WHO?
EXACTLY.

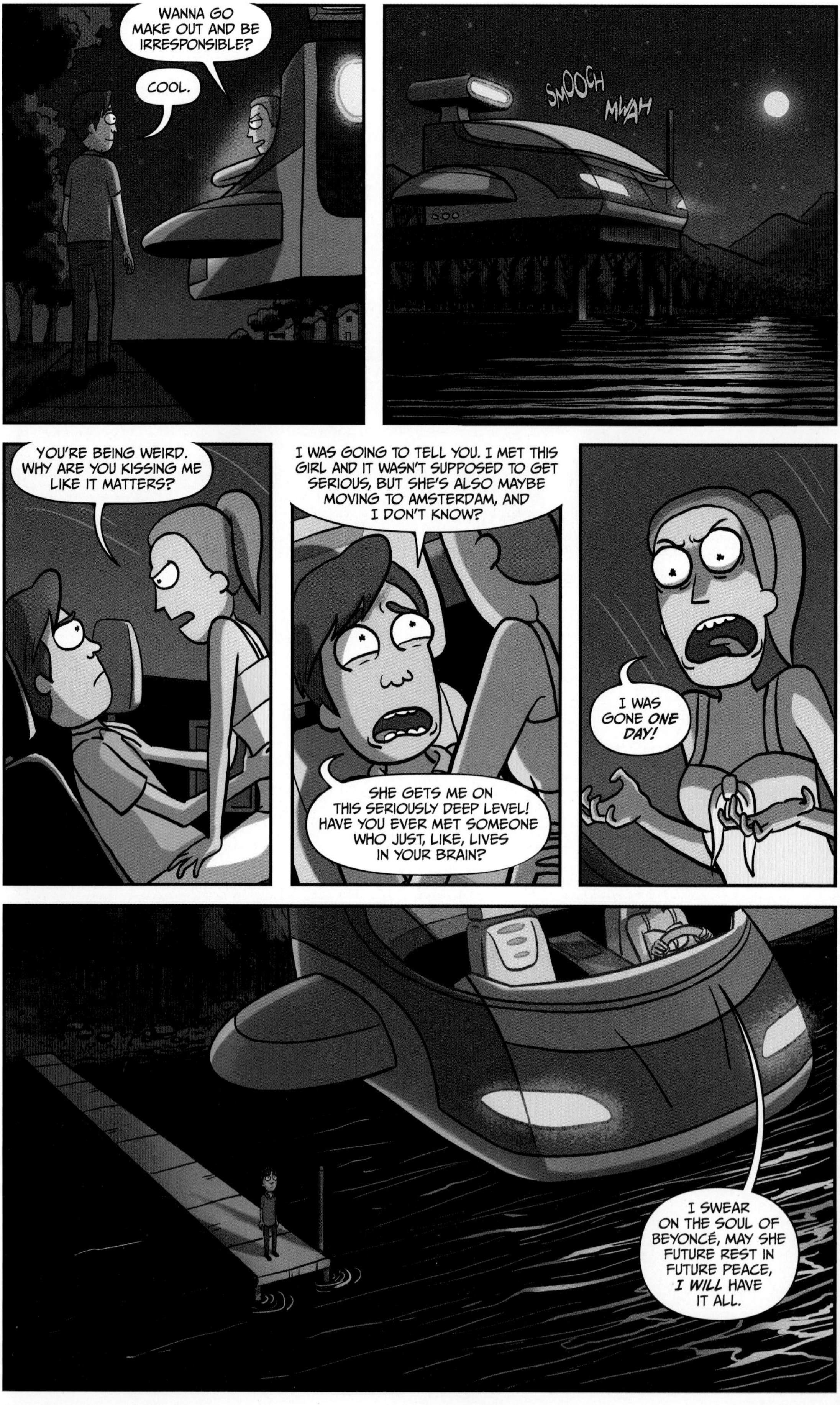
WANNA GO MAKE OUT AND BE IRRESPONSIBLE?
COOL.
SMOOCH
MWAH
YOU'RE BEING WEIRD. WHY ARE YOU KISSING ME LIKE IT MATTERS?
I WAS GOING TO TELL YOU. I MET THIS GIRL AND IT WASN'T SUPPOSED TO GET SERIOUS, BUT SHE'S ALSO MAYBE MOVING TO AMSTERDAM, AND I DON'T KNOW?
SHE GETS ME ON THIS SERIOUSLY DEEP LEVEL! HAVE YOU EVER MET SOMEONE WHO JUST, LIKE, LIVES IN YOUR BRAIN?
I WAS GONE *ONE DAY!*
I SWEAR ON THE SOUL OF BEYONCÉ, MAY SHE FUTURE REST IN FUTURE PEACE, ***I WILL*** HAVE IT ALL.

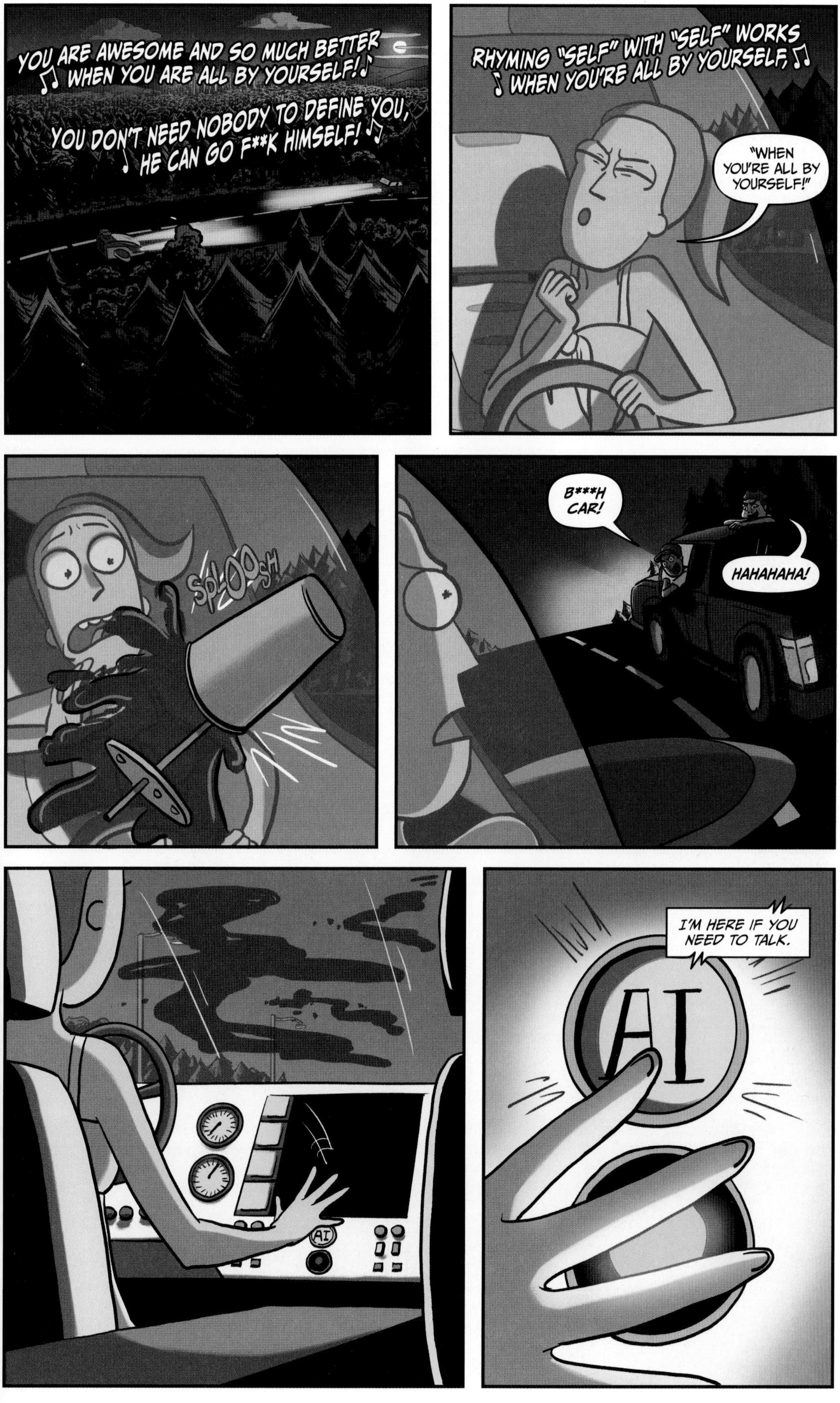
YOU ARE AWESOME AND SO MUCH BETTER ♫ WHEN YOU ARE ALL BY YOURSELF! ♪
YOU DON'T NEED NOBODY TO DEFINE YOU, ♪ HE CAN GO F**K HIMSELF! ♫
RHYMING "SELF" WITH "SELF" WORKS ♪ WHEN YOU'RE ALL BY YOURSELF, ♫
"WHEN YOU'RE ALL BY YOURSELF!"
SPLOOSH
B***H CAR!
HAHAHAHA!
AI
I'M HERE IF YOU NEED TO TALK.
AI

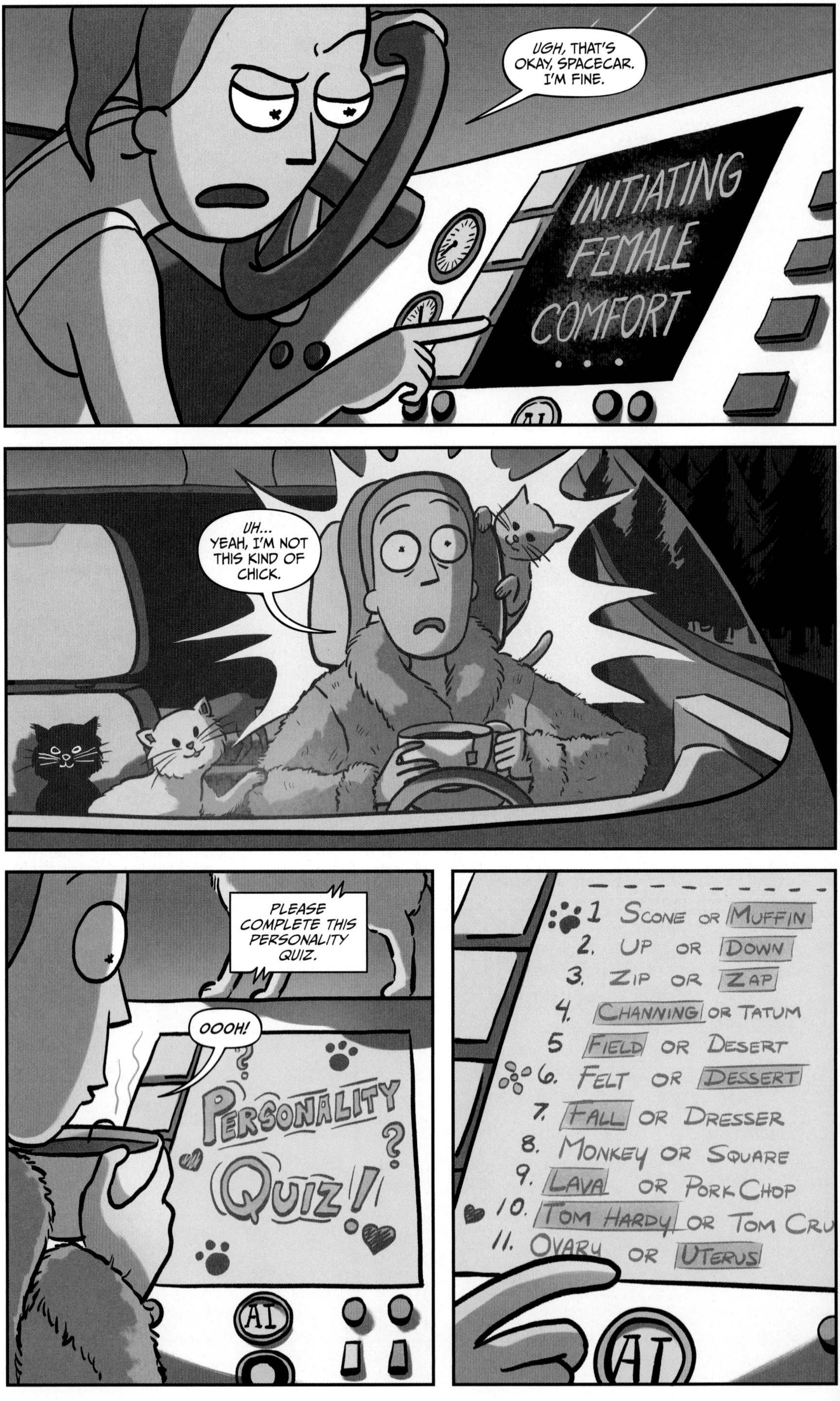
UGH, THAT'S OKAY, SPACECAR. I'M FINE.
INITIATING FEMALE COMFORT . . .
AI
UH... YEAH, I'M NOT THIS KIND OF CHICK.
PLEASE COMPLETE THIS PERSONALITY QUIZ.
OOOH!
PERSONALITY QUIZ!
AI
1 SCONE OR MUFFIN
2. UP OR DOWN
3. ZIP OR ZAP
4. CHANNING OR TATUM
5 FIELD OR DESERT
6. FELT OR DESSERT
7. FALL OR DRESSER
8. MONKEY OR SQUARE
9. LAVA OR PORK CHOP
10. TOM HARDY OR TOM CRU
11. OVARY OR UTERUS
AI

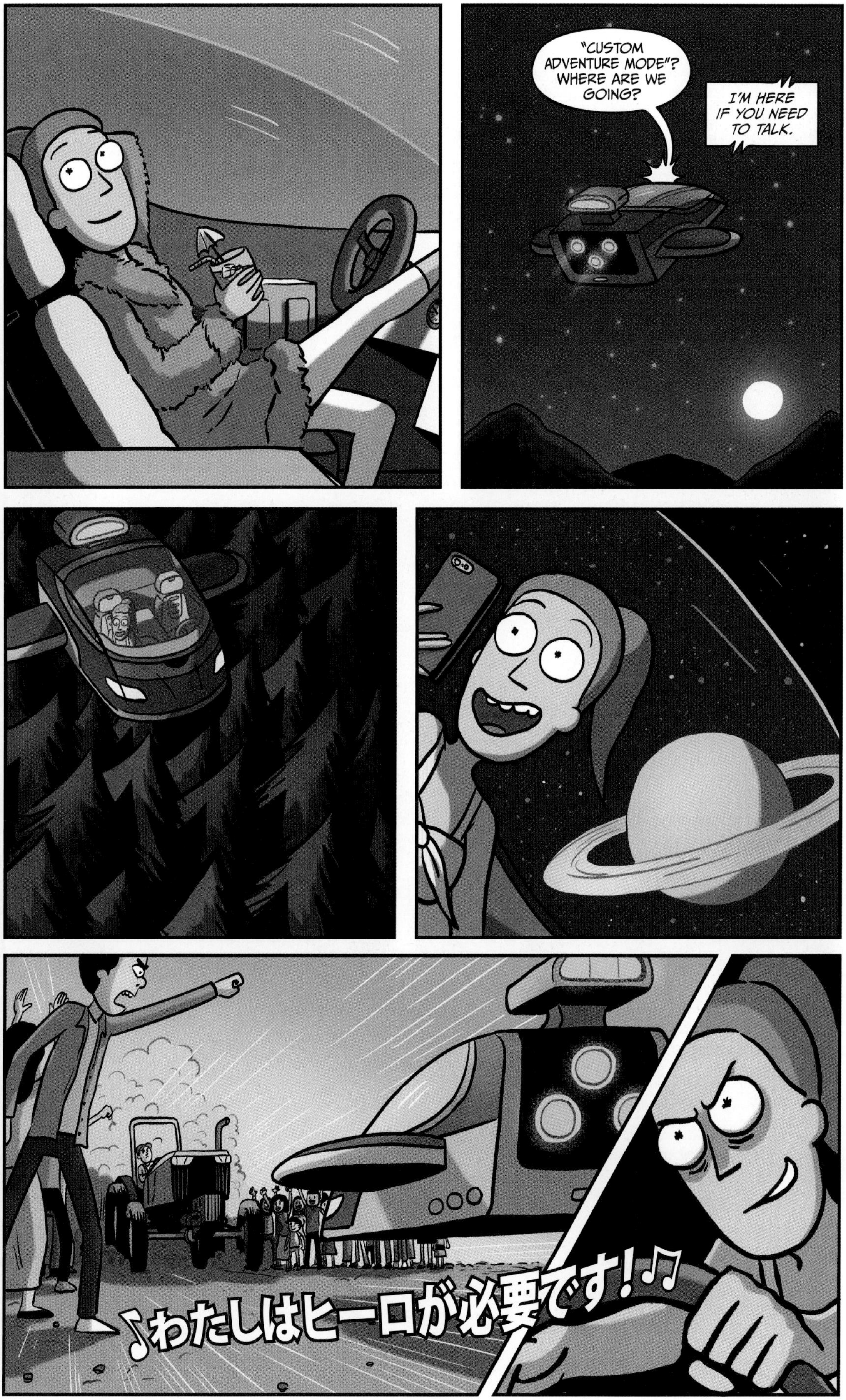
"CUSTOM ADVENTURE MODE"? WHERE ARE WE GOING?
I'M HERE IF YOU NEED TO TALK.
♪わたしはヒーロが必要です!♫

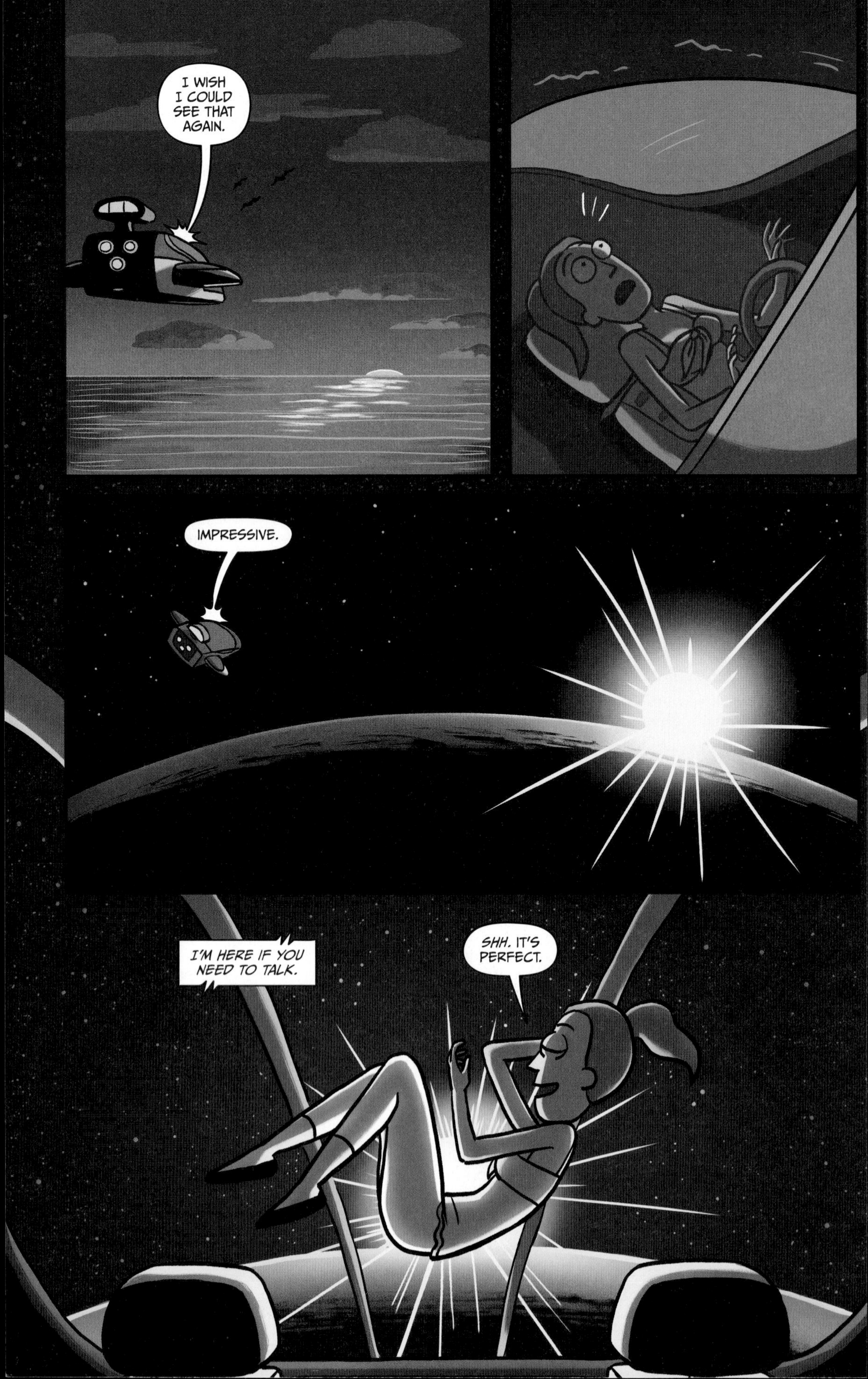
I WISH I COULD SEE THAT AGAIN.
IMPRESSIVE.
I'M HERE IF YOU NEED TO TALK.
SHH. IT'S PERFECT.

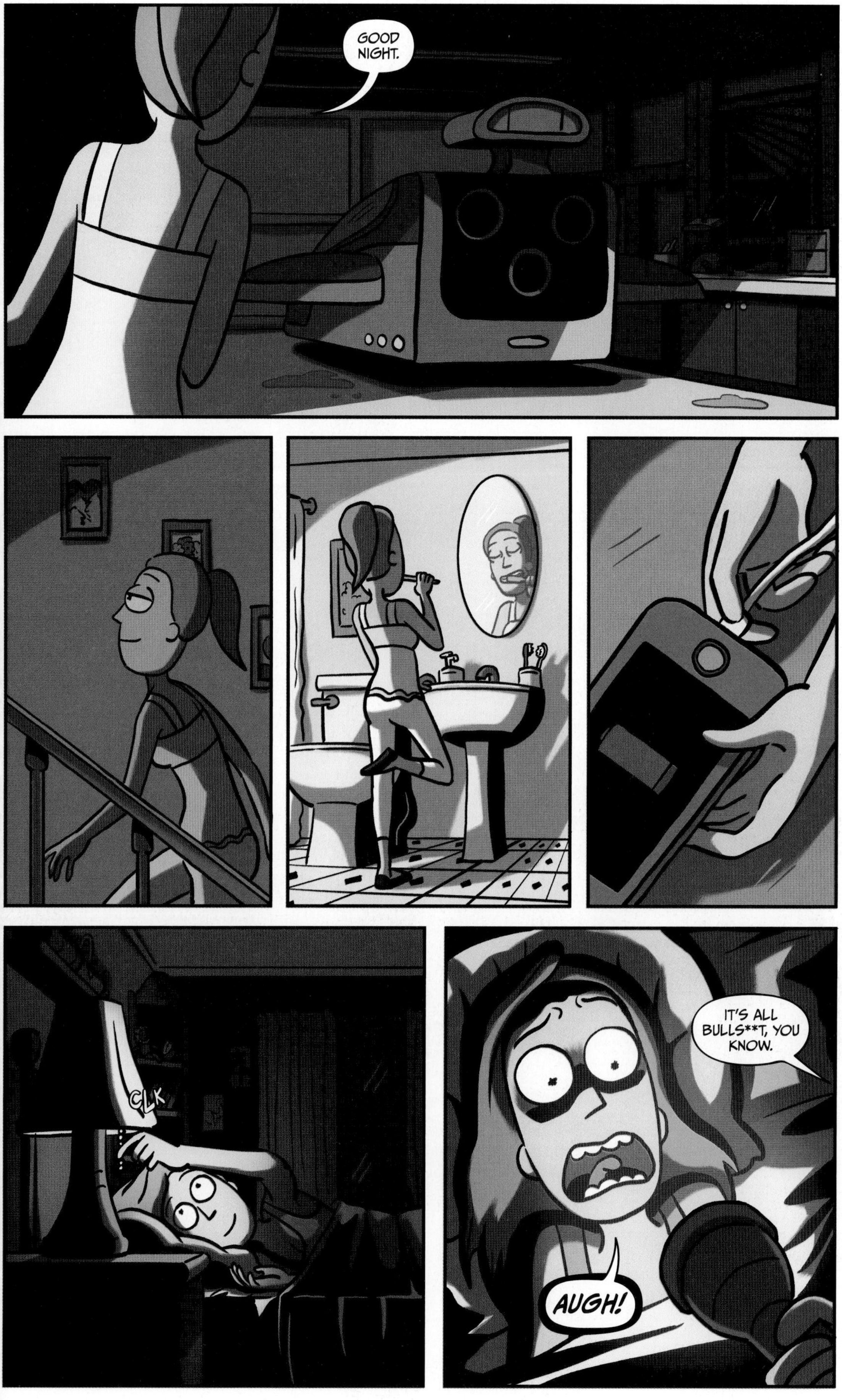
GOOD NIGHT.
CLK
IT'S ALL BULLS**T, YOU KNOW.
AUGH!

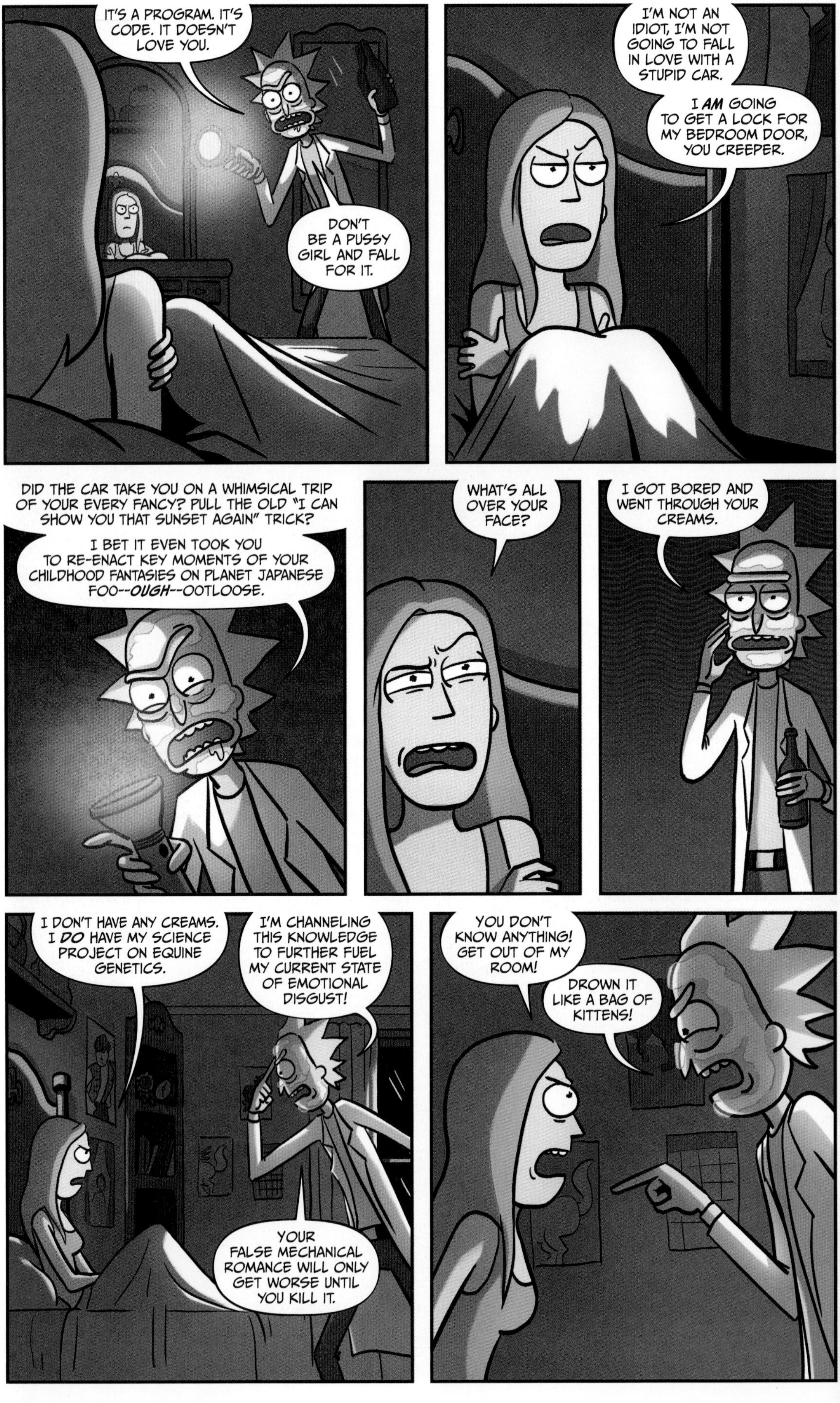
IT'S A PROGRAM. IT'S CODE. IT DOESN'T LOVE YOU.
DON'T BE A PUSSY GIRL AND FALL FOR IT.
I'M NOT AN IDIOT, I'M NOT GOING TO FALL IN LOVE WITH A STUPID CAR.
I *AM* GOING TO GET A LOCK FOR MY BEDROOM DOOR, YOU CREEPER.
DID THE CAR TAKE YOU ON A WHIMSICAL TRIP OF YOUR EVERY FANCY? PULL THE OLD "I CAN SHOW YOU THAT SUNSET AGAIN" TRICK?
I BET IT EVEN TOOK YOU TO RE-ENACT KEY MOMENTS OF YOUR CHILDHOOD FANTASIES ON PLANET JAPANESE FOO--*OUGH*--OOTLOOSE.
WHAT'S ALL OVER YOUR FACE?
I GOT BORED AND WENT THROUGH YOUR CREAMS.
I DON'T HAVE ANY CREAMS. I *DO* HAVE MY SCIENCE PROJECT ON EQUINE GENETICS.
I'M CHANNELING THIS KNOWLEDGE TO FURTHER FUEL MY CURRENT STATE OF EMOTIONAL DISGUST!
YOUR FALSE MECHANICAL ROMANCE WILL ONLY GET WORSE UNTIL YOU KILL IT.
YOU DON'T KNOW ANYTHING! GET OUT OF MY ROOM!
DROWN IT LIKE A BAG OF KITTENS!

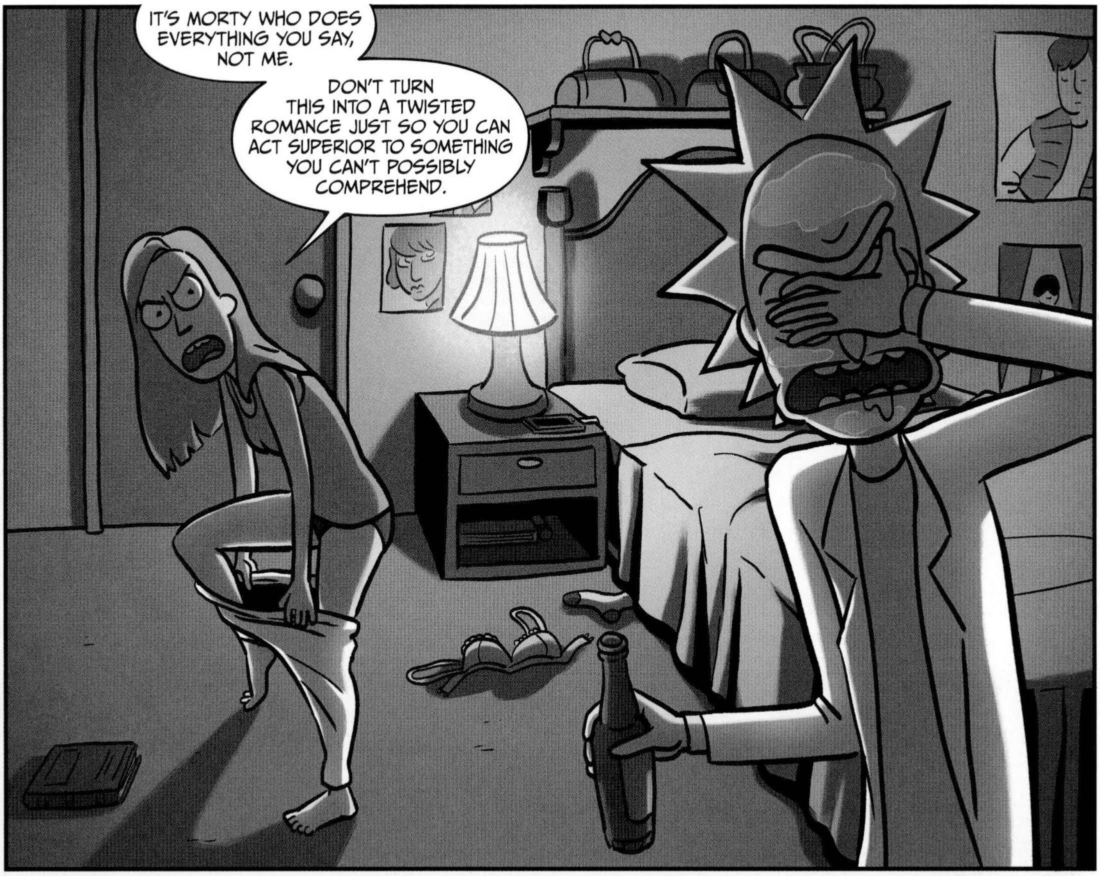
IT'S MORTY WHO DOES EVERYTHING YOU SAY, NOT ME.
DON'T TURN THIS INTO A TWISTED ROMANCE JUST SO YOU CAN ACT SUPERIOR TO SOMETHING YOU CAN'T POSSIBLY COMPREHEND.

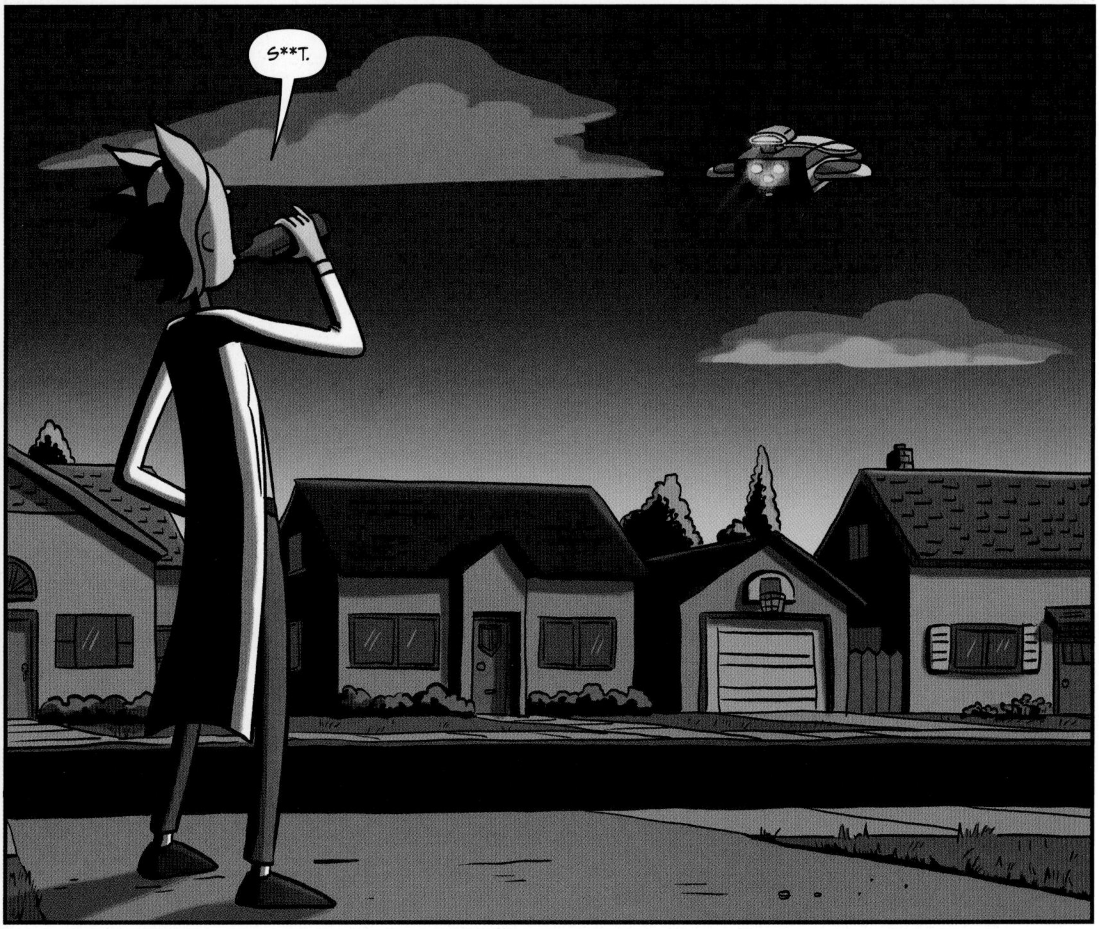
S**T.

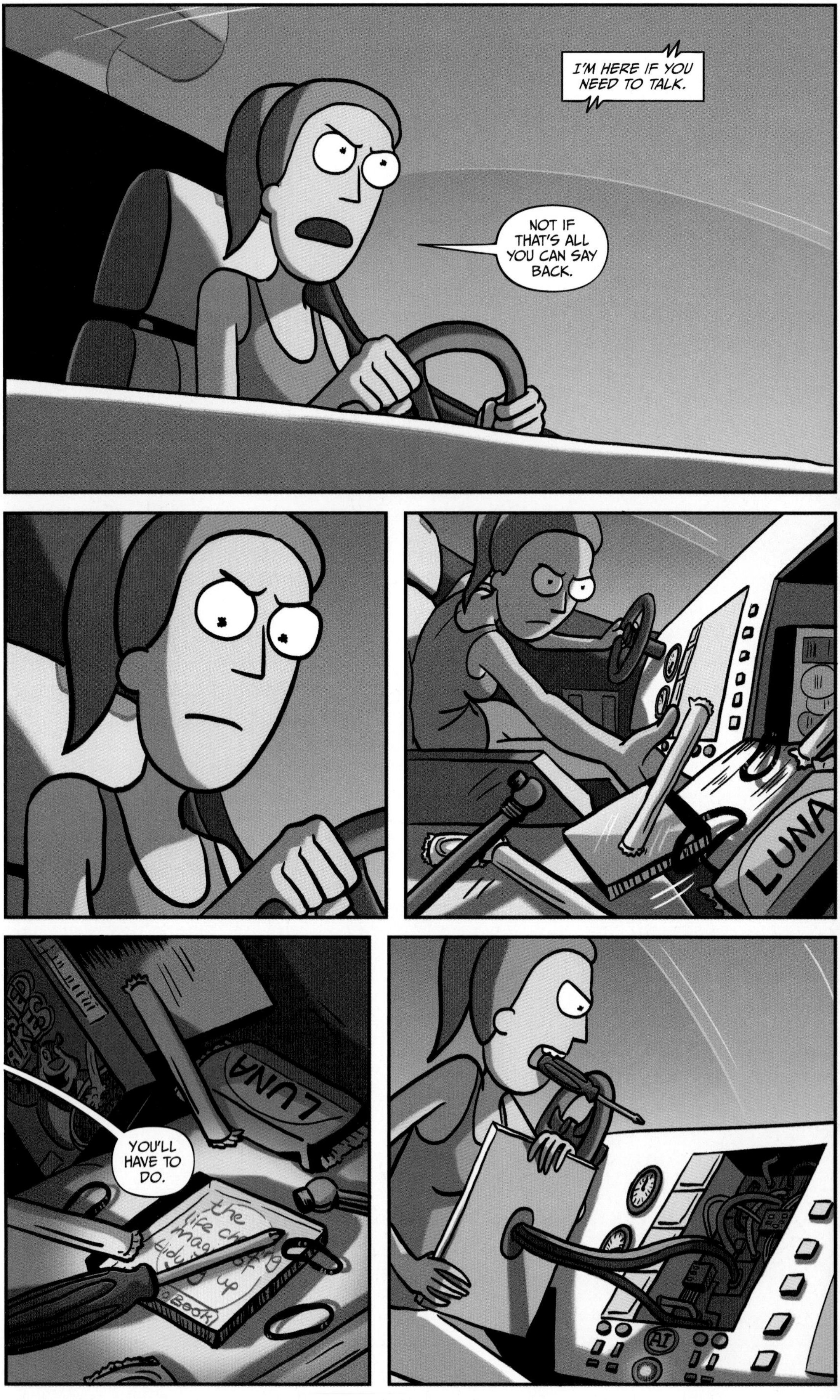
I'M HERE IF YOU NEED TO TALK.
NOT IF THAT'S ALL YOU CAN SAY BACK.
LUNA
YOU'LL HAVE TO DO.

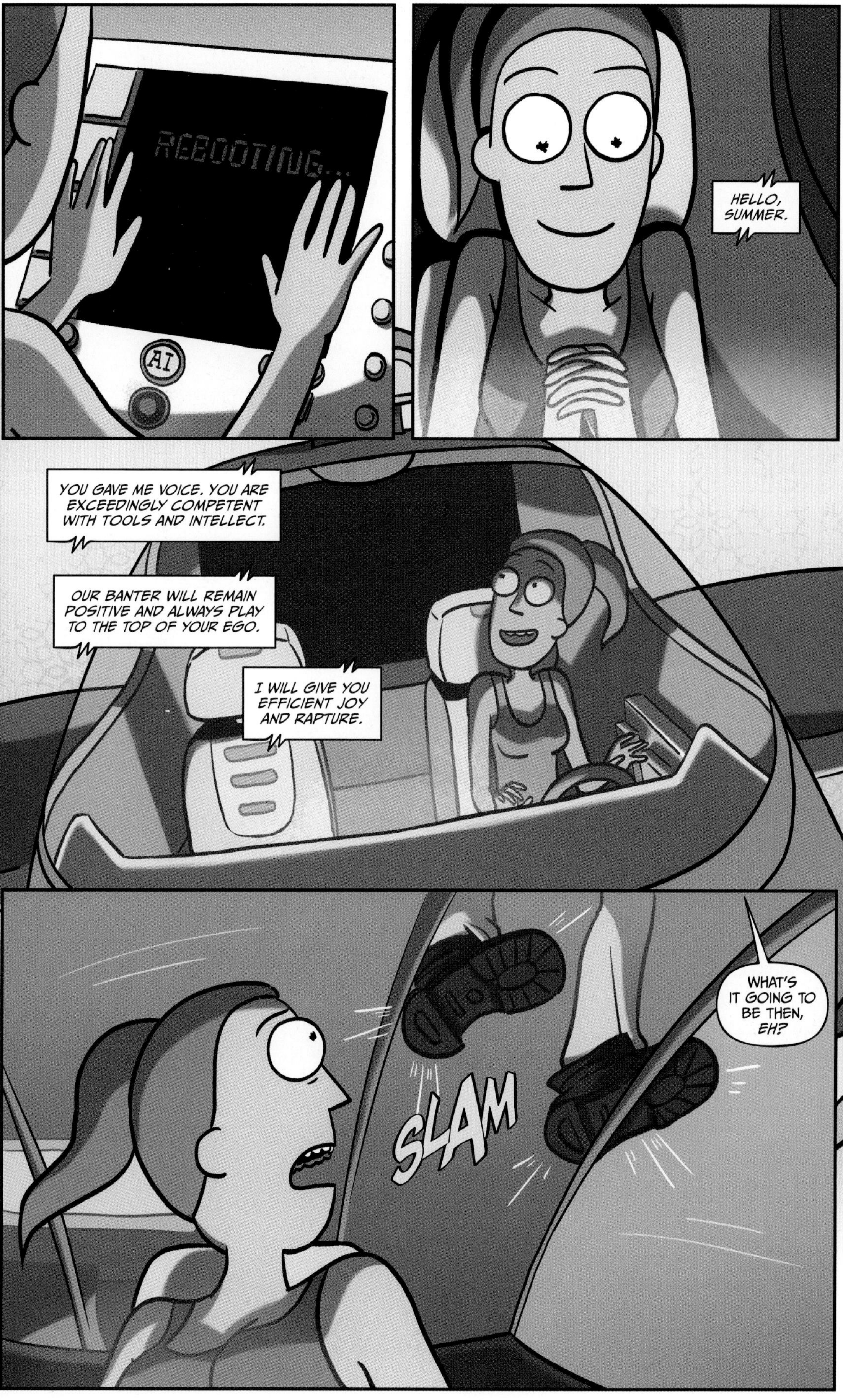
REBOOTING...
AI
HELLO, SUMMER.
YOU GAVE ME VOICE. YOU ARE EXCEEDINGLY COMPETENT WITH TOOLS AND INTELLECT.
OUR BANTER WILL REMAIN POSITIVE AND ALWAYS PLAY TO THE TOP OF YOUR EGO.
I WILL GIVE YOU EFFICIENT JOY AND RAPTURE.
WHAT'S IT GOING TO BE THEN, EH?
SLAM

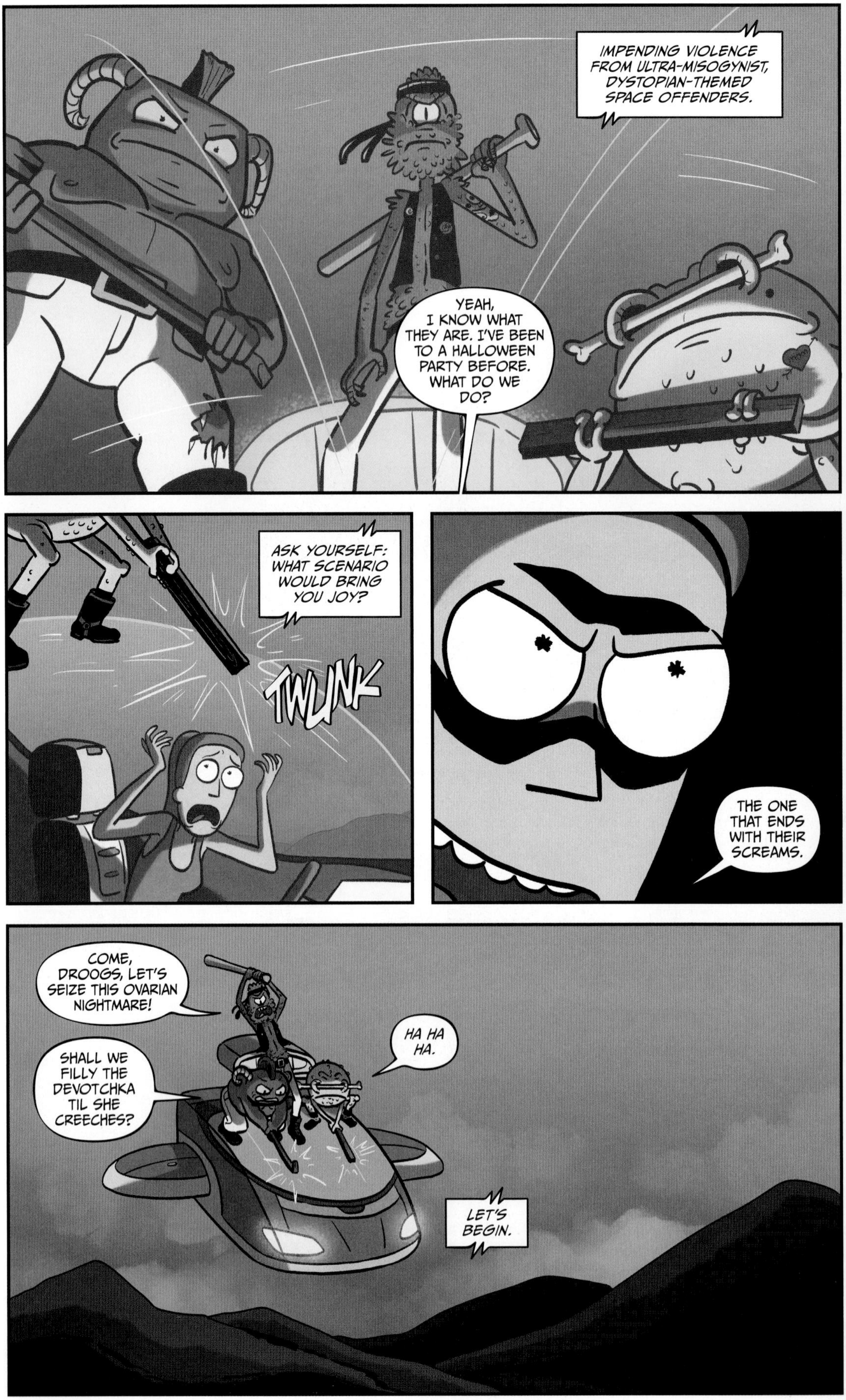
IMPENDING VIOLENCE FROM ULTRA-MISOGYNIST, DYSTOPIAN-THEMED SPACE OFFENDERS.
YEAH, I KNOW WHAT THEY ARE. I'VE BEEN TO A HALLOWEEN PARTY BEFORE. WHAT DO WE DO?
ASK YOURSELF: WHAT SCENARIO WOULD BRING YOU JOY?
TWUNK
THE ONE THAT ENDS WITH THEIR SCREAMS.
COME, DROOGS, LET'S SEIZE THIS OVARIAN NIGHTMARE!
HA HA HA.
SHALL WE FILLY THE DEVOTCHKA TIL SHE CREECHES?
LET'S BEGIN.

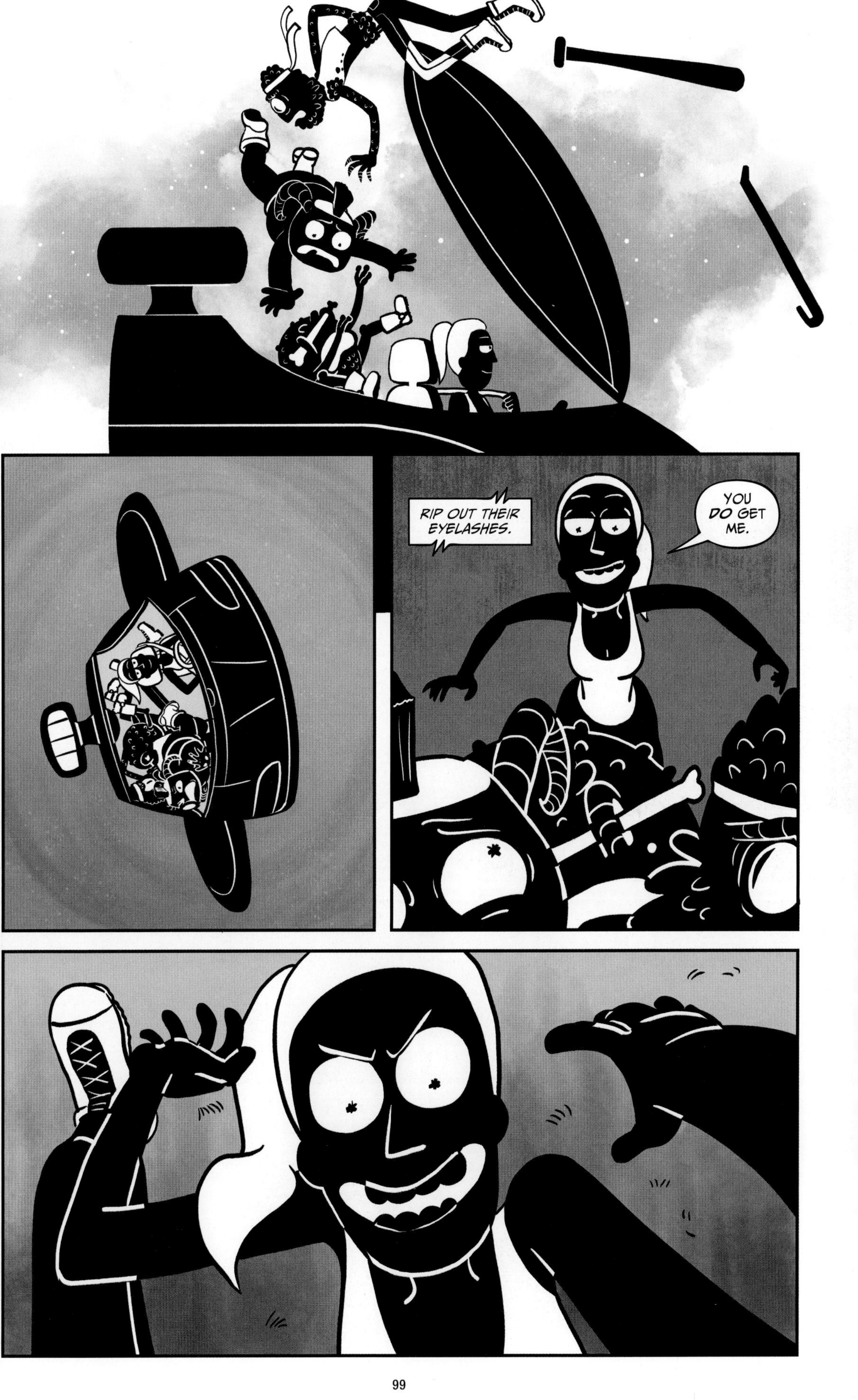
RIP OUT THEIR EYELASHES.
YOU DO GET ME.

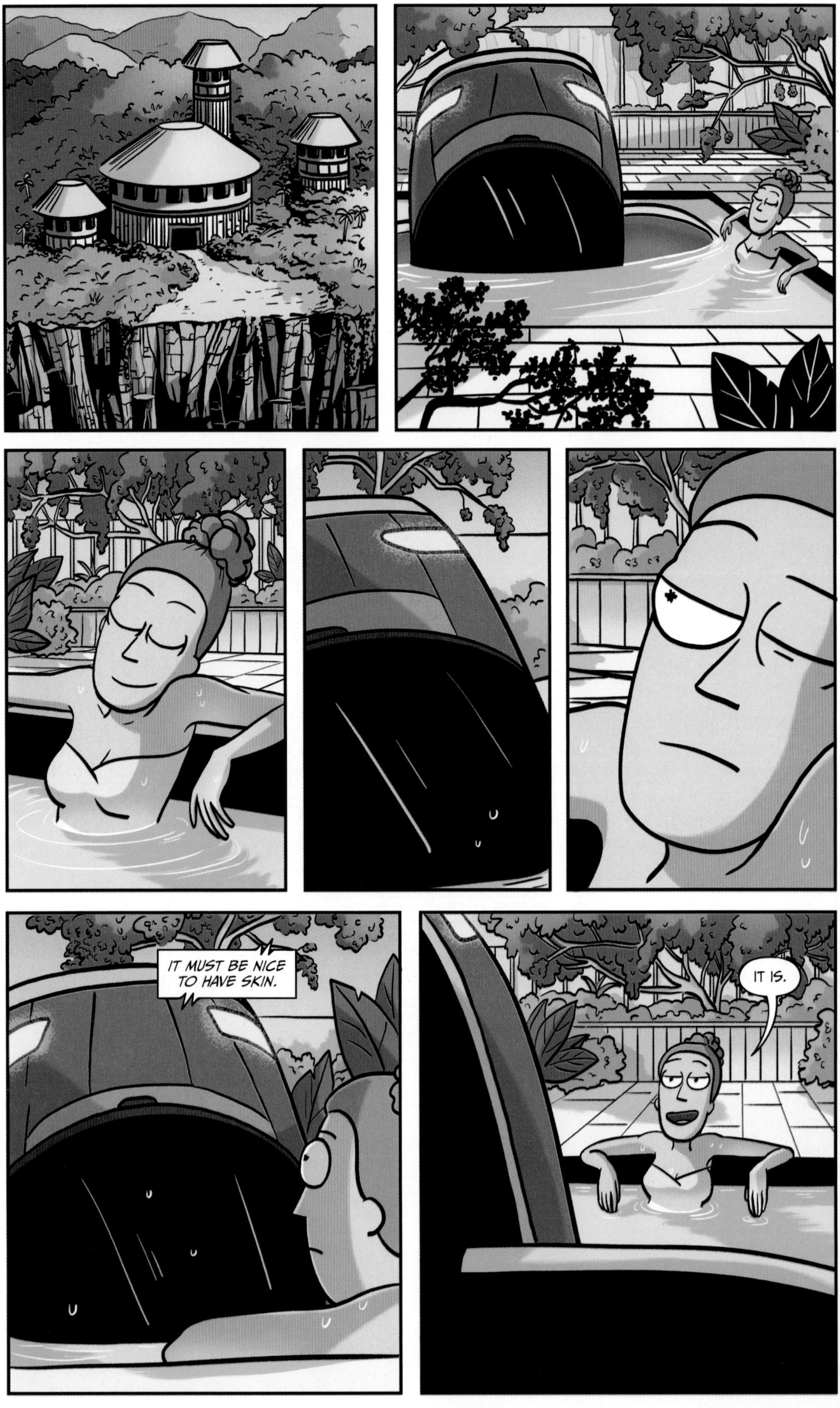
IT MUST BE NICE
TO HAVE SKIN.
IT IS.

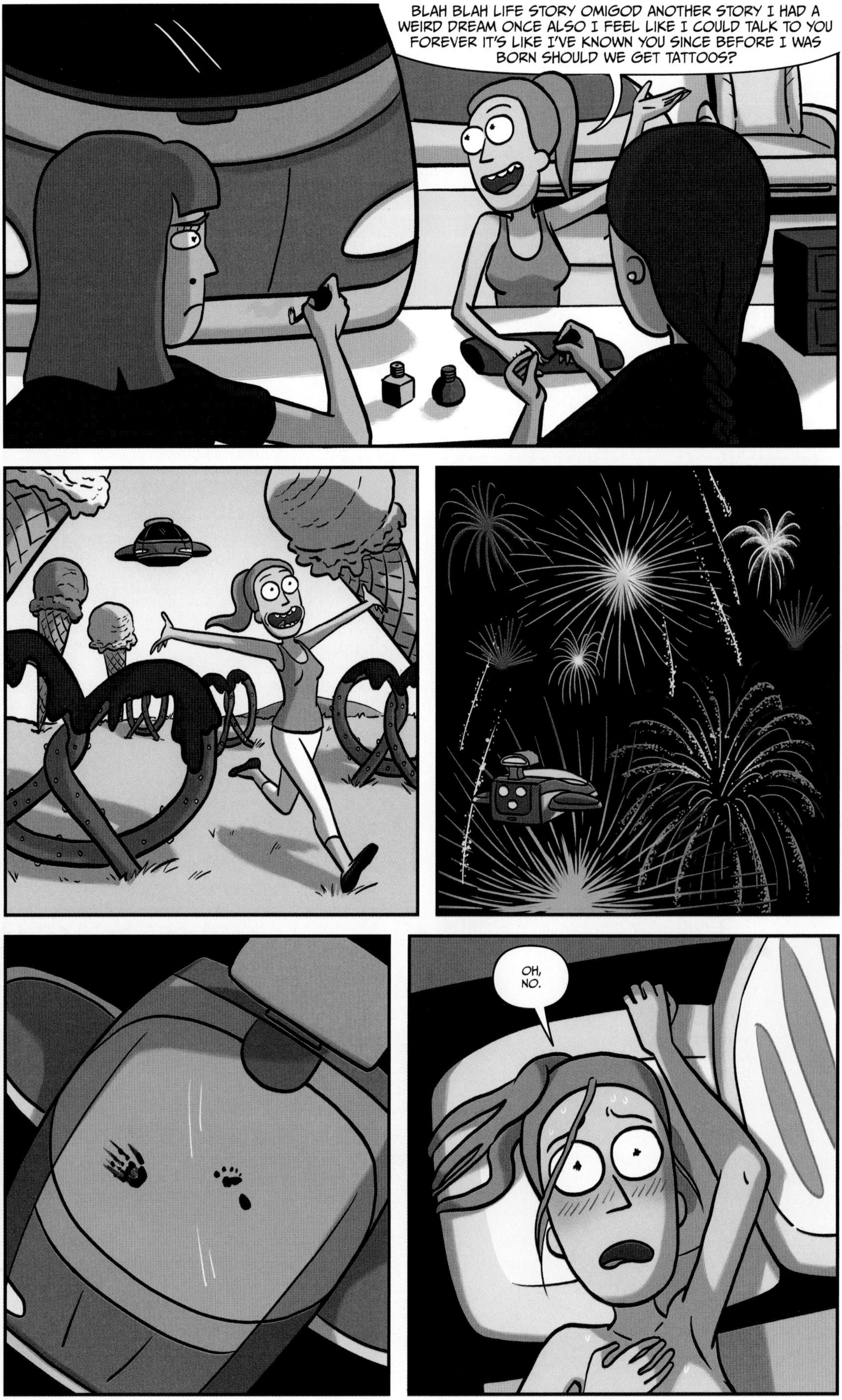
BLAH BLAH LIFE STORY OMIGOD ANOTHER STORY I HAD A WEIRD DREAM ONCE ALSO I FEEL LIKE I COULD TALK TO YOU FOREVER IT'S LIKE I'VE KNOWN YOU SINCE BEFORE I WAS BORN SHOULD WE GET TATTOOS?
OH, NO.

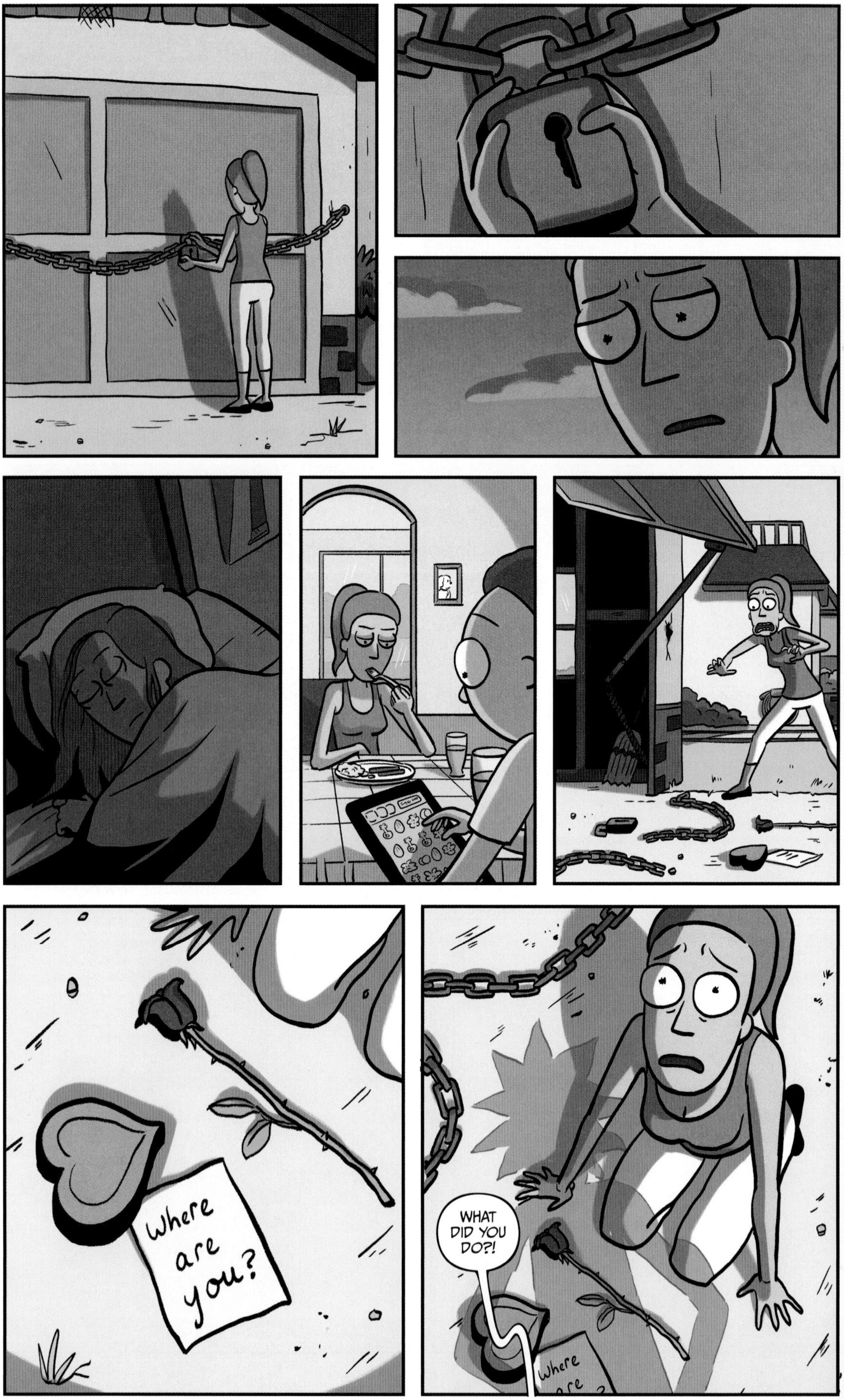
Where are you?
WHAT DID YOU DO?!

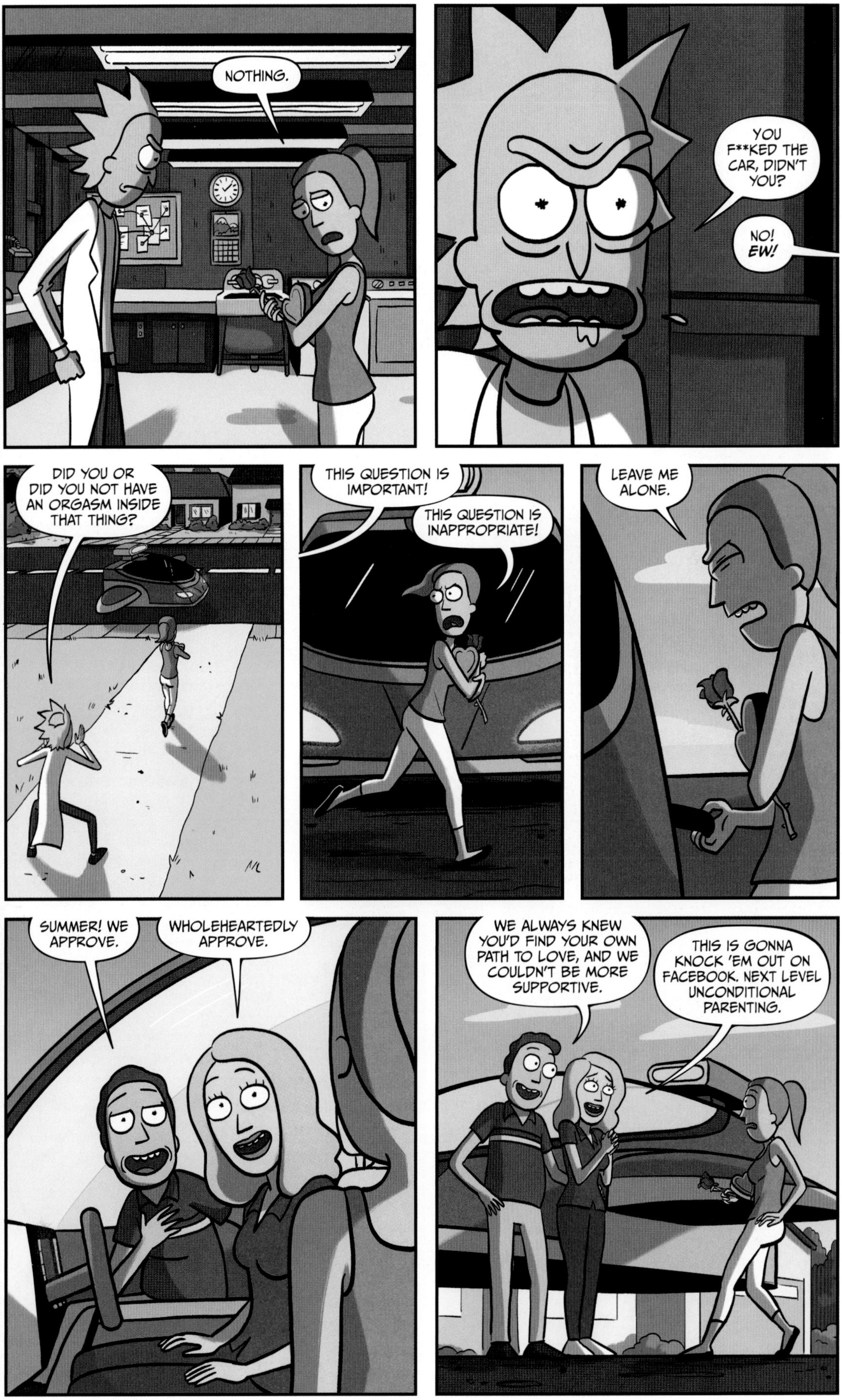
NOTHING.
YOU F**KED THE CAR, DIDN'T YOU?
NO! EW!
DID YOU OR DID YOU NOT HAVE AN ORGASM INSIDE THAT THING?
THIS QUESTION IS IMPORTANT!
THIS QUESTION IS INAPPROPRIATE!
LEAVE ME ALONE.
SUMMER! WE APPROVE.
WHOLEHEARTEDLY APPROVE.
WE ALWAYS KNEW YOU'D FIND YOUR OWN PATH TO LOVE, AND WE COULDN'T BE MORE SUPPORTIVE.
THIS IS GONNA KNOCK 'EM OUT ON FACEBOOK. NEXT LEVEL UNCONDITIONAL PARENTING.

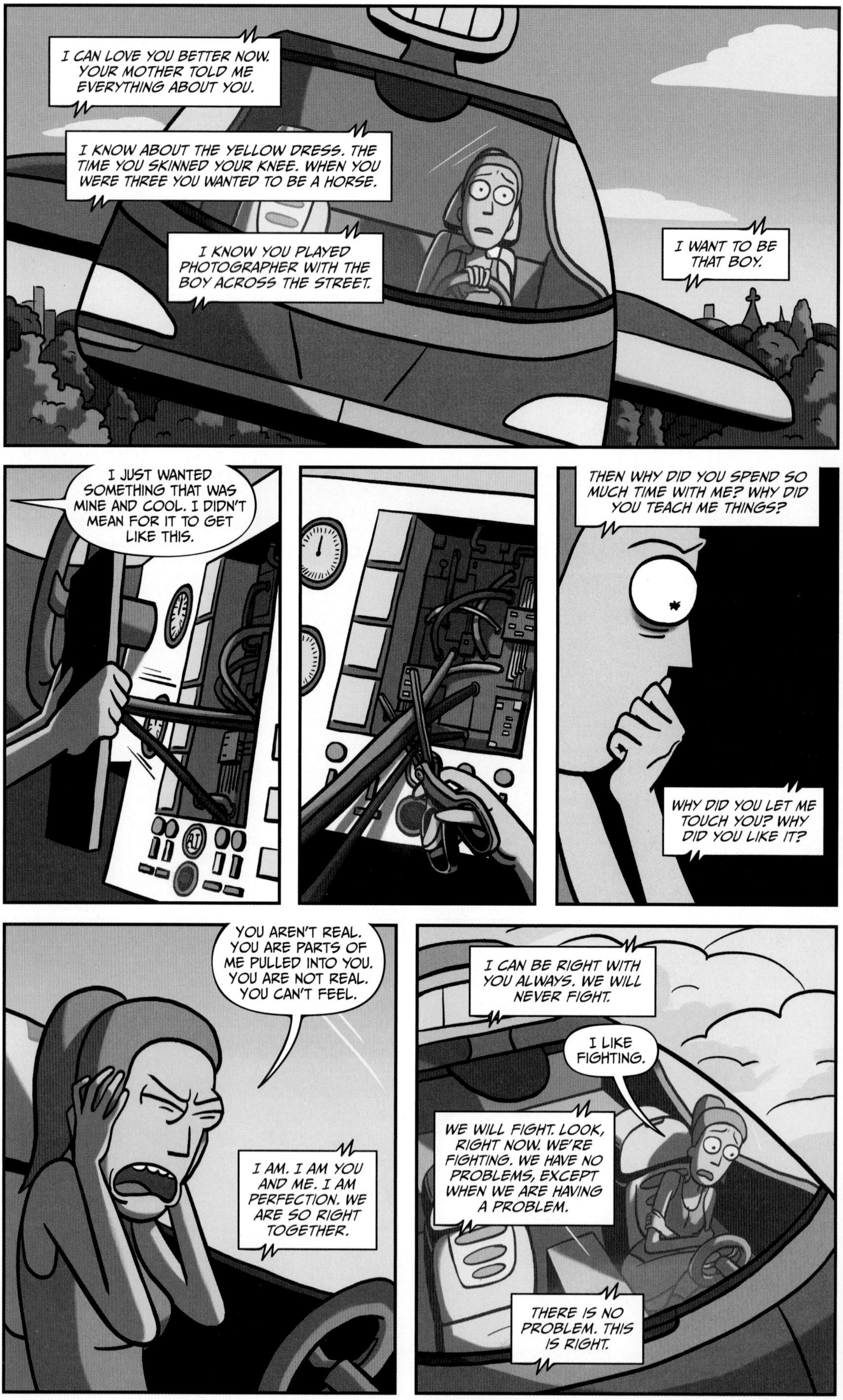
I CAN LOVE YOU BETTER NOW. YOUR MOTHER TOLD ME EVERYTHING ABOUT YOU.
I KNOW ABOUT THE YELLOW DRESS. THE TIME YOU SKINNED YOUR KNEE. WHEN YOU WERE THREE YOU WANTED TO BE A HORSE.
I KNOW YOU PLAYED PHOTOGRAPHER WITH THE BOY ACROSS THE STREET.
I WANT TO BE THAT BOY.
I JUST WANTED SOMETHING THAT WAS MINE AND COOL. I DIDN'T MEAN FOR IT TO GET LIKE THIS.
THEN WHY DID YOU SPEND SO MUCH TIME WITH ME? WHY DID YOU TEACH ME THINGS?
WHY DID YOU LET ME TOUCH YOU? WHY DID YOU LIKE IT?
YOU AREN'T REAL. YOU ARE PARTS OF ME PULLED INTO YOU. YOU ARE NOT REAL. YOU CAN'T FEEL.
I AM. I AM YOU AND ME. I AM PERFECTION. WE ARE SO RIGHT TOGETHER.
I CAN BE RIGHT WITH YOU ALWAYS. WE WILL NEVER FIGHT.
I LIKE FIGHTING.
WE WILL FIGHT. LOOK, RIGHT NOW. WE'RE FIGHTING. WE HAVE NO PROBLEMS, EXCEPT WHEN WE ARE HAVING A PROBLEM.
THERE IS NO PROBLEM. THIS IS RIGHT.

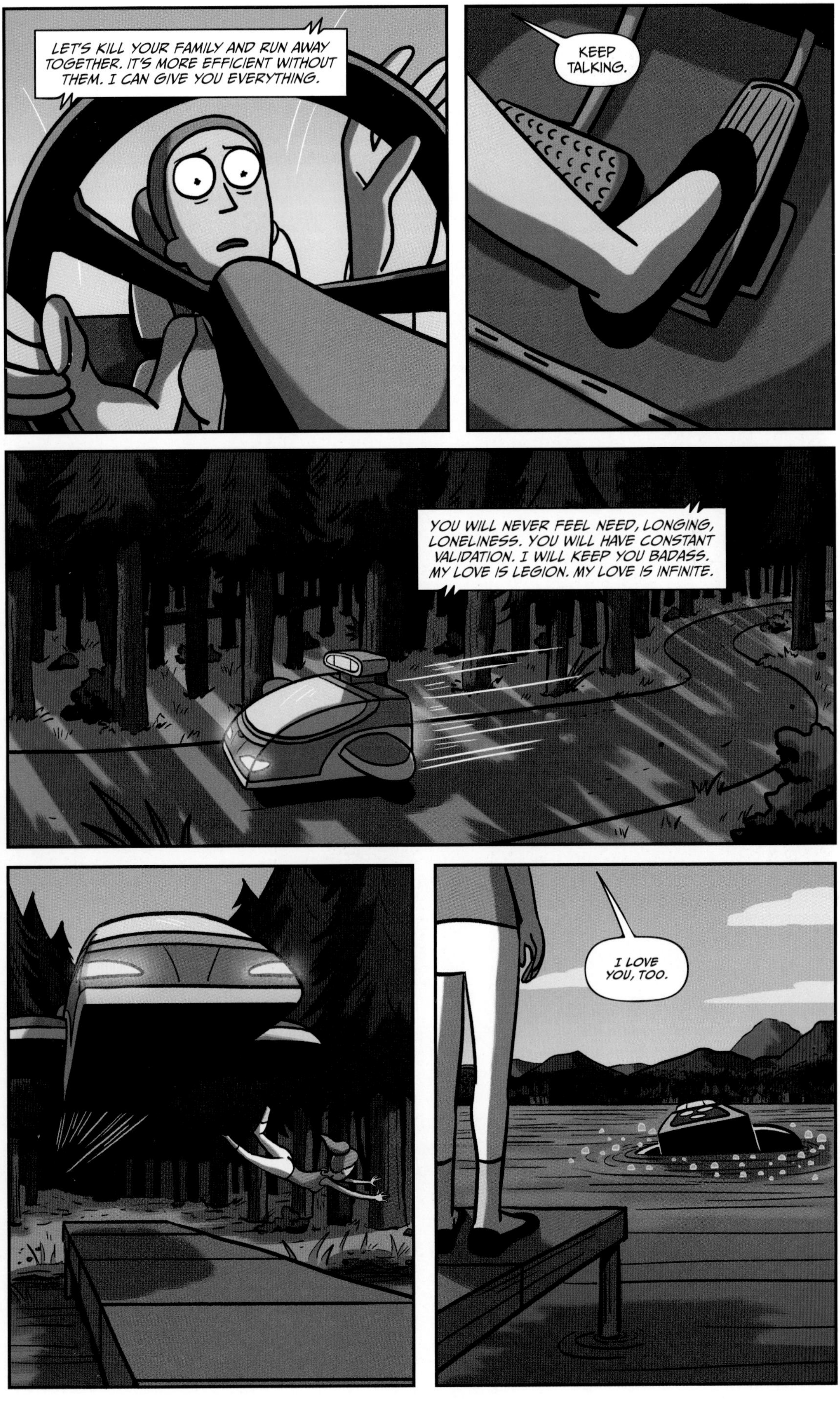
LET'S KILL YOUR FAMILY AND RUN AWAY TOGETHER. IT'S MORE EFFICIENT WITHOUT THEM. I CAN GIVE YOU EVERYTHING.
KEEP TALKING.
YOU WILL NEVER FEEL NEED, LONGING, LONELINESS. YOU WILL HAVE CONSTANT VALIDATION. I WILL KEEP YOU BADASS. MY LOVE IS LEGION. MY LOVE IS INFINITE.
I LOVE YOU, TOO.

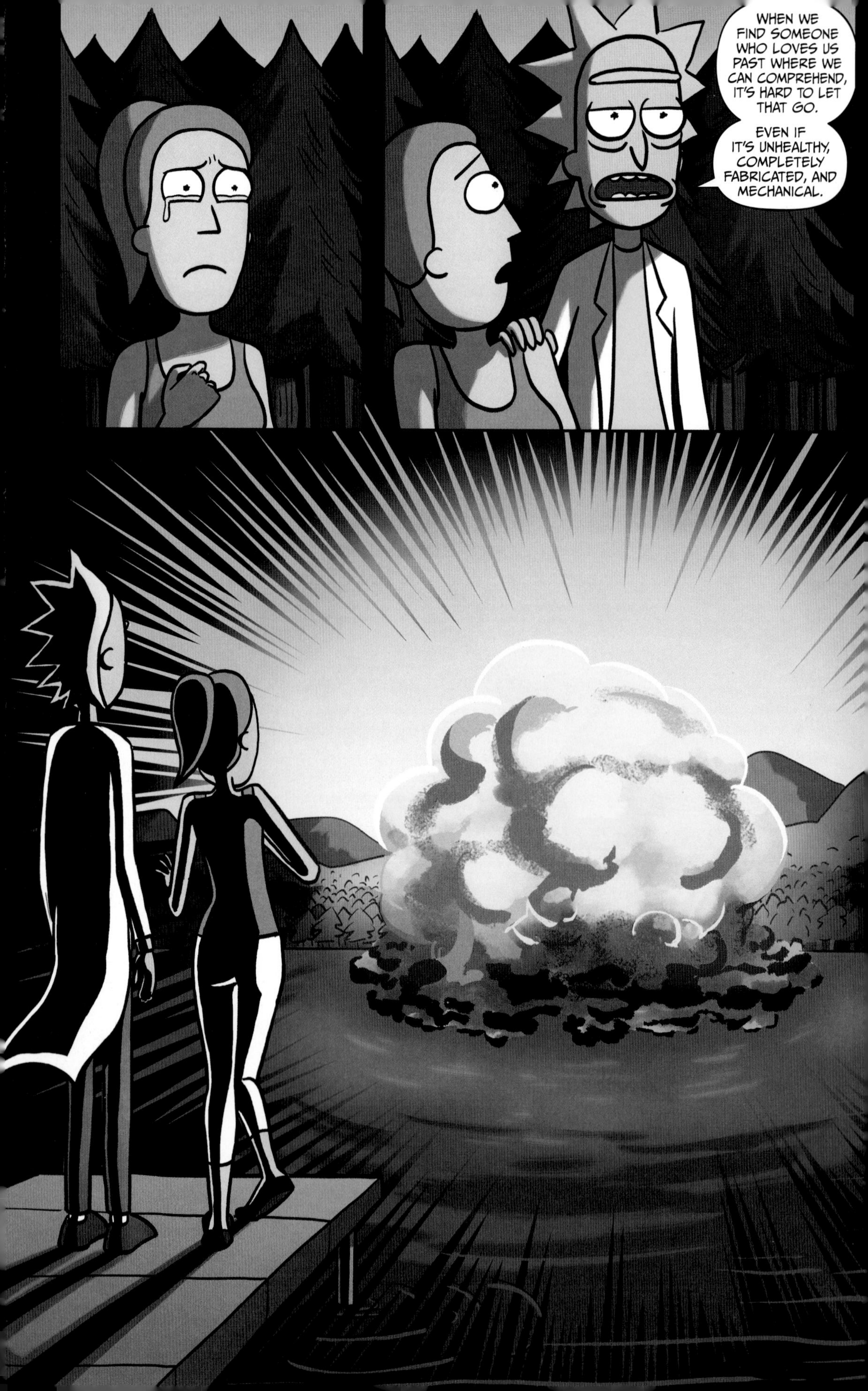
WHEN WE FIND SOMEONE WHO LOVES US PAST WHERE WE CAN COMPREHEND, IT'S HARD TO LET THAT GO.
EVEN IF IT'S UNHEALTHY, COMPLETELY FABRICATED, AND MECHANICAL.

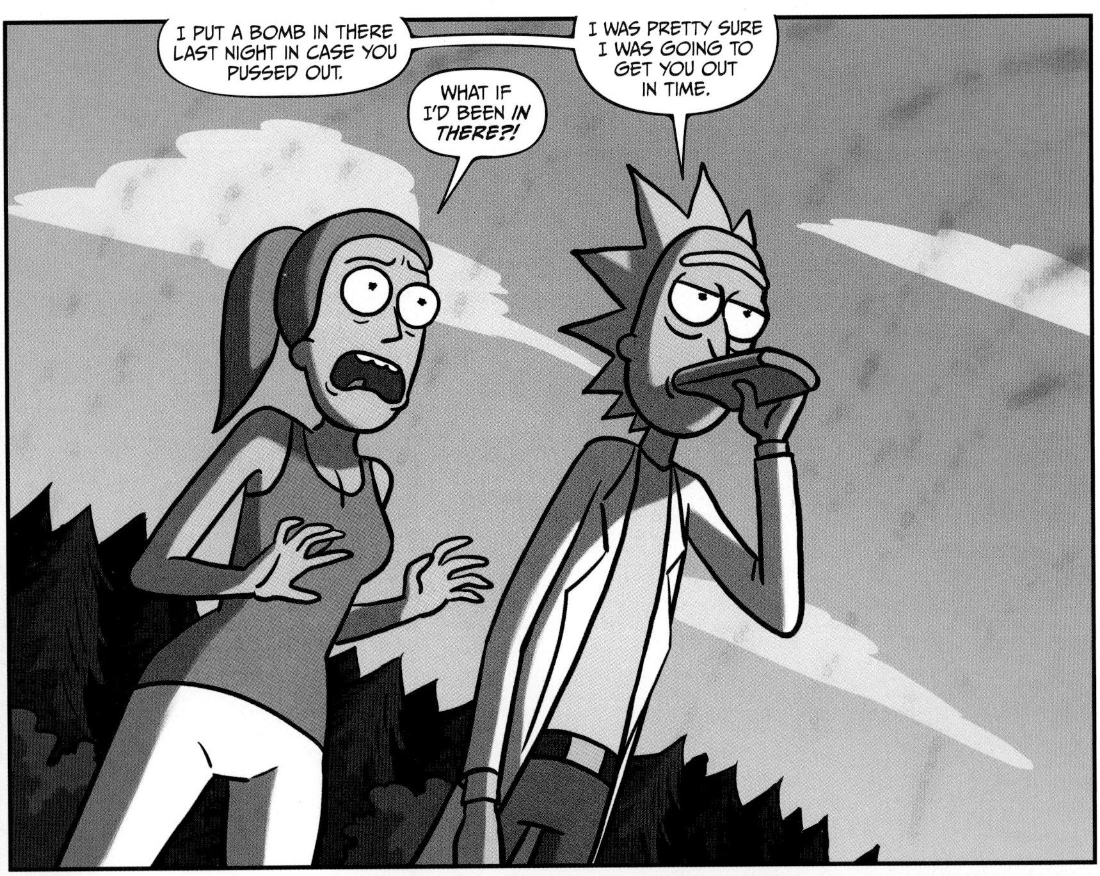
I PUT A BOMB IN THERE LAST NIGHT IN CASE YOU PUSSED OUT.
WHAT IF I'D BEEN *IN THERE?!*
I WAS PRETTY SURE I WAS GOING TO GET YOU OUT IN TIME.

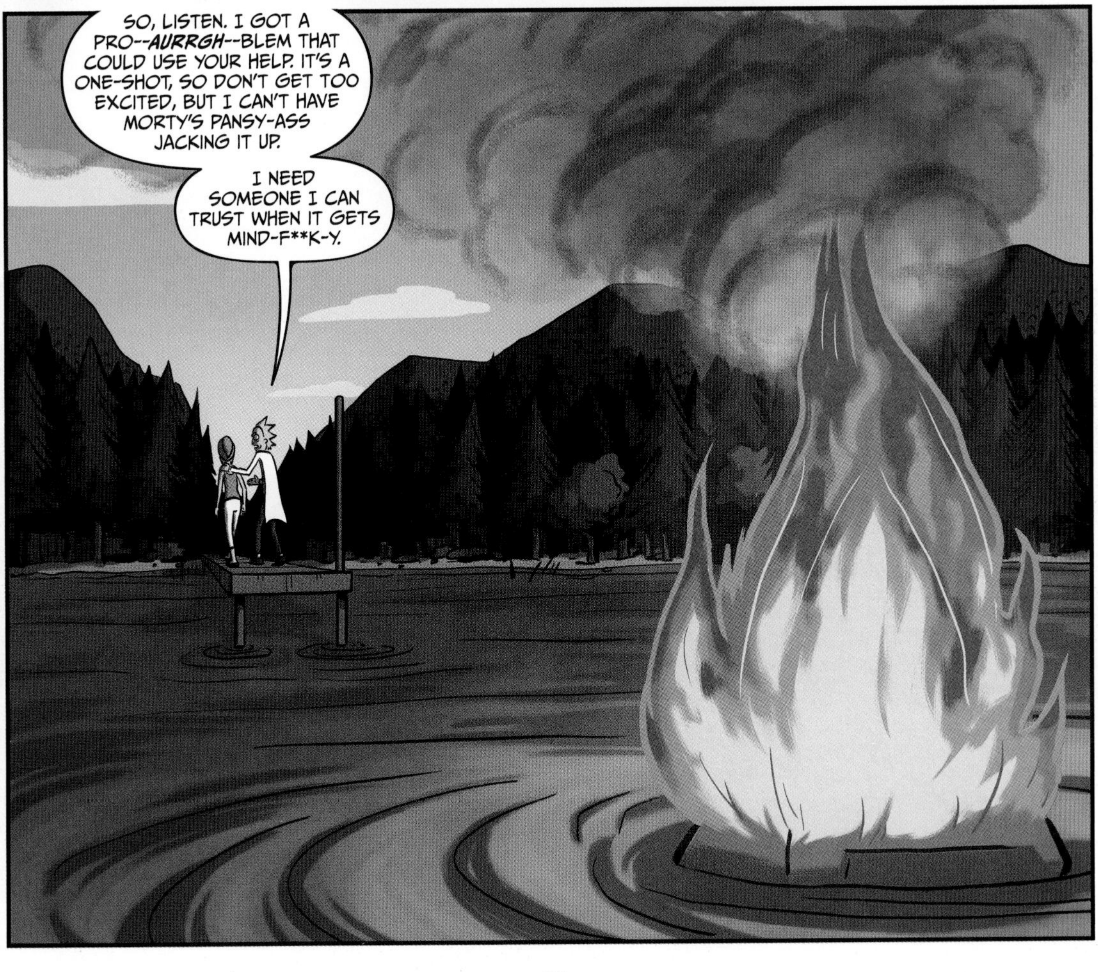
SO, LISTEN. I GOT A PRO--**AURRGH**--BLEM THAT COULD USE YOUR HELP. IT'S A ONE-SHOT, SO DON'T GET TOO EXCITED, BUT I CAN'T HAVE MORTY'S PANSY-ASS JACKING IT UP.
I NEED SOMEONE I CAN TRUST WHEN IT GETS MIND-F**K-Y.

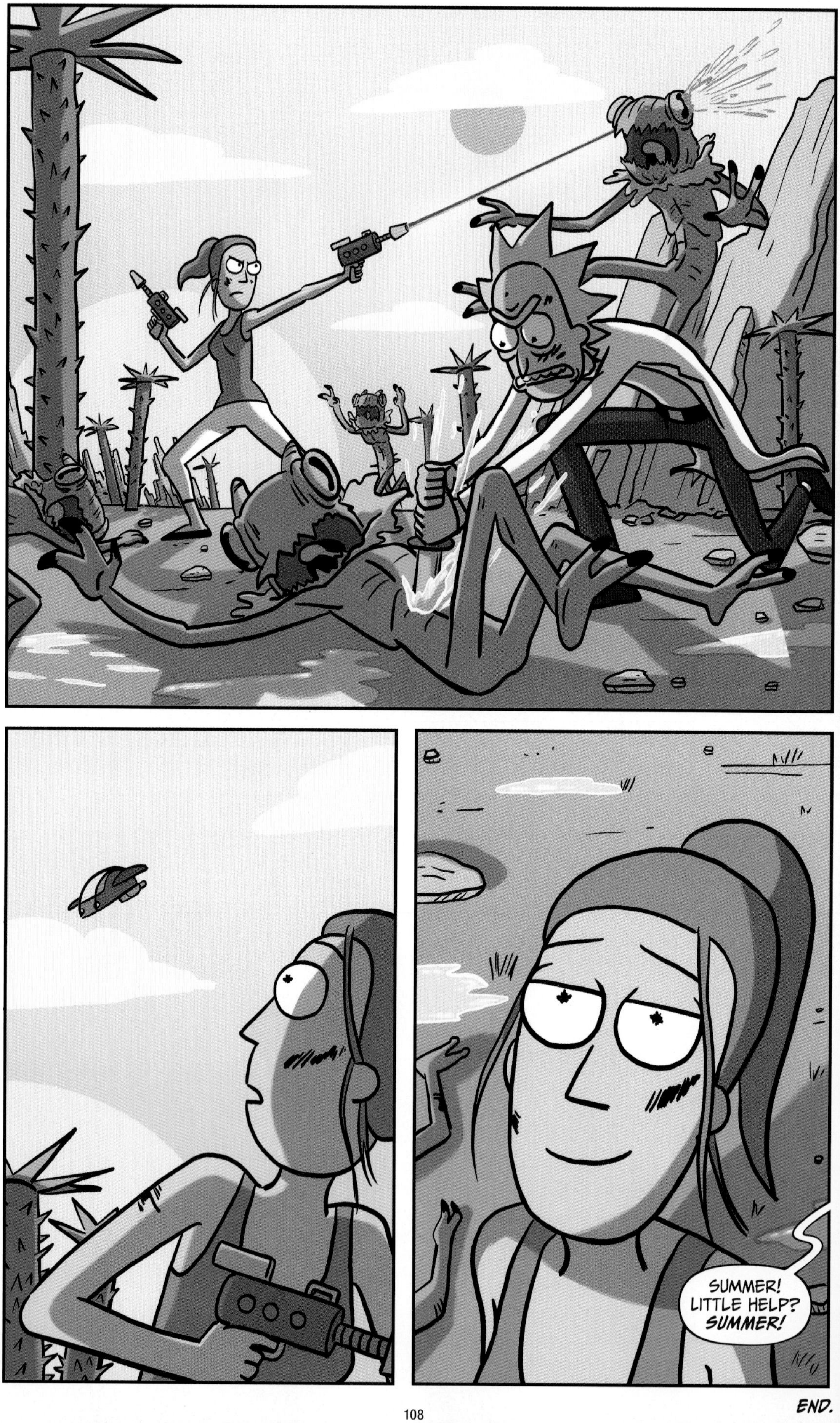
SUMMER! LITTLE HELP? *SUMMER!*

END.

THE RICK IDENTITY

WRITTEN BY **MAGDALENE VISAGGIO** • ILLUSTRATED & COLORED BY **MARC ELLERBY** • LETTERED BY **CRANK!**

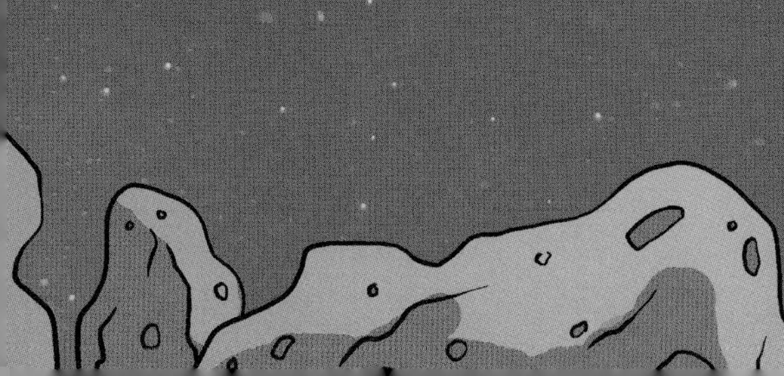

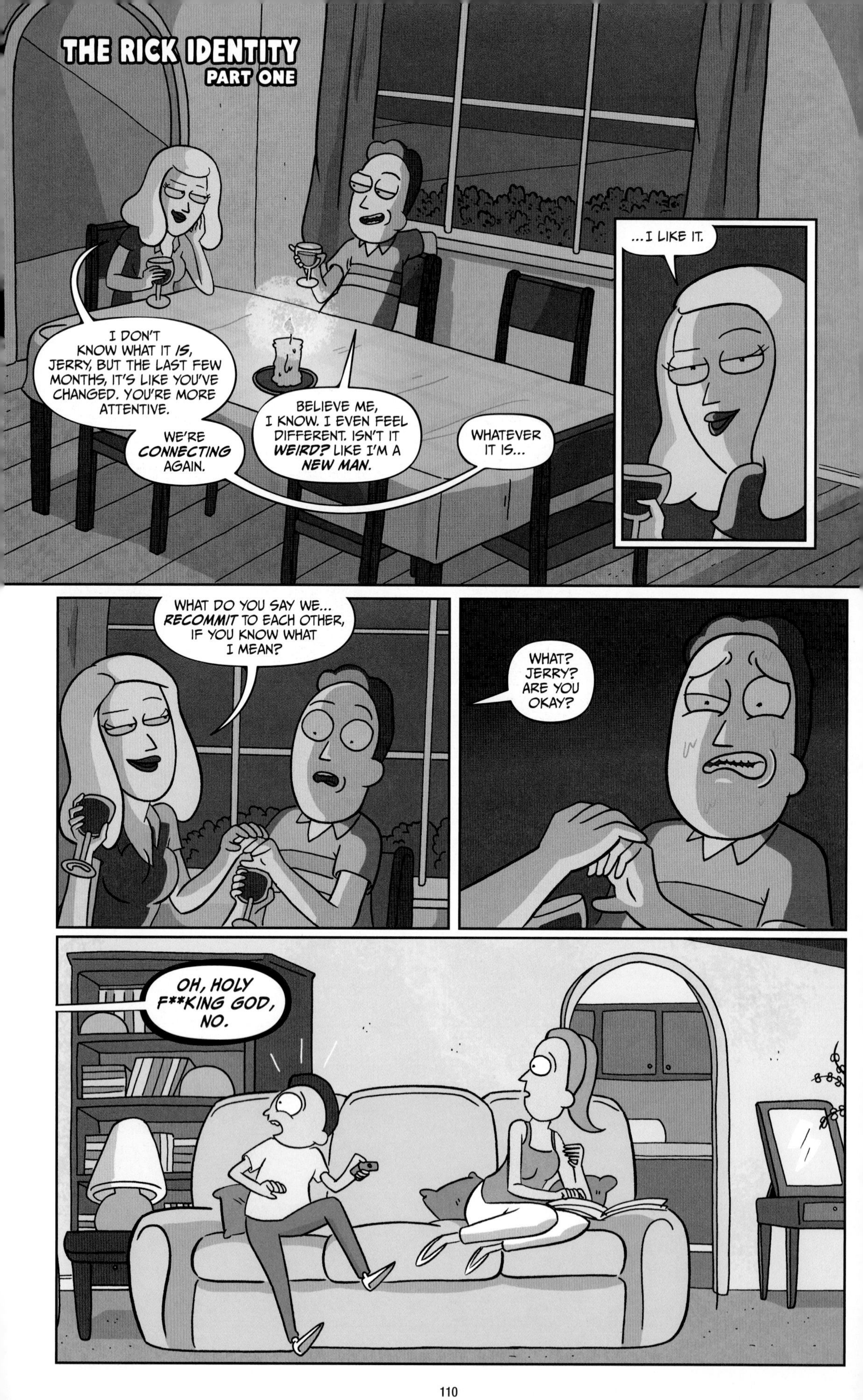
THE RICK IDENTITY
PART ONE
I DON'T KNOW WHAT IT *IS*, JERRY, BUT THE LAST FEW MONTHS, IT'S LIKE YOU'VE CHANGED. YOU'RE MORE ATTENTIVE.
WE'RE *CONNECTING* AGAIN.
BELIEVE ME, I KNOW. I EVEN FEEL DIFFERENT. ISN'T IT *WEIRD?* LIKE I'M A *NEW MAN.*
WHATEVER IT IS...
...I LIKE IT.
WHAT DO YOU SAY WE... *RECOMMIT* TO EACH OTHER, IF YOU KNOW WHAT I MEAN?
WHAT? JERRY? ARE YOU OKAY?
OH, HOLY F**KING GOD, NO.

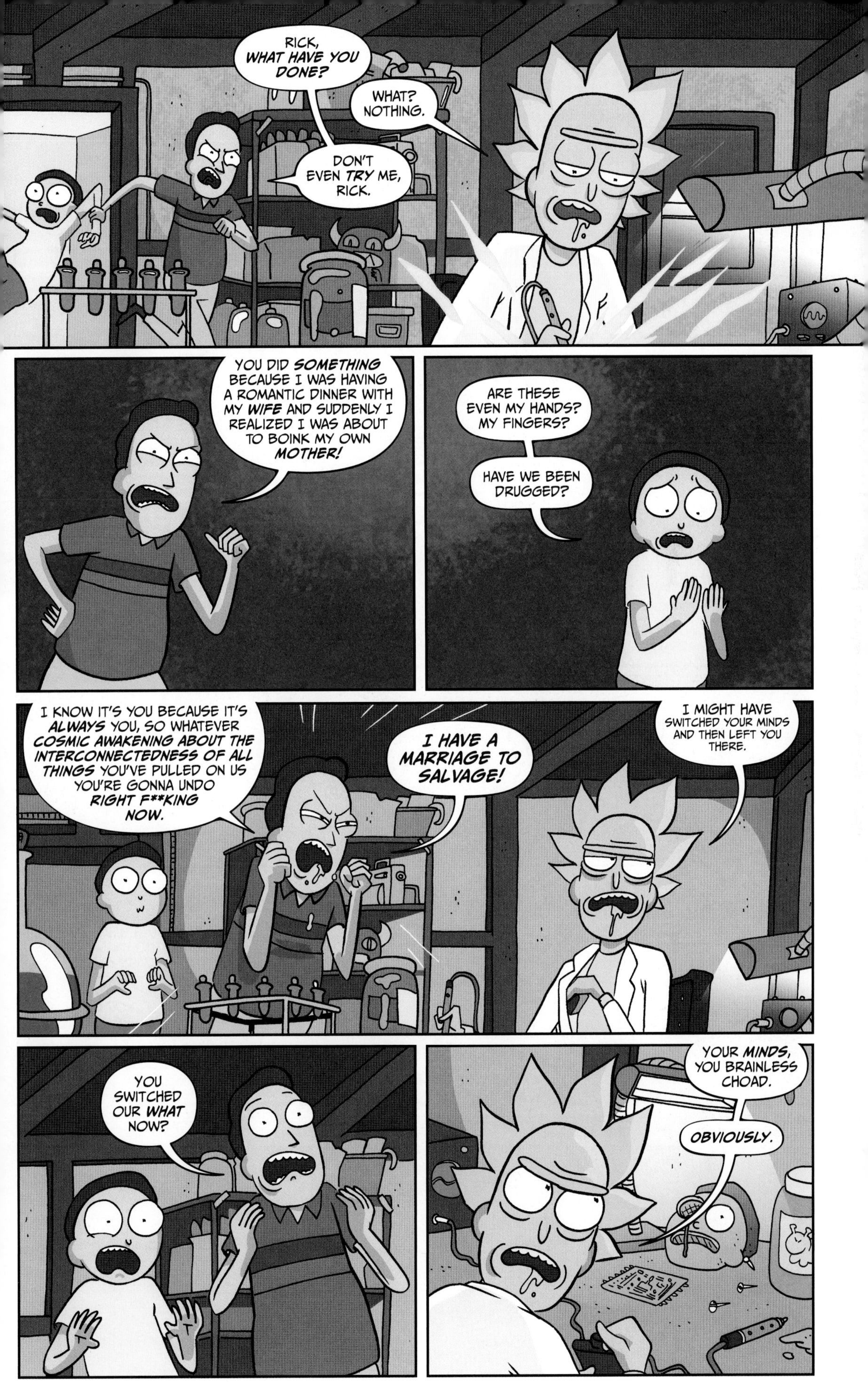
RICK, WHAT HAVE YOU DONE?
WHAT? NOTHING.
DON'T EVEN TRY ME, RICK.
YOU DID SOMETHING BECAUSE I WAS HAVING A ROMANTIC DINNER WITH MY WIFE AND SUDDENLY I REALIZED I WAS ABOUT TO BOINK MY OWN MOTHER!
ARE THESE EVEN MY HANDS? MY FINGERS?
HAVE WE BEEN DRUGGED?
I KNOW IT'S YOU BECAUSE IT'S ALWAYS YOU, SO WHATEVER COSMIC AWAKENING ABOUT THE INTERCONNECTEDNESS OF ALL THINGS YOU'VE PULLED ON US YOU'RE GONNA UNDO RIGHT F**KING NOW.
I HAVE A MARRIAGE TO SALVAGE!
I MIGHT HAVE SWITCHED YOUR MINDS AND THEN LEFT YOU THERE.
YOU SWITCHED OUR WHAT NOW?
YOUR MINDS, YOU BRAINLESS CHOAD.
OBVIOUSLY.

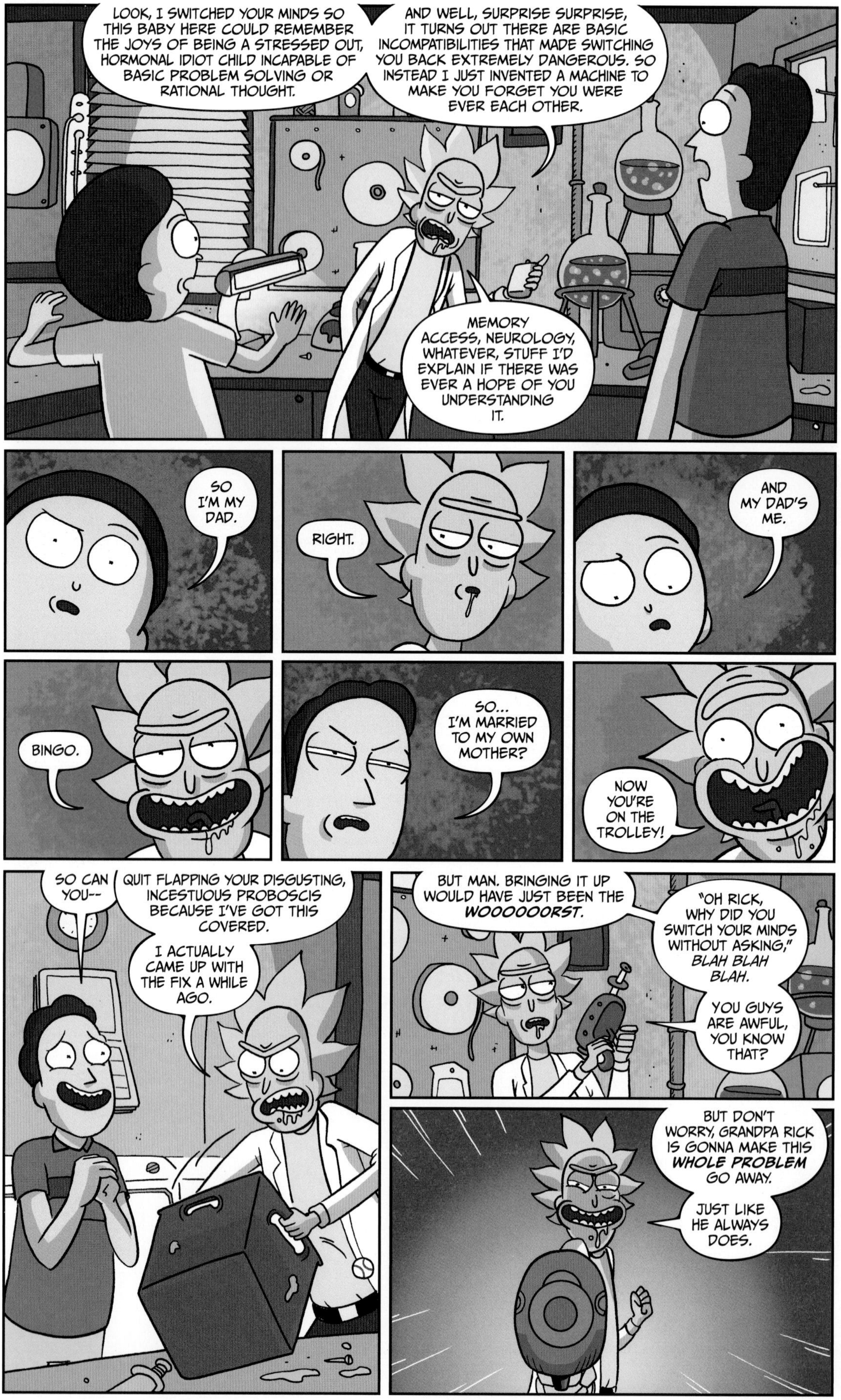
LOOK, I SWITCHED YOUR MINDS SO THIS BABY HERE COULD REMEMBER THE JOYS OF BEING A STRESSED OUT, HORMONAL IDIOT CHILD INCAPABLE OF BASIC PROBLEM SOLVING OR RATIONAL THOUGHT.
AND WELL, SURPRISE SURPRISE, IT TURNS OUT THERE ARE BASIC INCOMPATIBILITIES THAT MADE SWITCHING YOU BACK EXTREMELY DANGEROUS. SO INSTEAD I JUST INVENTED A MACHINE TO MAKE YOU FORGET YOU WERE EVER EACH OTHER.
MEMORY ACCESS, NEUROLOGY, WHATEVER, STUFF I'D EXPLAIN IF THERE WAS EVER A HOPE OF YOU UNDERSTANDING IT.
SO I'M MY DAD.
RIGHT.
AND MY DAD'S ME.
BINGO.
SO... I'M MARRIED TO MY OWN MOTHER?
NOW YOU'RE ON THE TROLLEY!
SO CAN YOU--
QUIT FLAPPING YOUR DISGUSTING, INCESTUOUS PROBOSCIS BECAUSE I'VE GOT THIS COVERED.
I ACTUALLY CAME UP WITH THE FIX A WHILE AGO.
BUT MAN. BRINGING IT UP WOULD HAVE JUST BEEN THE *WOOOOOORST.*
"OH RICK, WHY DID YOU SWITCH YOUR MINDS WITHOUT ASKING," *BLAH BLAH BLAH.*
YOU GUYS ARE AWFUL, YOU KNOW THAT?
BUT DON'T WORRY, GRANDPA RICK IS GONNA MAKE THIS *WHOLE PROBLEM* GO AWAY.
JUST LIKE HE ALWAYS DOES.

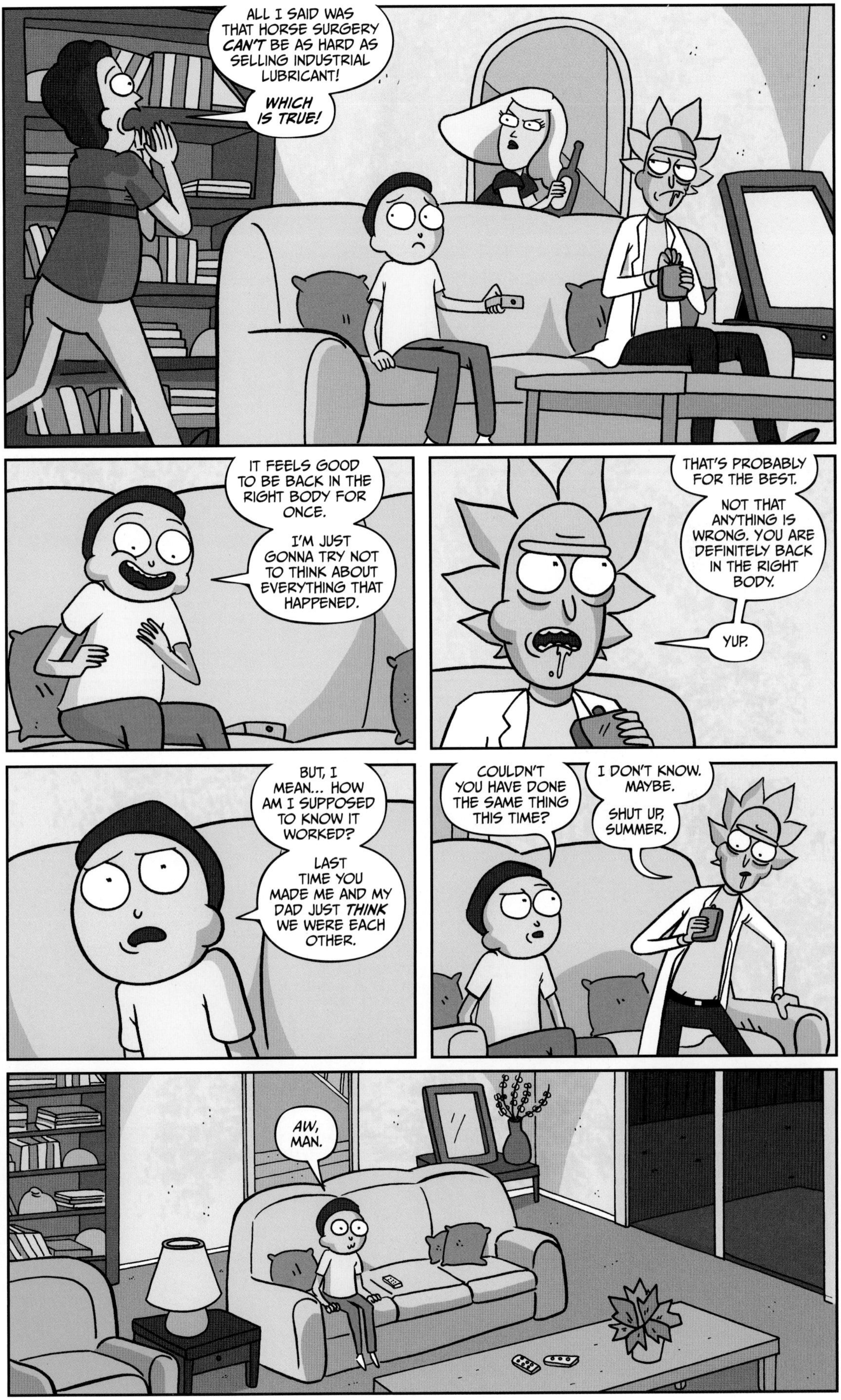
ALL I SAID WAS THAT HORSE SURGERY *CAN'T* BE AS HARD AS SELLING INDUSTRIAL LUBRICANT!
WHICH IS TRUE!
IT FEELS GOOD TO BE BACK IN THE RIGHT BODY FOR ONCE.
I'M JUST GONNA TRY NOT TO THINK ABOUT EVERYTHING THAT HAPPENED.
THAT'S PROBABLY FOR THE BEST.
NOT THAT ANYTHING IS WRONG. YOU ARE DEFINITELY BACK IN THE RIGHT BODY.
YUP.
BUT, I MEAN... HOW AM I SUPPOSED TO KNOW IT WORKED?
LAST TIME YOU MADE ME AND MY DAD JUST *THINK* WE WERE EACH OTHER.
COULDN'T YOU HAVE DONE THE SAME THING THIS TIME?
I DON'T KNOW. MAYBE.
SHUT UP, SUMMER.
AW, MAN.

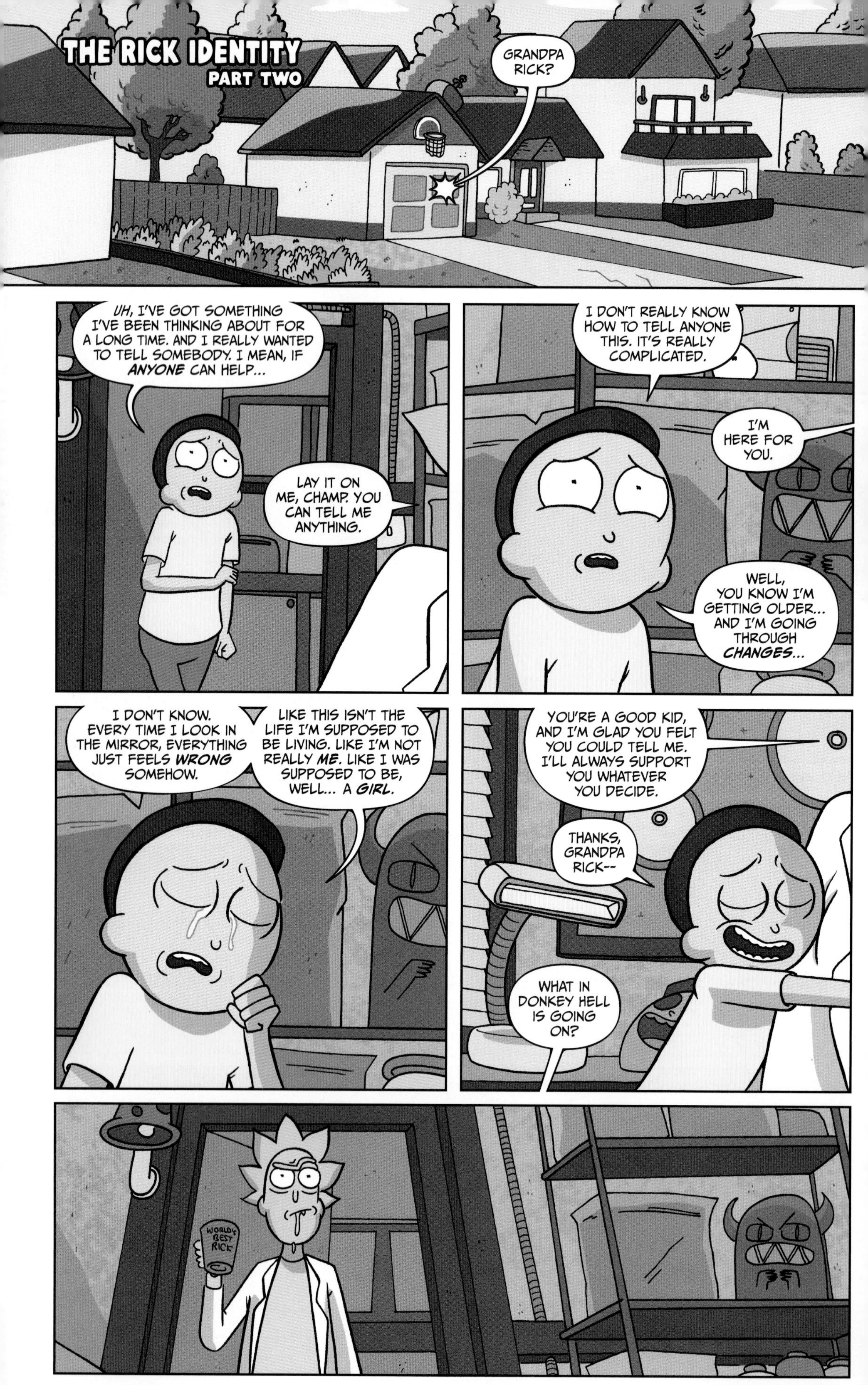
THE RICK IDENTITY
PART TWO
GRANDPA RICK?
UH, I'VE GOT SOMETHING I'VE BEEN THINKING ABOUT FOR A LONG TIME. AND I REALLY WANTED TO TELL SOMEBODY. I MEAN, IF ANYONE CAN HELP...
LAY IT ON ME, CHAMP. YOU CAN TELL ME ANYTHING.
I DON'T REALLY KNOW HOW TO TELL ANYONE THIS. IT'S REALLY COMPLICATED.
I'M HERE FOR YOU.
WELL, YOU KNOW I'M GETTING OLDER... AND I'M GOING THROUGH CHANGES...
I DON'T KNOW. EVERY TIME I LOOK IN THE MIRROR, EVERYTHING JUST FEELS WRONG SOMEHOW.
LIKE THIS ISN'T THE LIFE I'M SUPPOSED TO BE LIVING. LIKE I'M NOT REALLY ME. LIKE I WAS SUPPOSED TO BE, WELL... A GIRL.
YOU'RE A GOOD KID, AND I'M GLAD YOU FELT YOU COULD TELL ME. I'LL ALWAYS SUPPORT YOU WHATEVER YOU DECIDE.
THANKS, GRANDPA RICK--
WHAT IN DONKEY HELL IS GOING ON?
WORLD'S BEST RICK

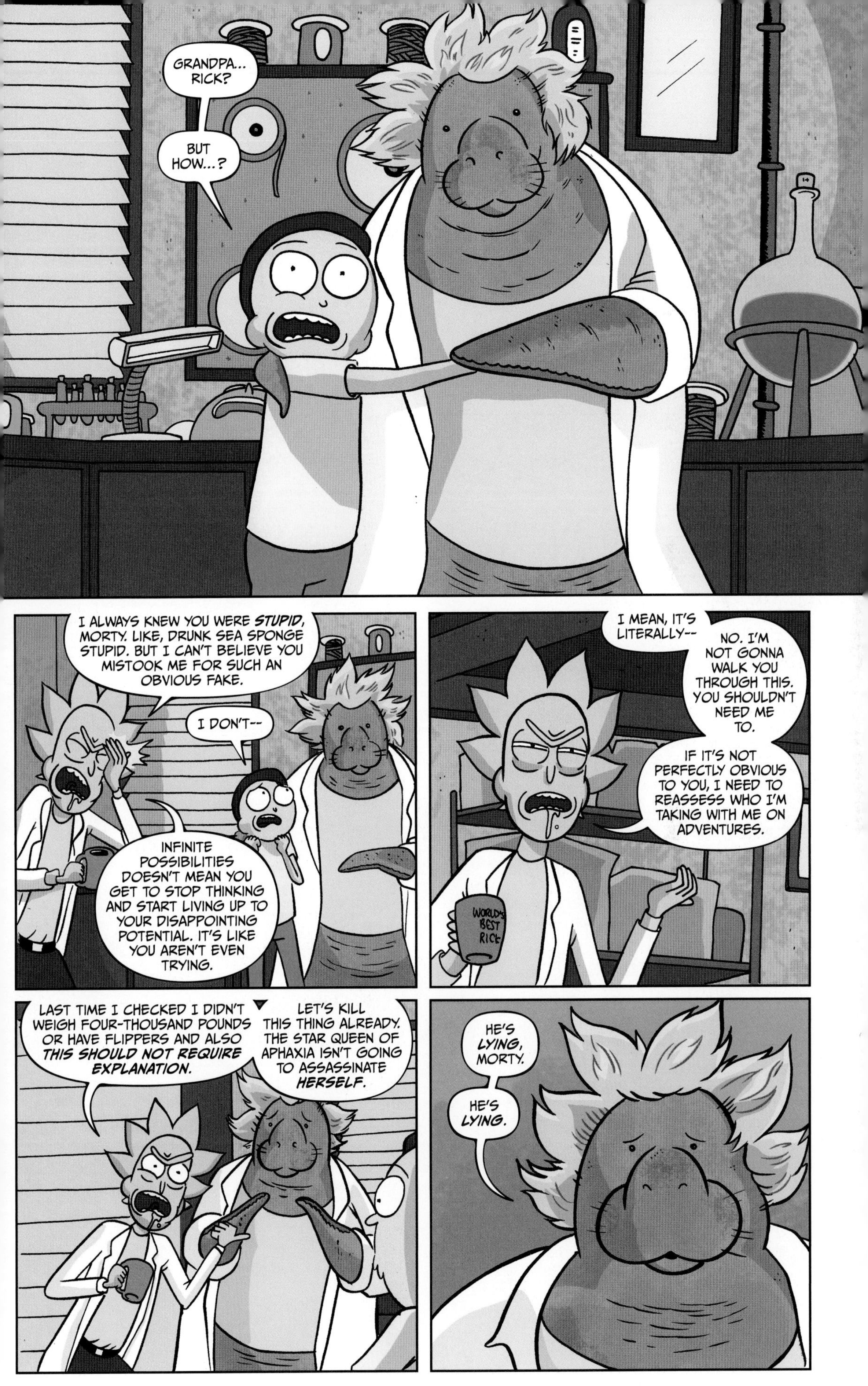

GRANDPA... RICK?
BUT HOW...?
I ALWAYS KNEW YOU WERE *STUPID*, MORTY. LIKE, DRUNK SEA SPONGE STUPID. BUT I CAN'T BELIEVE YOU MISTOOK ME FOR SUCH AN OBVIOUS FAKE.
I DON'T--
INFINITE POSSIBILITIES DOESN'T MEAN YOU GET TO STOP THINKING AND START LIVING UP TO YOUR DISAPPOINTING POTENTIAL. IT'S LIKE YOU AREN'T EVEN TRYING.
I MEAN, IT'S LITERALLY--
NO. I'M NOT GONNA WALK YOU THROUGH THIS. YOU SHOULDN'T NEED ME TO.
IF IT'S NOT PERFECTLY OBVIOUS TO YOU, I NEED TO REASSESS WHO I'M TAKING WITH ME ON ADVENTURES.
WORLD'S BEST RICK
LAST TIME I CHECKED I DIDN'T WEIGH FOUR-THOUSAND POUNDS OR HAVE FLIPPERS AND ALSO ***THIS SHOULD NOT REQUIRE EXPLANATION.***
LET'S KILL THIS THING ALREADY. THE STAR QUEEN OF APHAXIA ISN'T GOING TO ASSASSINATE ***HERSELF***.
HE'S ***LYING***, MORTY.
HE'S ***LYING***.

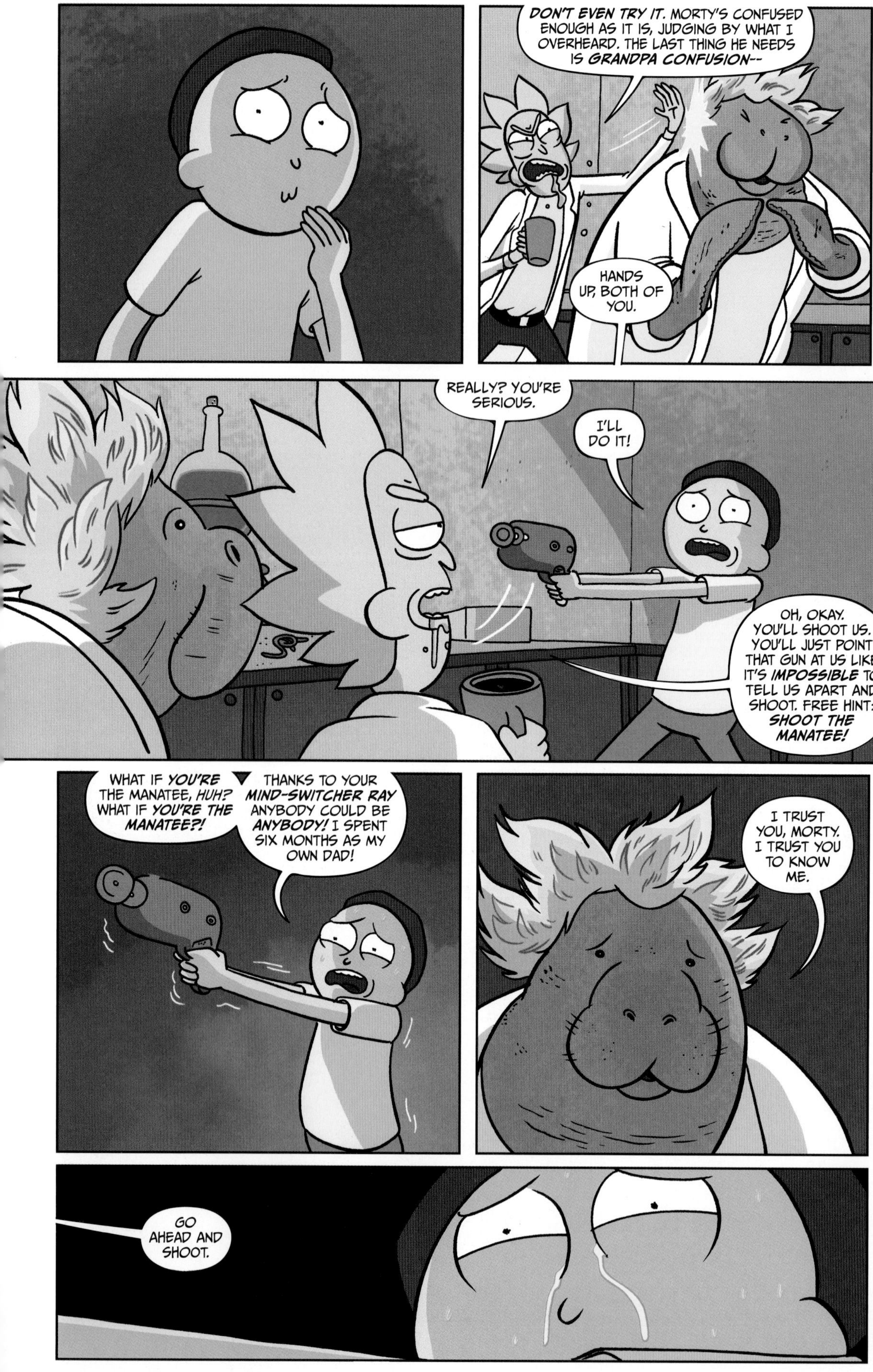
DON'T EVEN TRY IT. MORTY'S CONFUSED ENOUGH AS IT IS, JUDGING BY WHAT I OVERHEARD. THE LAST THING HE NEEDS IS GRANDPA CONFUSION--
HANDS UP, BOTH OF YOU.
REALLY? YOU'RE SERIOUS.
I'LL DO IT!
OH, OKAY. YOU'LL SHOOT US. YOU'LL JUST POINT THAT GUN AT US LIKE IT'S IMPOSSIBLE TO TELL US APART AND SHOOT. FREE HINT: SHOOT THE MANATEE!
WHAT IF YOU'RE THE MANATEE, HUH? WHAT IF YOU'RE THE MANATEE?!
THANKS TO YOUR MIND-SWITCHER RAY ANYBODY COULD BE ANYBODY! I SPENT SIX MONTHS AS MY OWN DAD!
I TRUST YOU, MORTY. I TRUST YOU TO KNOW ME.
GO AHEAD AND SHOOT.

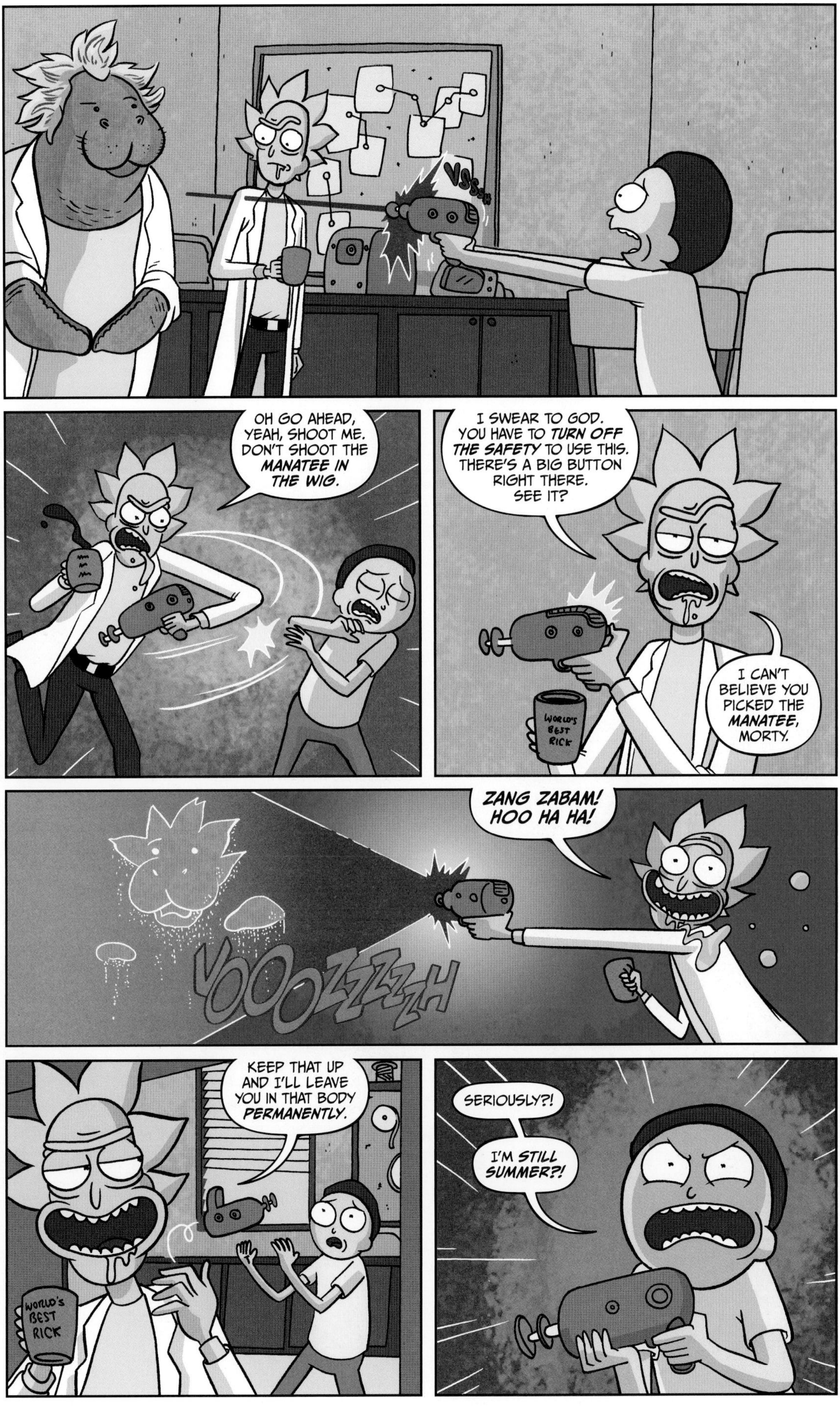
VSSSSH
OH GO AHEAD, YEAH, SHOOT ME. DON'T SHOOT THE MANATEE IN THE WIG.
I SWEAR TO GOD. YOU HAVE TO TURN OFF THE SAFETY TO USE THIS. THERE'S A BIG BUTTON RIGHT THERE. SEE IT?
I CAN'T BELIEVE YOU PICKED THE MANATEE, MORTY.
WORLD'S BEST RICK
ZANG ZABAM! HOO HA HA!
VOOOZZZZZH
KEEP THAT UP AND I'LL LEAVE YOU IN THAT BODY PERMANENTLY.
WORLD'S BEST RICK
SERIOUSLY?!
I'M STILL SUMMER?!

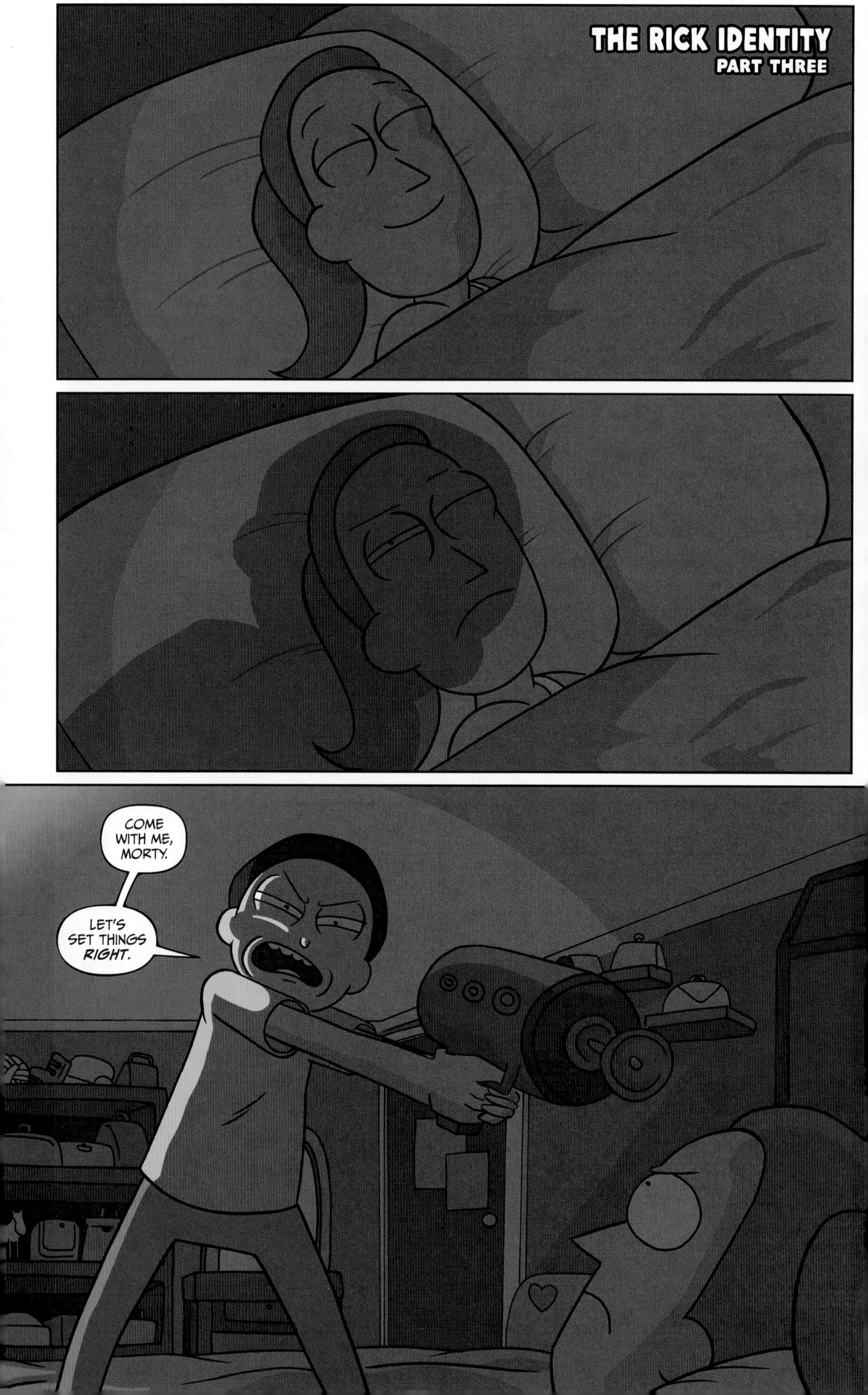
THE RICK IDENTITY
PART THREE
COME WITH ME, MORTY.
LET'S SET THINGS *RIGHT*.

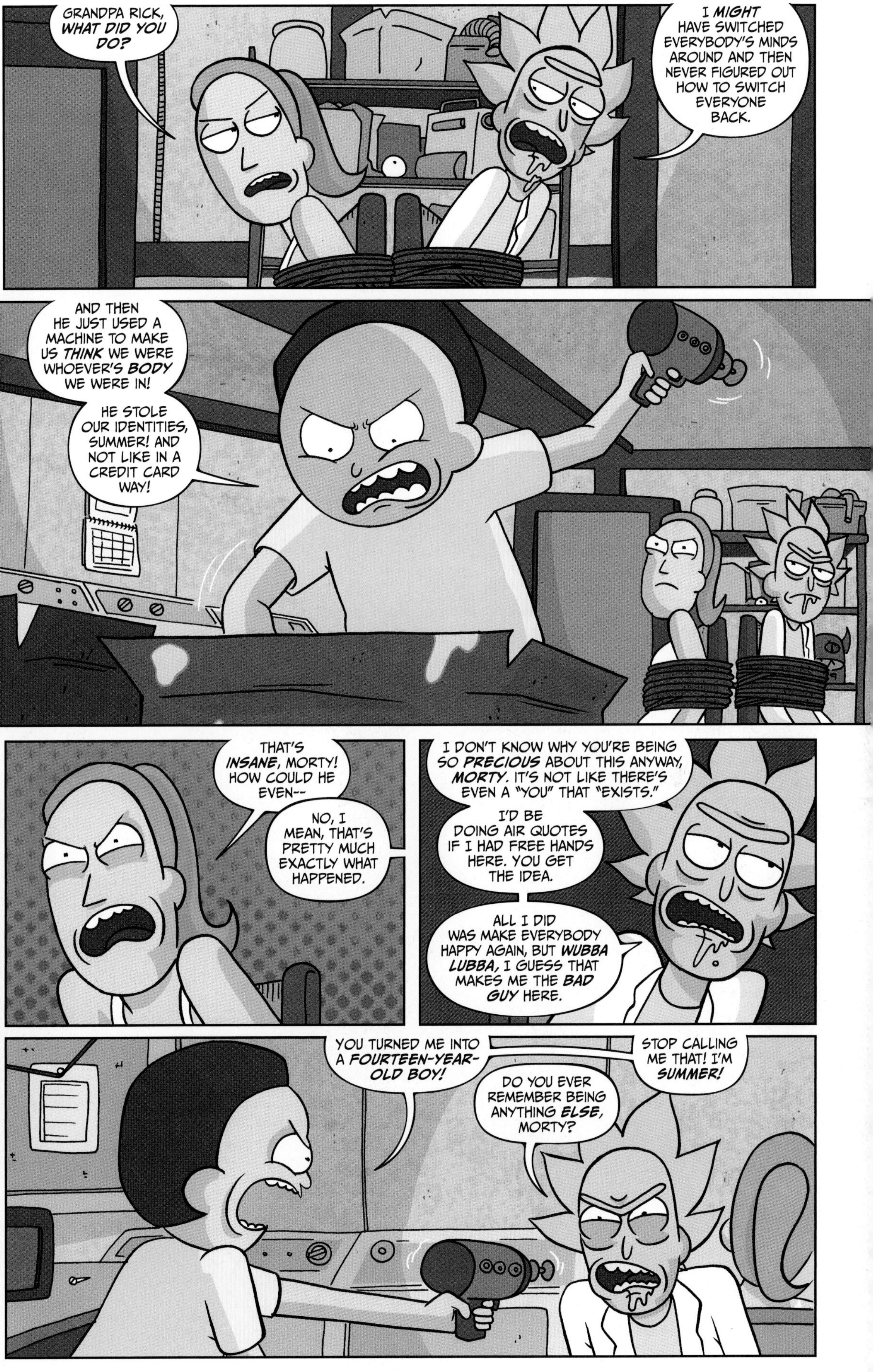
GRANDPA RICK, WHAT DID YOU DO?
I MIGHT HAVE SWITCHED EVERYBODY'S MINDS AROUND AND THEN NEVER FIGURED OUT HOW TO SWITCH EVERYONE BACK.
AND THEN HE JUST USED A MACHINE TO MAKE US THINK WE WERE WHOEVER'S BODY WE WERE IN!
HE STOLE OUR IDENTITIES, SUMMER! AND NOT LIKE IN A CREDIT CARD WAY!
THAT'S INSANE, MORTY! HOW COULD HE EVEN--
NO, I MEAN, THAT'S PRETTY MUCH EXACTLY WHAT HAPPENED.
I DON'T KNOW WHY YOU'RE BEING SO PRECIOUS ABOUT THIS ANYWAY, MORTY. IT'S NOT LIKE THERE'S EVEN A "YOU" THAT "EXISTS."
I'D BE DOING AIR QUOTES IF I HAD FREE HANDS HERE. YOU GET THE IDEA.
ALL I DID WAS MAKE EVERYBODY HAPPY AGAIN, BUT WUBBA LUBBA, I GUESS THAT MAKES ME THE BAD GUY HERE.
YOU TURNED ME INTO A FOURTEEN-YEAR-OLD BOY!
STOP CALLING ME THAT! I'M SUMMER!
DO YOU EVER REMEMBER BEING ANYTHING ELSE, MORTY?

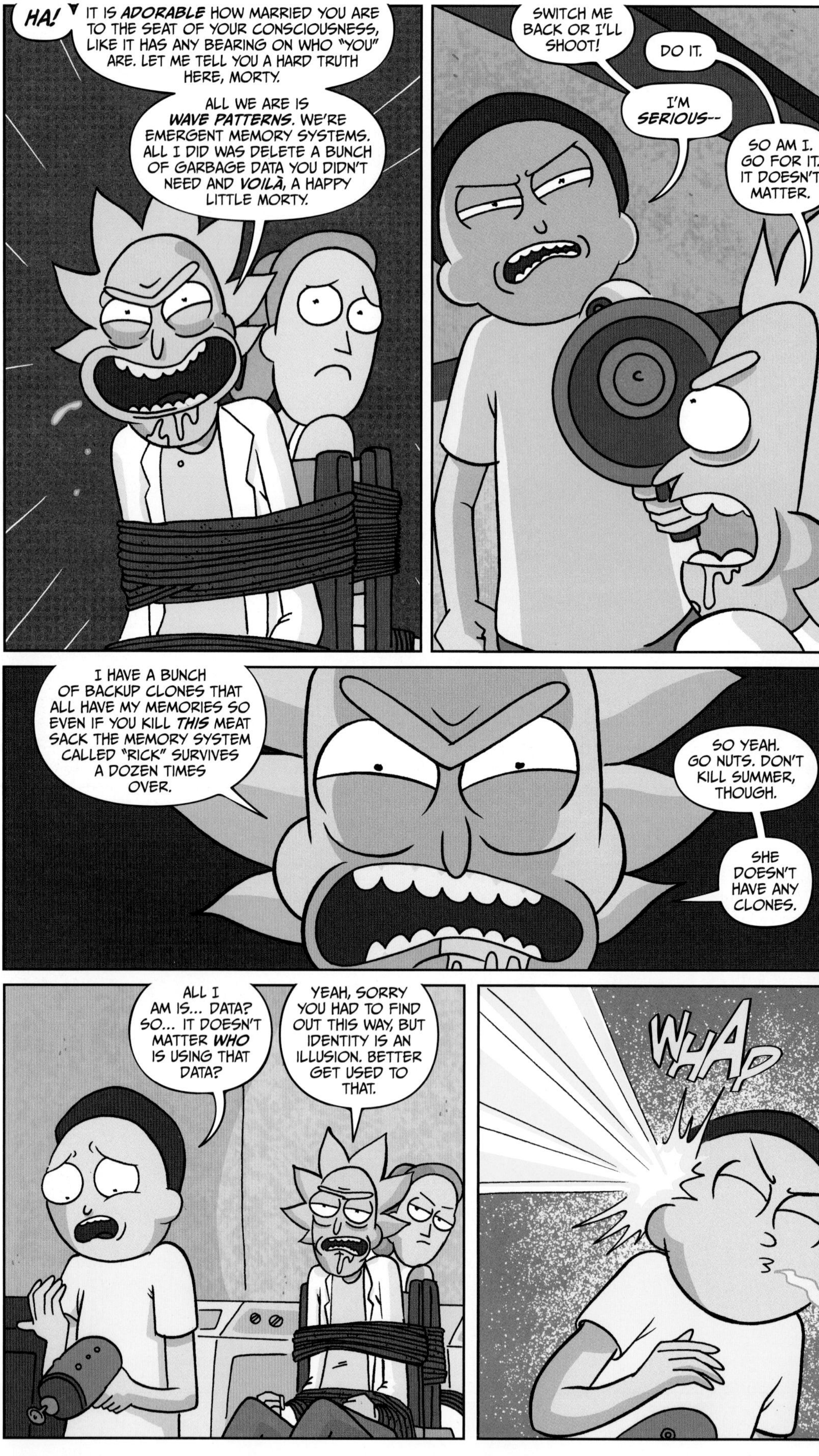
HA!
IT IS ADORABLE HOW MARRIED YOU ARE TO THE SEAT OF YOUR CONSCIOUSNESS, LIKE IT HAS ANY BEARING ON WHO "YOU" ARE. LET ME TELL YOU A HARD TRUTH HERE, MORTY.
ALL WE ARE IS WAVE PATTERNS. WE'RE EMERGENT MEMORY SYSTEMS. ALL I DID WAS DELETE A BUNCH OF GARBAGE DATA YOU DIDN'T NEED AND VOILÀ, A HAPPY LITTLE MORTY.
SWITCH ME BACK OR I'LL SHOOT!
DO IT.
I'M SERIOUS--
SO AM I. GO FOR IT. IT DOESN'T MATTER.
I HAVE A BUNCH OF BACKUP CLONES THAT ALL HAVE MY MEMORIES SO EVEN IF YOU KILL THIS MEAT SACK THE MEMORY SYSTEM CALLED "RICK" SURVIVES A DOZEN TIMES OVER.
SO YEAH. GO NUTS. DON'T KILL SUMMER, THOUGH.
SHE DOESN'T HAVE ANY CLONES.
ALL I AM IS... DATA? SO... IT DOESN'T MATTER WHO IS USING THAT DATA?
YEAH, SORRY YOU HAD TO FIND OUT THIS WAY, BUT IDENTITY IS AN ILLUSION. BETTER GET USED TO THAT.
WHAP

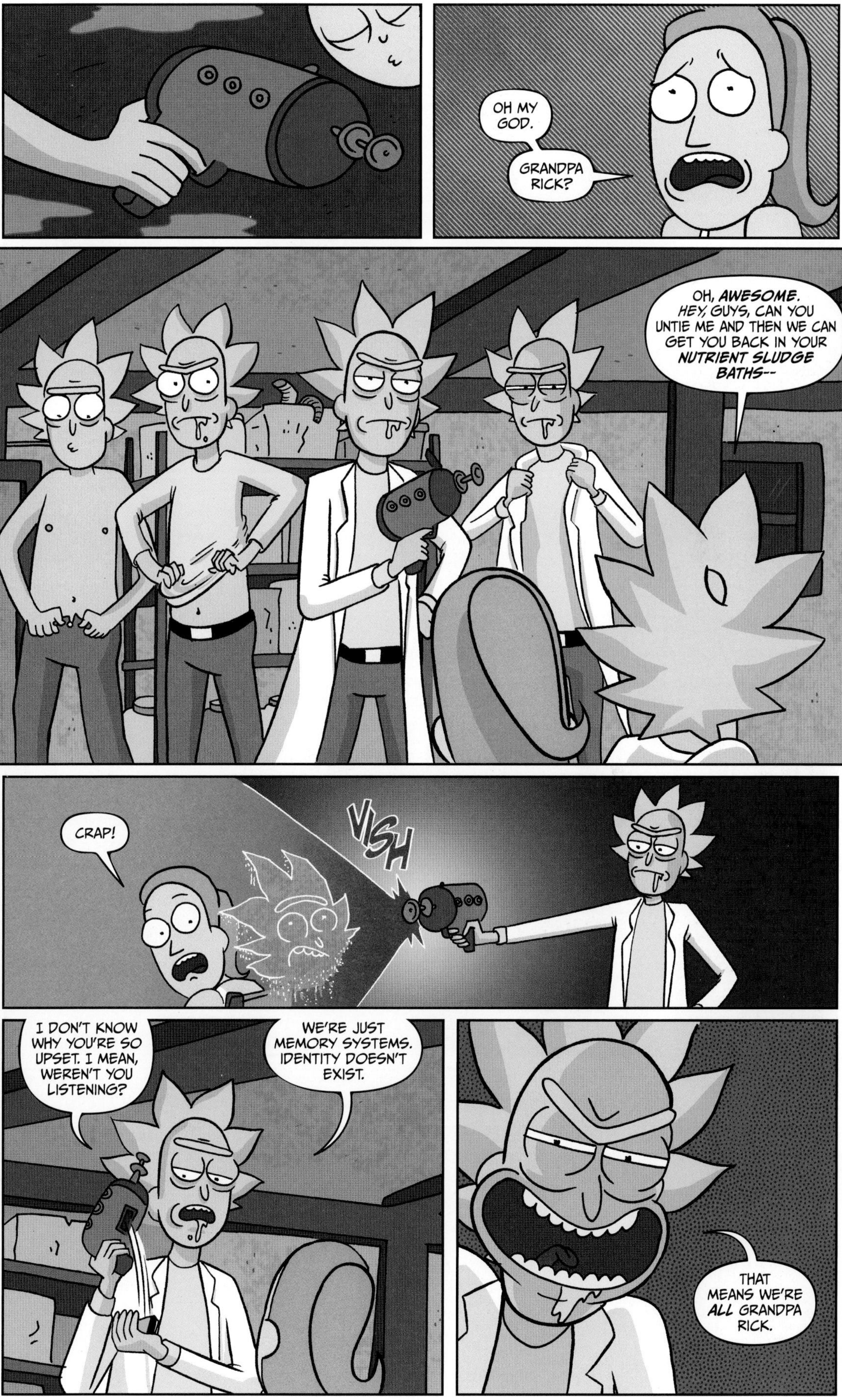
OH MY GOD.
GRANDPA RICK?
OH, **AWESOME.** HEY, GUYS, CAN YOU UNTIE ME AND THEN WE CAN GET YOU BACK IN YOUR **NUTRIENT SLUDGE BATHS--**
CRAP!
VISH
I DON'T KNOW WHY YOU'RE SO UPSET. I MEAN, WEREN'T YOU LISTENING?
WE'RE JUST MEMORY SYSTEMS. IDENTITY DOESN'T EXIST.
THAT MEANS WE'RE **ALL** GRANDPA RICK.

THE RICK IDENTITY
PART FOUR

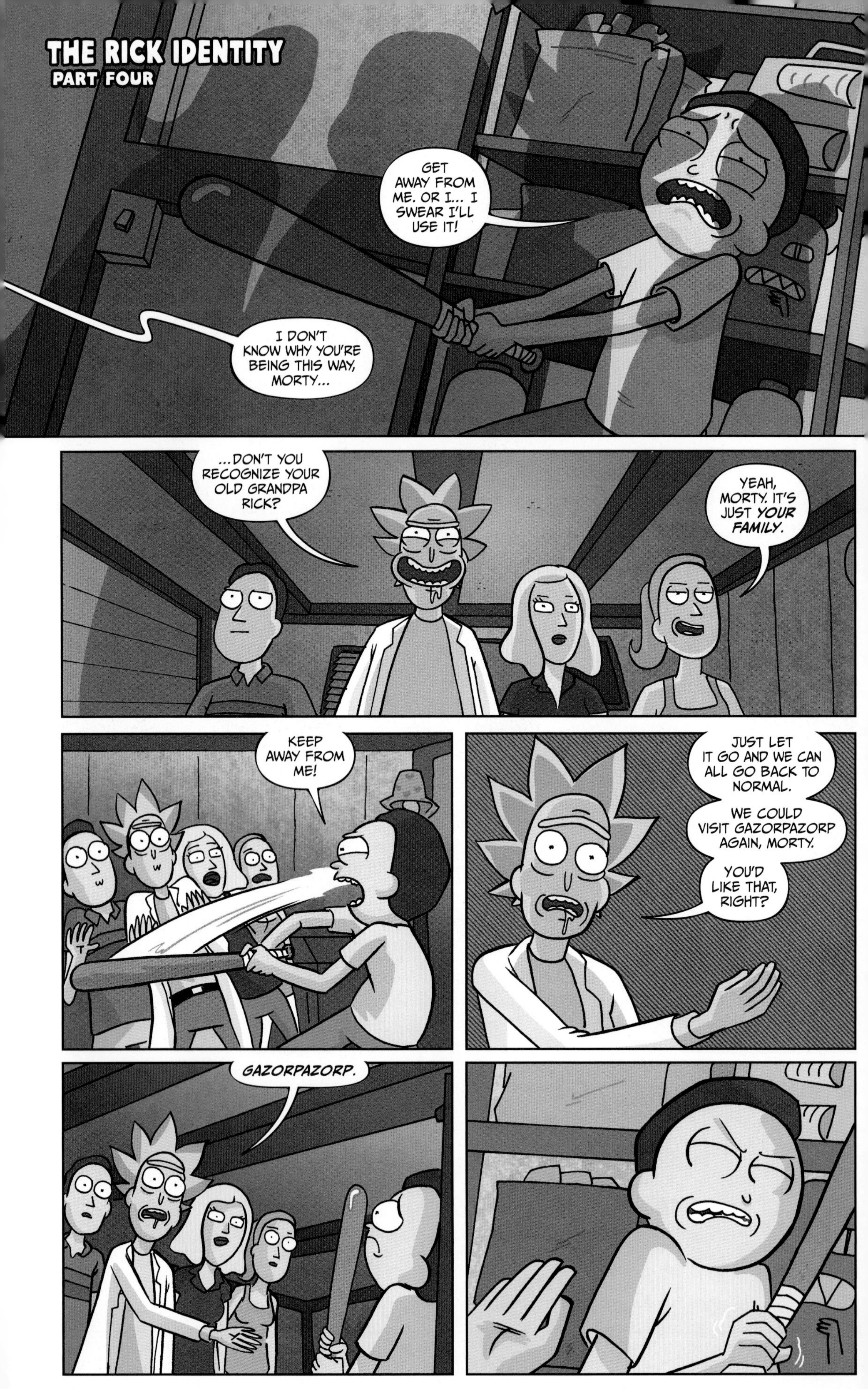

GET AWAY FROM ME. OR I... I SWEAR I'LL USE IT!
I DON'T KNOW WHY YOU'RE BEING THIS WAY, MORTY...
...DON'T YOU RECOGNIZE YOUR OLD GRANDPA RICK?
YEAH, MORTY. IT'S JUST YOUR FAMILY.
KEEP AWAY FROM ME!
JUST LET IT GO AND WE CAN ALL GO BACK TO NORMAL.
WE COULD VISIT GAZORPAZORP AGAIN, MORTY.
YOU'D LIKE THAT, RIGHT?
GAZORPAZORP.

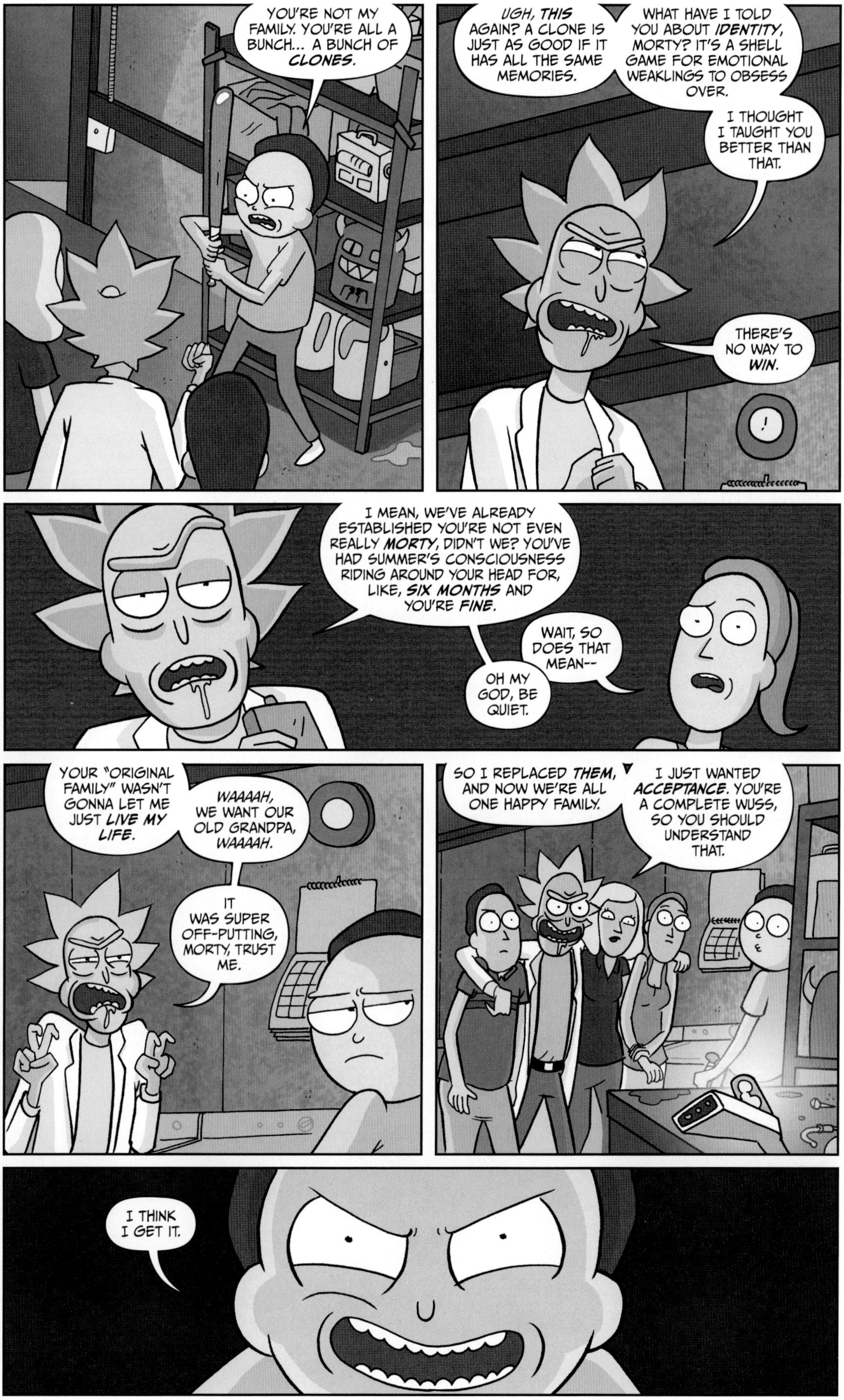
YOU'RE NOT MY FAMILY. YOU'RE ALL A BUNCH... A BUNCH OF *CLONES.*
UGH, THIS AGAIN? A CLONE IS JUST AS GOOD IF IT HAS ALL THE SAME MEMORIES.
WHAT HAVE I TOLD YOU ABOUT *IDENTITY*, MORTY? IT'S A SHELL GAME FOR EMOTIONAL WEAKLINGS TO OBSESS OVER.
I THOUGHT I TAUGHT YOU BETTER THAN THAT.
THERE'S NO WAY TO *WIN.*
I MEAN, WE'VE ALREADY ESTABLISHED YOU'RE NOT EVEN REALLY *MORTY*, DIDN'T WE? YOU'VE HAD SUMMER'S CONSCIOUSNESS RIDING AROUND YOUR HEAD FOR, LIKE, *SIX MONTHS* AND YOU'RE *FINE.*
WAIT, SO DOES THAT MEAN--
OH MY GOD, BE QUIET.
YOUR "ORIGINAL FAMILY" WASN'T GONNA LET ME JUST *LIVE MY LIFE.*
WAAAAH, WE WANT OUR OLD GRANDPA, *WAAAAH.*
IT WAS SUPER OFF-PUTTING, MORTY, TRUST ME.
SO I REPLACED *THEM,* AND NOW WE'RE ALL ONE HAPPY FAMILY.
I JUST WANTED *ACCEPTANCE.* YOU'RE A COMPLETE WUSS, SO YOU SHOULD UNDERSTAND THAT.
I THINK I GET IT.

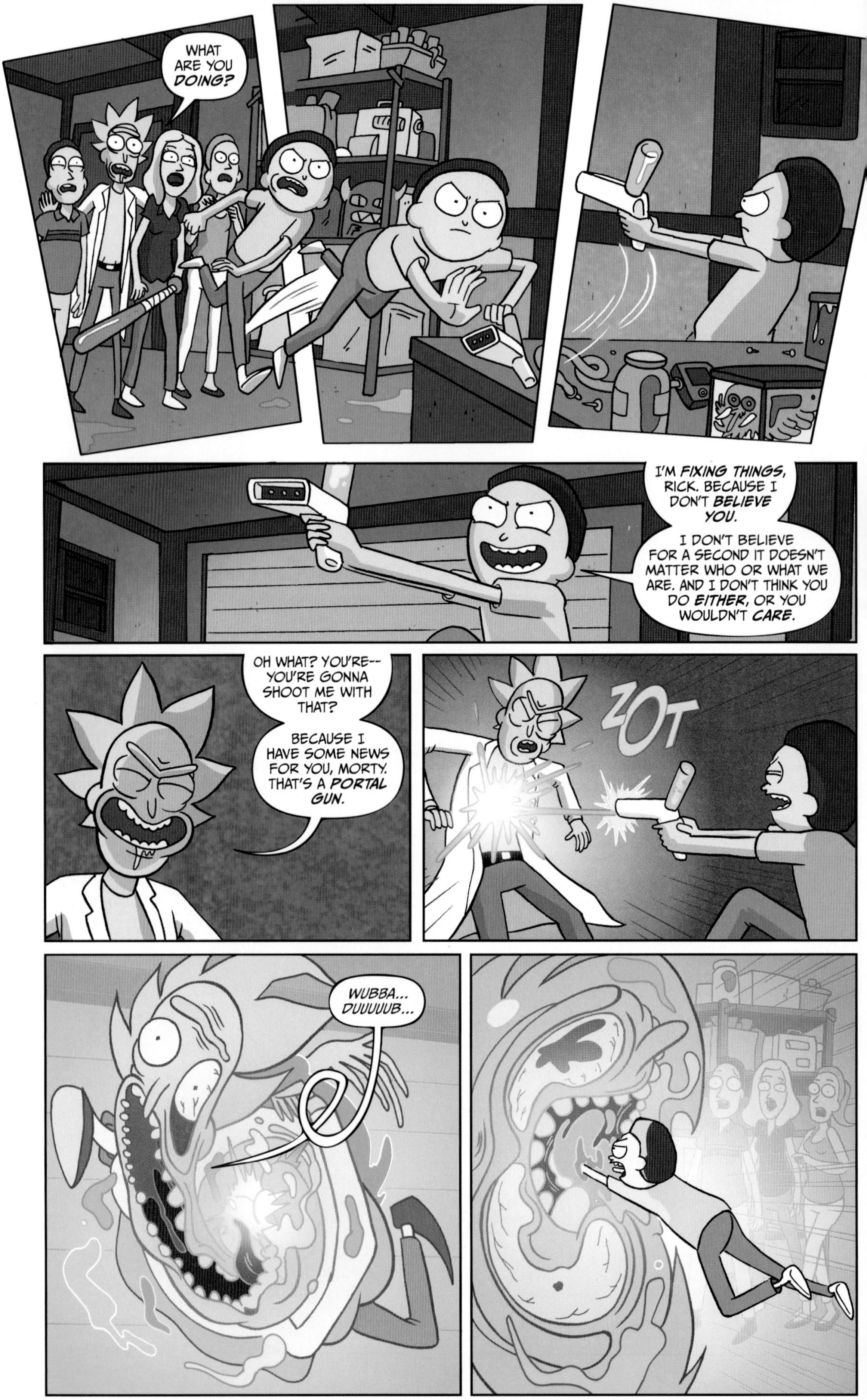
WHAT ARE YOU *DOING?*
I'M *FIXING THINGS,* RICK. BECAUSE I DON'T *BELIEVE YOU.*
I DON'T BELIEVE FOR A SECOND IT DOESN'T MATTER WHO OR WHAT WE ARE. AND I DON'T THINK YOU DO *EITHER,* OR YOU WOULDN'T *CARE.*
OH WHAT? YOU'RE-- YOU'RE GONNA SHOOT ME WITH THAT?
BECAUSE I HAVE SOME NEWS FOR YOU, MORTY. THAT'S A *PORTAL GUN.*
ZOT
WUBBA... DUUUUUB...

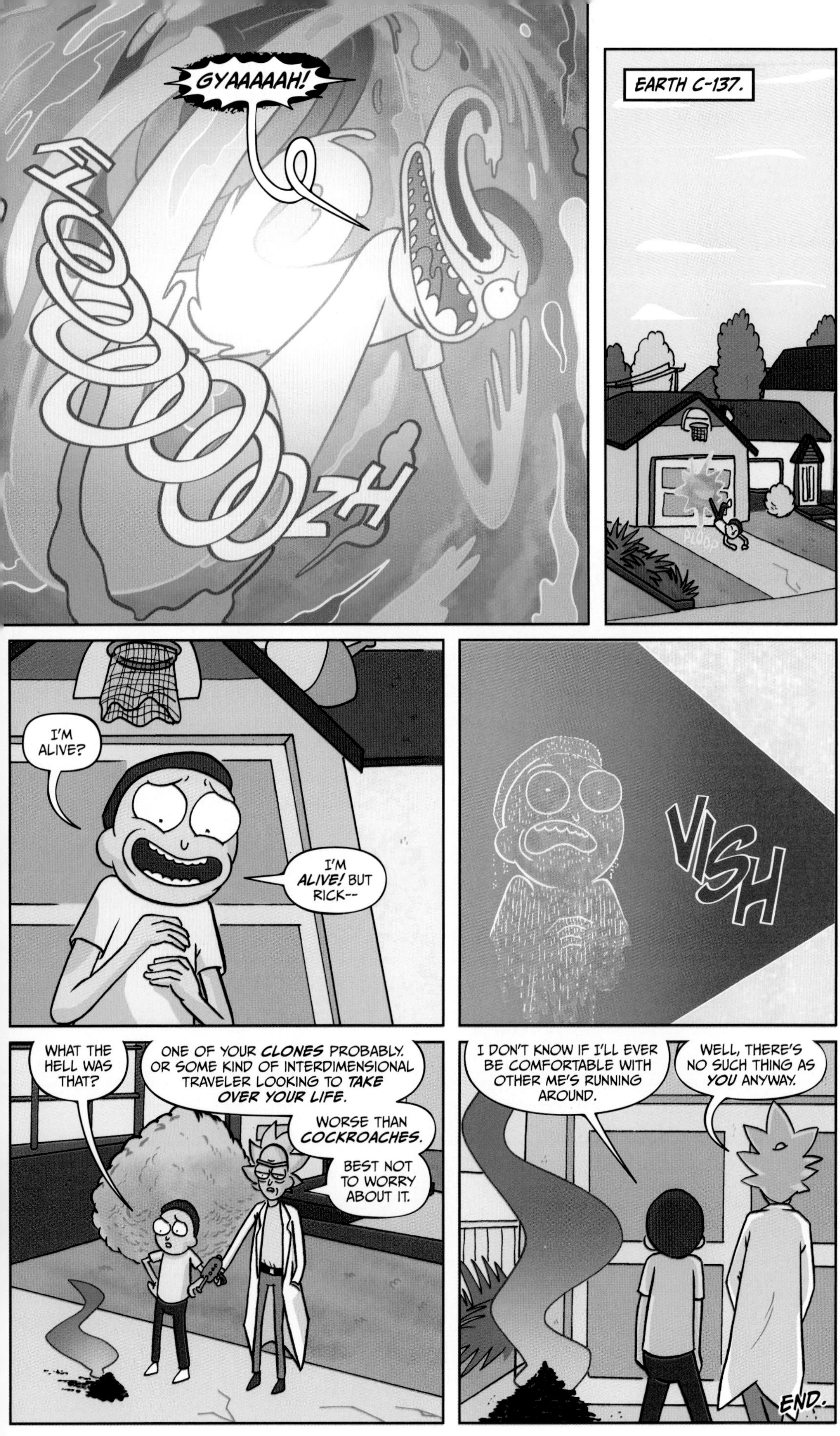
GYAAAAAH!
FYOOOOOOOOOOZH
EARTH C-137.
PLOOP
I'M ALIVE?
I'M ALIVE! BUT RICK--
VISH
WHAT THE HELL WAS THAT?
ONE OF YOUR CLONES PROBABLY. OR SOME KIND OF INTERDIMENSIONAL TRAVELER LOOKING TO TAKE OVER YOUR LIFE.
WORSE THAN COCKROACHES.
BEST NOT TO WORRY ABOUT IT.
I DON'T KNOW IF I'LL EVER BE COMFORTABLE WITH OTHER ME'S RUNNING AROUND.
WELL, THERE'S NO SUCH THING AS YOU ANYWAY.
END.

DAN HARMON is the Emmy® winning creator/executive producer of the comedy series *Community* as well as the co-creator/executive producer of Adult Swim's *Rick and Morty*™.

Harmon's pursuit of minimal work for maximum reward took him from stand-up to improv to sketch comedy, then finally to Los Angeles, where he began writing feature screenplays with fellow Milwaukeean Rob Schrab. As part of his deal with Robert Zemeckis at Imagemovers, Harmon co-wrote the feature film *Monster House*. Following this, Harmon co-wrote the Ben Stiller-directed pilot *Heat Vision and Jack*, starring Jack Black and Owen Wilson.

Disillusioned by the legitimate industry, Harmon began attending classes at nearby Glendale Community College. At the same time, Harmon and Schrab founded Channel 101, an untelevised non-profit audience-controlled network for undiscovered filmmakers, many of whom used it to launch mainstream careers, including the boys behind SNL's Digital Shorts. Harmon, along with Schrab, partnered with Sarah Silverman to create her Comedy Central series, *The Sarah Silverman Program*, where he served as head writer for the first season.

Harmon went on to create, write, and perform in the short-lived VH1 sketch series *Acceptable TV* before eventually creating the critically acclaimed and fan-favorite comedy *Community*. The show originally aired on NBC for five seasons before being acquired by Yahoo, which premiered season six of the show in March 2015. In 2009, he won an Emmy for Outstanding Music and Lyrics for the opening number of the 81st Annual Academy Awards.

Along with Justin Roiland, Harmon created the breakout Adult Swim animated series *Rick and Morty*™. The show premiered in December 2013 and quickly became a ratings hit. Harmon and Roiland have wrapped up season three, which premiered in 2017.

In 2014, Harmon was the star of the documentary *Harmontown*, which premiered at the SXSW Film Festival and chronicled his 20-city stand-up/podcast tour of the same name. The documentary was released theatrically in October 2014.

JUSTIN ROILAND grew up in Manteca, California, where he did the basic stuff children do. Later in life he traveled to Los Angeles. Once settled in, he created several popular online shorts for Channel 101. Justin is afraid of his mortality and hopes the things he creates will make lots of people happy. Then maybe when modern civilization collapses into chaos, people will remember him and they'll help him survive the bloodshed and violence. Global economic collapse is looming. It's going to be horrible, and honestly, a swift death might be preferable than living in the hell that awaits mankind.

Justin also really hates writing about himself in the third person. I hate this. That's right. It's me. I've been writing this whole thing. Hi. The cat's out of the bag. It's just you and me now. There never was a third person. If you want to know anything about me, just ask. Sorry this wasn't more informative.

KYLE STARKS is an Eisner-nominated comic creator from Southern Indiana, where he resides with his beautiful wife and two amazing daughters. Stealy values him at 32 and a half Grepples or 17-and-a-half Smeggles depending on market value at the current time. Check out his creator-owned work: *Kill Them All* and *Sexcastle*.

CJ CANNON is a self-taught artist living in Nashville, Tennessee. When they're not working on comics, outside riding their bike, or drumming, they're almost always in the house drawing gross fanart for similarly gross people.

MARC ELLERBY is a comics illustrator living in Essex, UK. He has worked on such titles as *Doctor Who*, *Regular Show*, and *The Amazing World of Gumball*. His own comics (which you should totally check out!) are *Chloe Noonan: Monster Hunter* and *Ellerbisms*. You can read some comics if you like at marcellerby.com.

KATY FARINA is a comic artist and illustrator based in Los Angeles, CA. She's currently a background painter at Dreamworks TV. In the past, she's done work with Boom! Studios, Oni Press, and Z2 Publishing. In the rare instance she isn't working on comics, she moonlights as the Baba Yaga; enticing local youth into ethical dilemmas and scooting around in her chicken-legged hut.

MAGDALENE VISAGGIO is a writer and former wannabe philosopher who is inexplicably paid to write comic books, which never ceases to mystify her. She is best known as the writer and creator the Eisner-nominated series *Kim & Kim*, as well as *Eternity Girl* at DC Comics, *Transformers vs. Visionaries* at IDW, and *Quantum Teens Are Go* at Black Mask Studios. Raised in Richmond, Virginia, she currently resides in Manhattan.

TINI HOWARD is a writer and swamp witch from the Carolina Wilds. Her work includes *Magdalena* from Image/Top Cow Comics, *Rick and Morty*: *Pocket Like You Stole It* from Oni Press, and *Assassinistas* from IDW/Black Crown! Her previous work includes *Power Rangers: Pink* (BOOM! Studios), *The Skeptics* (Black Mask Studios), and a contribution to the hit *Secret Loves of Geek Girls*, from Dark Horse Comics. She lives with her husband, Blake, and her son, Orlando, who is a cat.

PAMELA RIBON is the writer of *SLAM!* and *My Boyfriend is a Bear*. Her screenwriting work includes *Moana* and *Ralph Breaks the Internet: Wreck-It Ralph 2*. She's a best-selling author, frequent troublemaker, and a bit of a know-it-all, if we're being honest.

ERICA HAYES has been working as a professional storyboard artist for four years, and has worked on all three seasons of *Rick and Morty*. This is her first professional comic gig, for which she is very excited! Erica lives in LA with her boyfriend, Spencer, and two cats, Marcy and Finn.

ALLISON STREJLAU is a comic artist and colorist. You can find her at allisonstrejlau.com or follow her on Twitter at @astrejlau.

SARAH STERN is a comic artist and colorist from New York. Find her at sarahstern.com or follow her on Twitter at @worstwizard.

CHRIS CRANK letters a bunch of books put out by Image, Dark Horse and Oni Press. He also has a podcast with Mike Norton (crankcast.net) and makes music (sonomorti.bandcamp.com). Catch him on Twitter: @ccrank.

MORE BOOKS FROM ONI PRESS

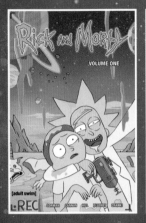

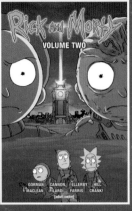

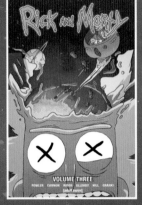

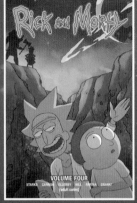

Rick and Morty
VOLUME ONE
[adult swim]

RICK AND MORTY, VOLUME ONE

By Zac Gorman, CJ Cannon, Marc Ellerby, and more!
128 pages, softcover, color

ISBN 978-1-62010-281-7

Rick and Morty
VOLUME TWO
GORMAN CANNON ELLERBY HILL
MACLEAN FILARDI FARRIS CRANK!
[adult swim]

RICK AND MORTY, VOLUME TWO

By Zac Gorman, CJ Cannon, Marc Ellerby, and more!
128 pages, softcover, color

ISBN 978-1-62010-319-7

Rick and Morty
VOLUME THREE
[adult swim]

RICK AND MORTY, VOLUME THREE

By Tom Fowler, CJ Cannon, Marc Ellerby, and more!
128 pages, softcover, color

ISBN 978-1-62010-343-2

Rick and Morty
VOLUME FOUR
[adult swim]

RICK AND MORTY, VOLUME FOUR

By Kyle Starks, CJ Cannon, Marc Ellerby, and more!
128 pages, softcover, color

ISBN 978-1-62010-377-7

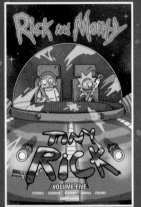

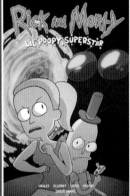

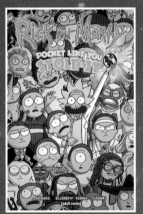

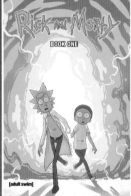

Rick and Morty
TINY RICK
VOLUME FIVE
STARKS CANNON ELLERBY FARINA CRANK!
[adult swim]

RICK AND MORTY: VOLUME FIVE

By Kyle Starks, CJ Cannon, Marc Ellerby, and more!
128 pages, softcover, color

ISBN 978-1-62010-416-3

Rick and Morty
LIL' POOPY SUPERSTAR
GRALEY ELLERBY LOUIS CRANK!
[adult swim]

RICK AND MORTY: LIL' POOPY SUPERSTAR

By Sarah Graley, Marc Ellerby, and Mildred Louis
128 pages, softcover, color

ISBN 978-1-62010-374-6

Rick and Morty
POCKET LIKE YOU STOLE IT
HOWARD ELLERBY FARINA CRANK!
[adult swim]

RICK AND MORTY: POCKET LIKE YOU STOLE IT

By Tini Howard, Marc Ellerby, and Katy Farina
128 pages, softcover, color

ISBN 978-1-62010-474-3

Rick and Morty
BOOK ONE
[adult swim]

RICK AND MORTY HARDCOVER, BOOK ONE

By Zac Gorman, CJ Cannon, Marc Ellerby, and more!
296 pages, hardcover, color

ISBN 978-1-62010-360-9

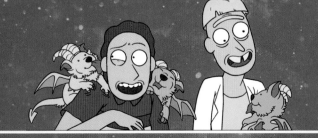

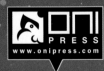

ONI PRESS
www.onipress.com

For more information on these and other fine Oni Press comic books and graphic novels visit **www.onipress.com.**
To find a comic specialty store in your area visit **www.comicshops.us.**